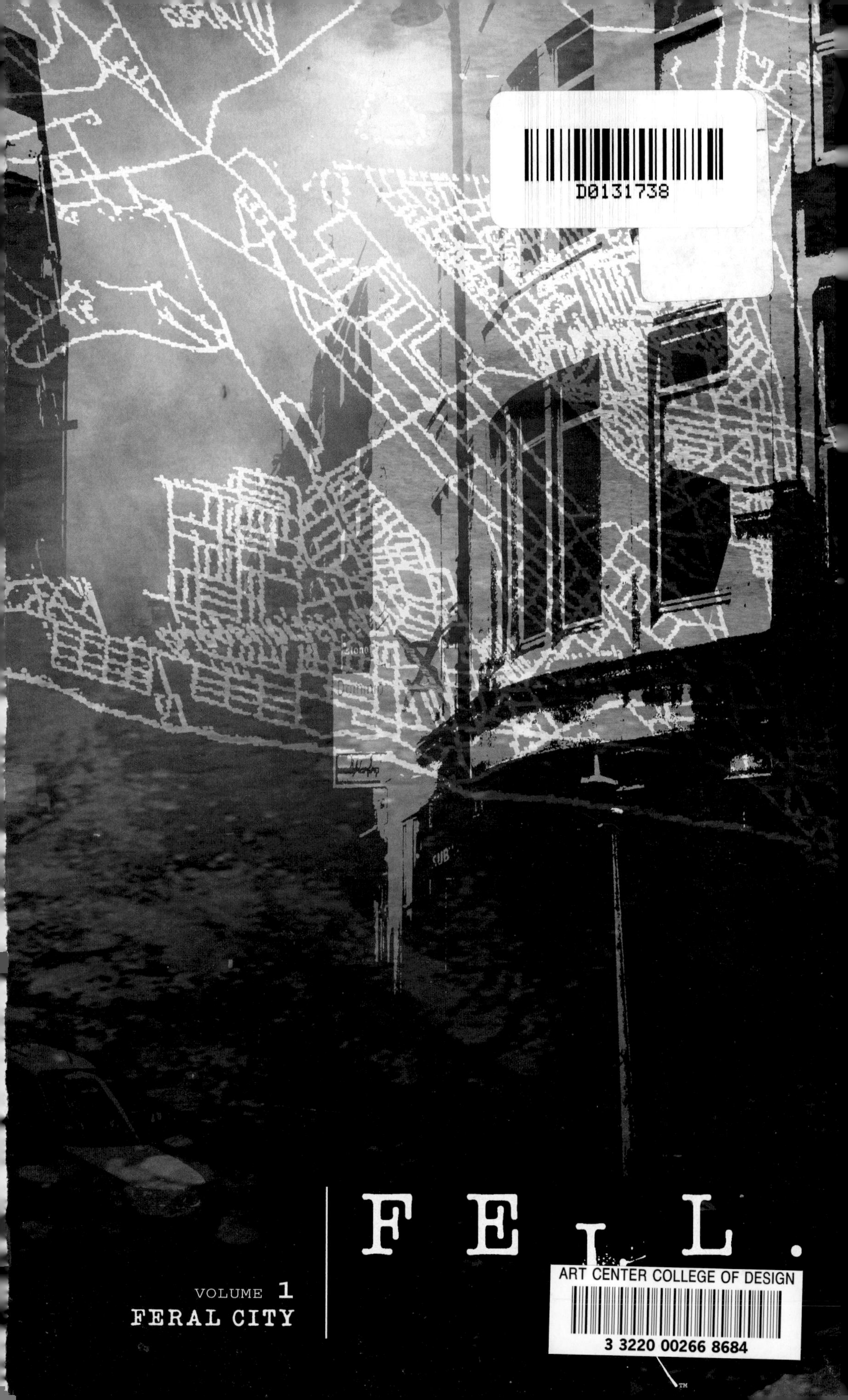

# FELL.

VOLUME 1
FERAL CITY

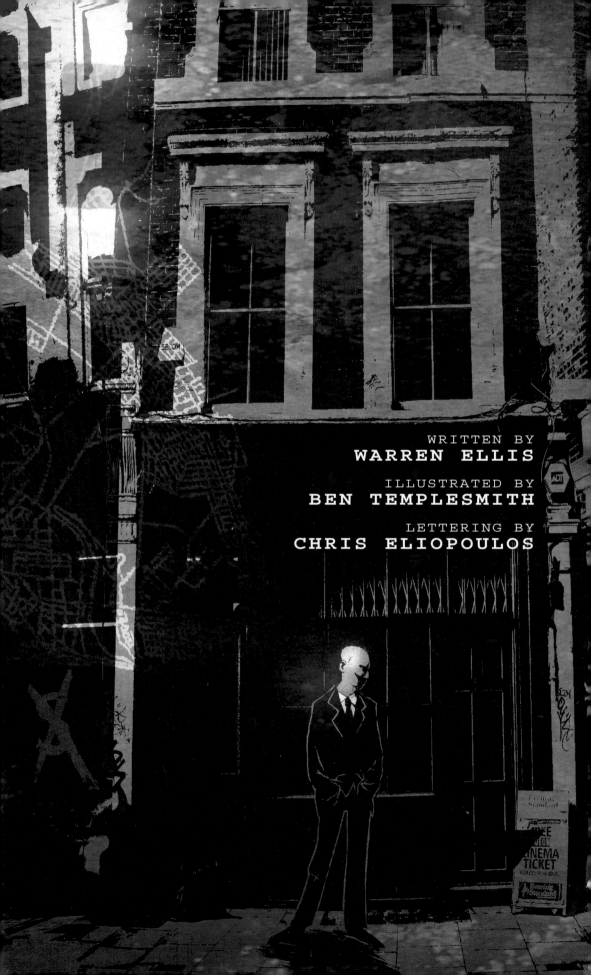

WRITTEN BY
**WARREN ELLIS**

ILLUSTRATED BY
**BEN TEMPLESMITH**

LETTERING BY
**CHRIS ELIOPOULOS**

IMAGE COMICS, INC.

PUBLISHER
ERIK LARSEN

PRESIDENT
TODD McFARLANE

CEO
MARC SILVESTRI

VICE-PRESIDENT
JIM VALENTINO

EXECUTIVE DIRECTOR
ERIC STEPHENSON

DIRECTOR OF MARKETING
MARK HAVEN BRITT

ACCOUNTS MANAGER
THAO LE

ACCOUNTING ASSISTANT
ROSEMARY CAO

ADMINISTRATIVE ASSISTANT
TRACI HUI

TRAFFIC MANAGER
JOE KEATINGE

PRODUCTION MANAGER
ALLEN HUI

PRODUCTION ARTIST
JONATHAN CHAN

PRODUCTION ARTIST
DREW GILL

PRODUCTION ARTIST
CHRIS GIARRUSSO

WWW.IMAGECOMICS.COM

FELL, VOL. 1: FERAL CITY

ISBN: 978-1-58240-693-0 (PAPERBACK)
ISBN: 978-1-58240-808-8 (HARDCOVER)

FIRST PRINTING

PUBLISHED BY IMAGE COMICS, INC. OFFICE OF
PUBLICATION: 1942 UNIVERSITY AVENUE, SUITE
305, BERKELEY, CALIFORNIA 94704. COPYRIGHT
© 2007 WARREN ELLIS & BEN TEMPLESMITH.
ORIGINALLY PUBLISHED IN SINGLE MAGAZINE FORM
AS FELL #1-8. ALL RIGHTS RESERVED. FELL™
(INCLUDING ALL PROMINENT CHARACTERS FEATURED
HEREIN), ITS LOGO AND ALL CHARACTER
LIKENESSES ARE TRADEMARKS OF WARREN ELLIS
& BEN TEMPLESMITH, UNLESS OTHERWISE NOTED.
IMAGE COMICS® IS A TRADEMARK OF IMAGE COMICS,
INC. ALL RIGHTS RESERVED. NO PART OF THIS
PUBLICATION MAY BE REPRODUCED OR TRANSMITTED,
IN ANY FORM OR BY ANY MEANS (EXCEPT FOR SHORT
EXCERPTS FOR REVIEW PURPOSES) WITHOUT THE
EXPRESS WRITTEN PERMISSION OF IMAGE COMICS,
INC. ALL NAMES, CHARACTERS, EVENTS AND LOCALES
IN THIS PUBLICATION ARE ENTIRELY FICTIONAL.
ANY RESEMBLANCE TO ACTUAL PERSONS (LIVING
OR DEAD), EVENTS OR PLACES, WITHOUT SATIRIC
INTENT, IS COINCIDENTAL.

PRINTED IN CANADA

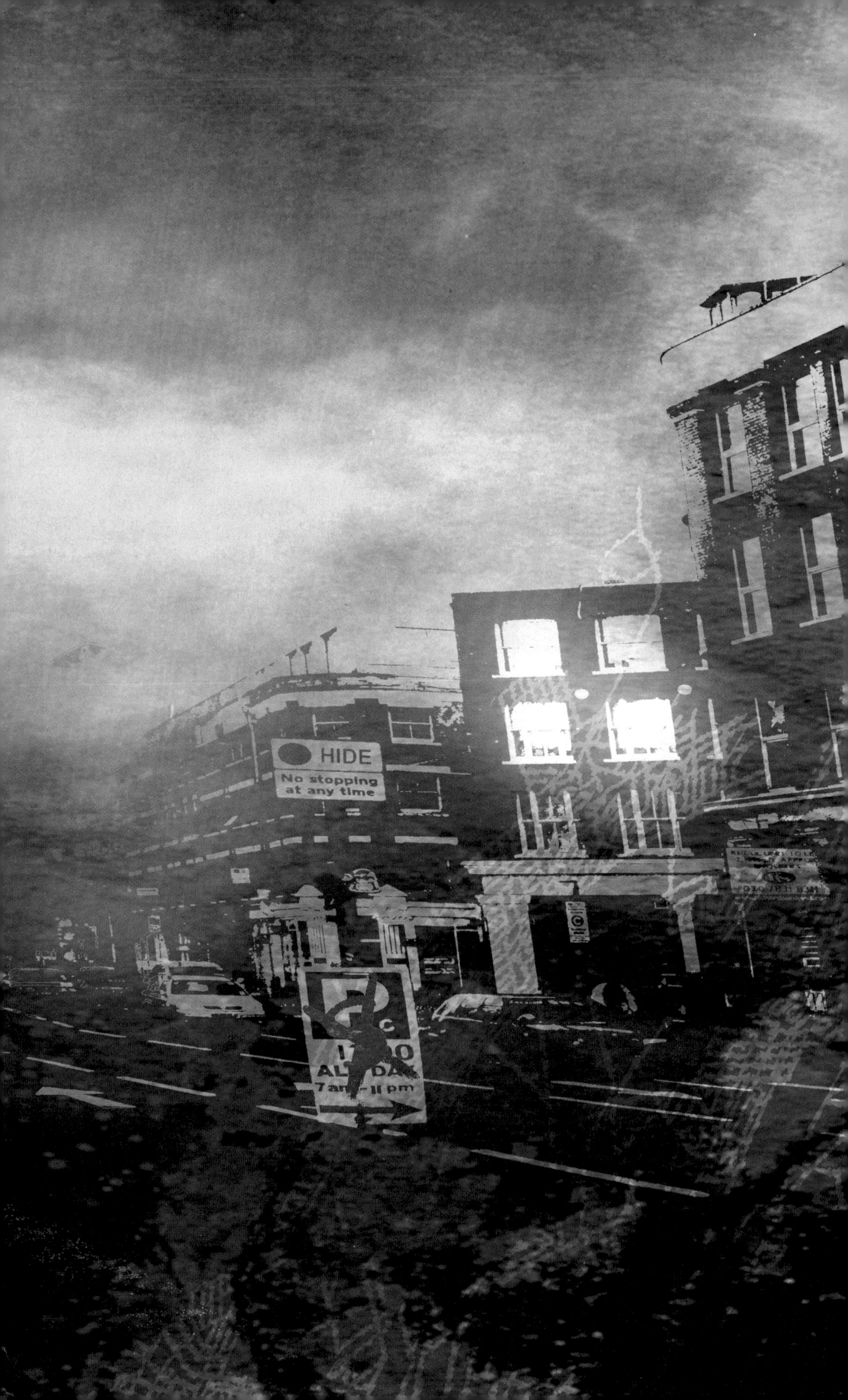
HIDE
No stopping
at any time

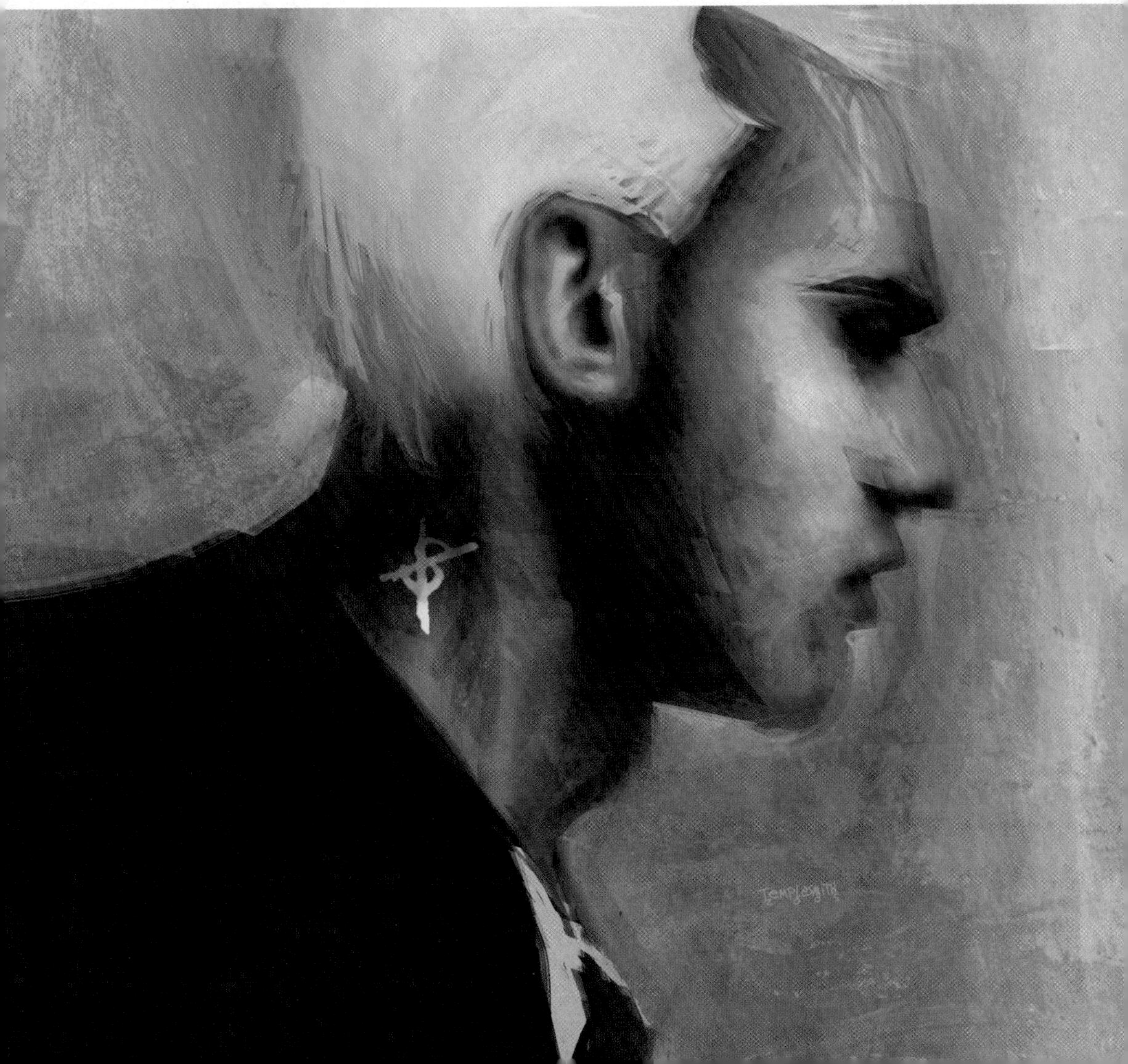
TEMPLESMITH

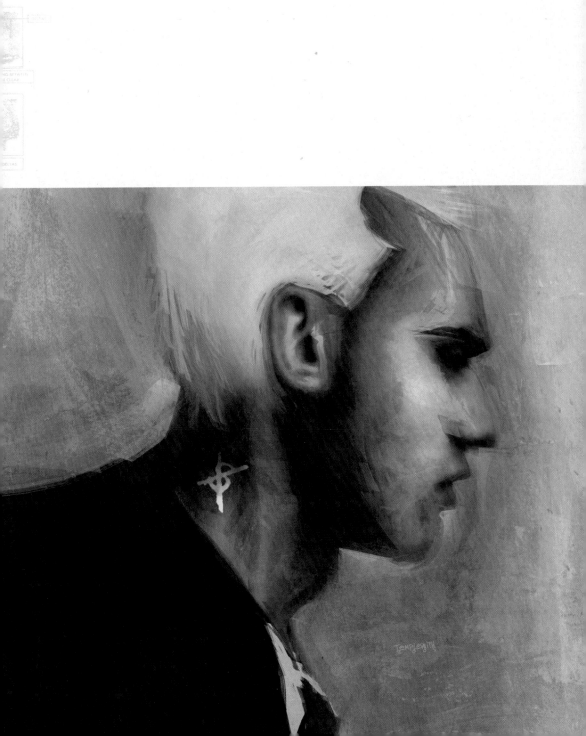

# FELL.™

## CHAPTER 1

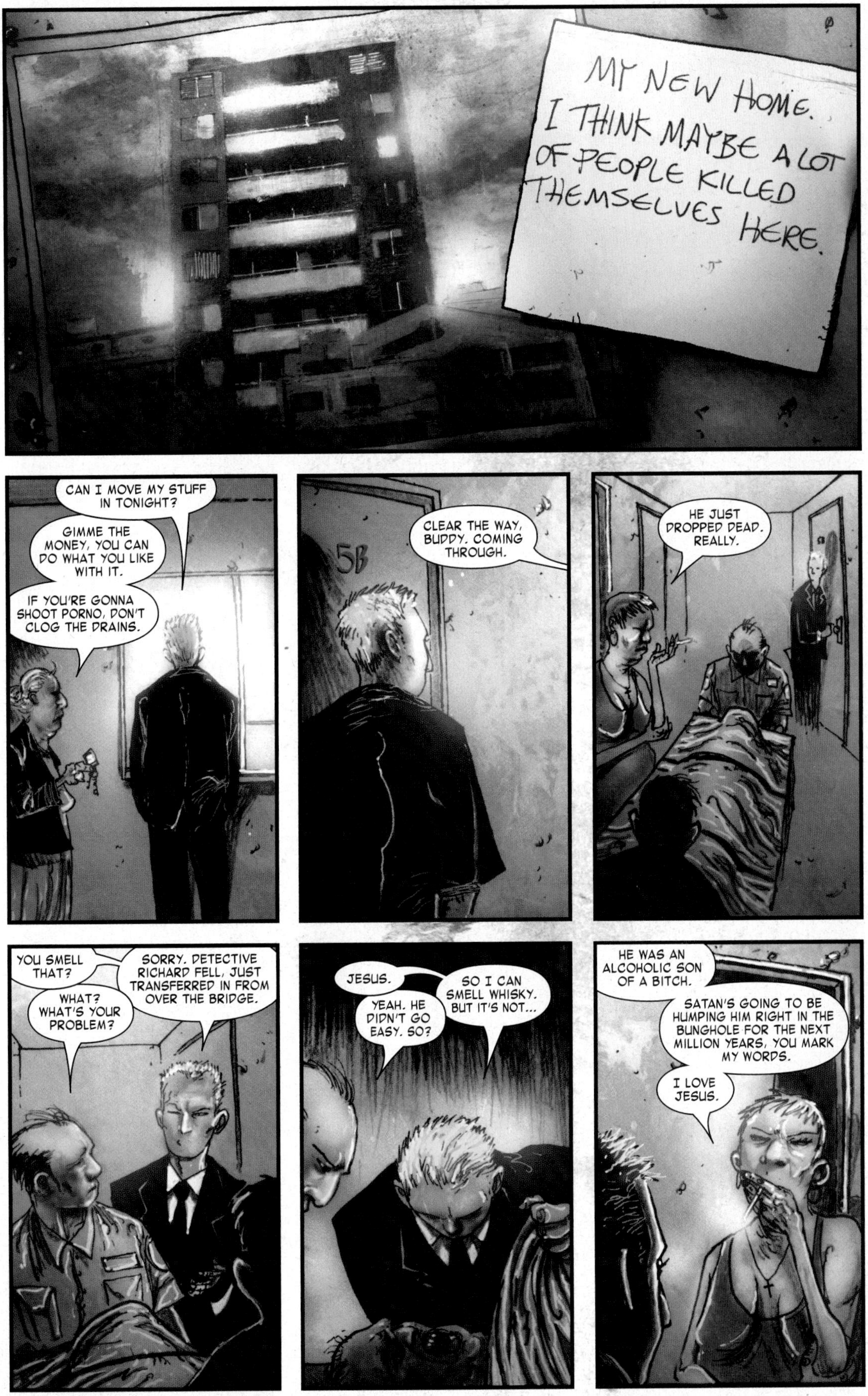
MY NEW HOME. I THINK MAYBE A LOT OF PEOPLE KILLED THEMSELVES HERE.
CAN I MOVE MY STUFF IN TONIGHT?
GIMME THE MONEY, YOU CAN DO WHAT YOU LIKE WITH IT.
IF YOU'RE GONNA SHOOT PORNO, DON'T CLOG THE DRAINS.
5B
CLEAR THE WAY, BUDDY. COMING THROUGH.
HE JUST DROPPED DEAD. REALLY.
YOU SMELL THAT?
SORRY. DETECTIVE RICHARD FELL, JUST TRANSFERRED IN FROM OVER THE BRIDGE.
WHAT? WHAT'S YOUR PROBLEM?
JESUS.
SO I CAN SMELL WHISKY. BUT IT'S NOT...
YEAH. HE DIDN'T GO EASY. SO?
HE WAS AN ALCOHOLIC SON OF A BITCH.
SATAN'S GOING TO BE HUMPING HIM RIGHT IN THE BUNGHOLE FOR THE NEXT MILLION YEARS, YOU MARK MY WORDS.
I LOVE JESUS.

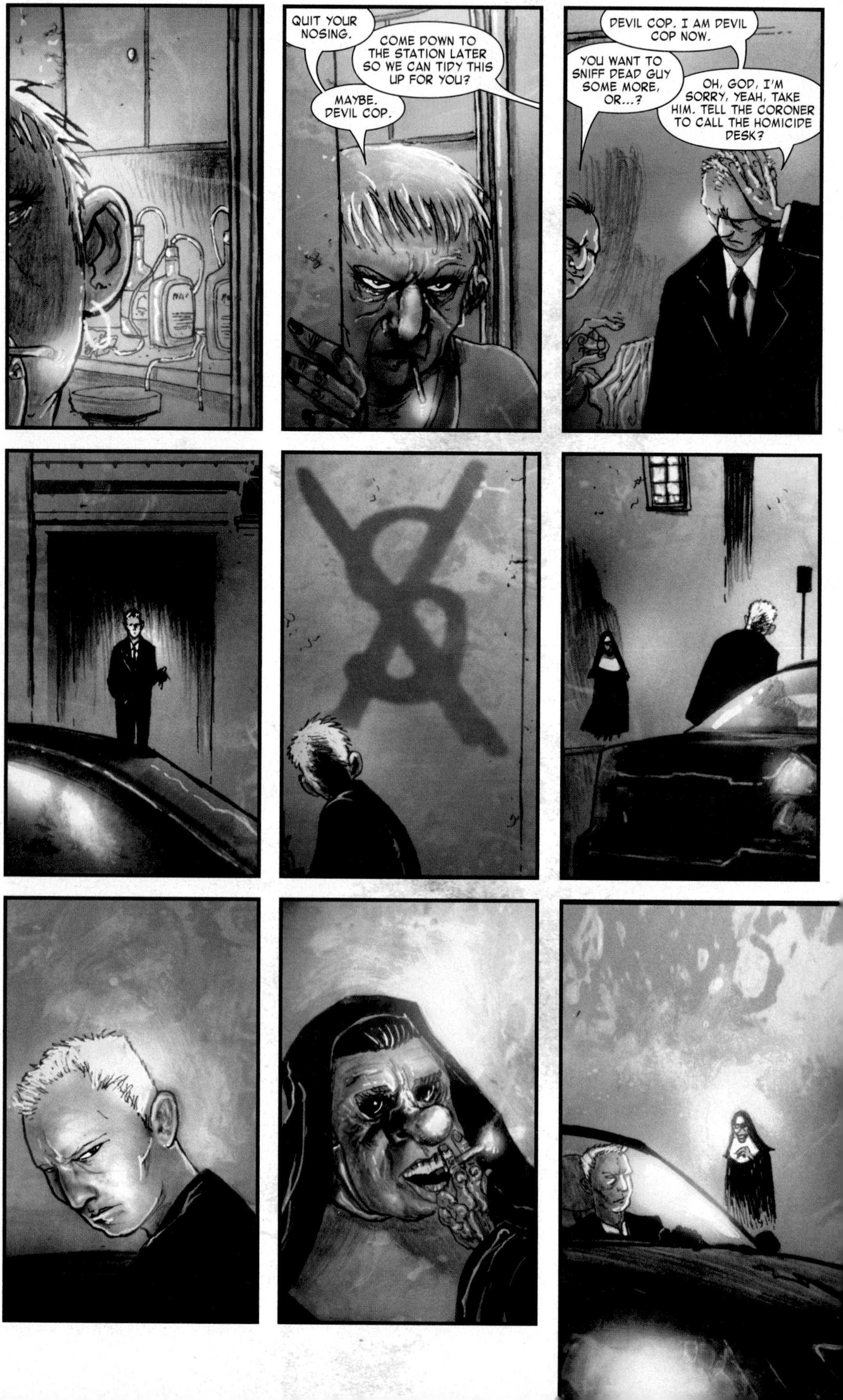
QUIT YOUR NOSING.
COME DOWN TO THE STATION LATER SO WE CAN TIDY THIS UP FOR YOU?
MAYBE. DEVIL COP.
DEVIL COP. I AM DEVIL COP NOW.
YOU WANT TO SNIFF DEAD GUY SOME MORE, OR...?
OH, GOD, I'M SORRY, YEAH, TAKE HIM. TELL THE CORONER TO CALL THE HOMICIDE DESK?

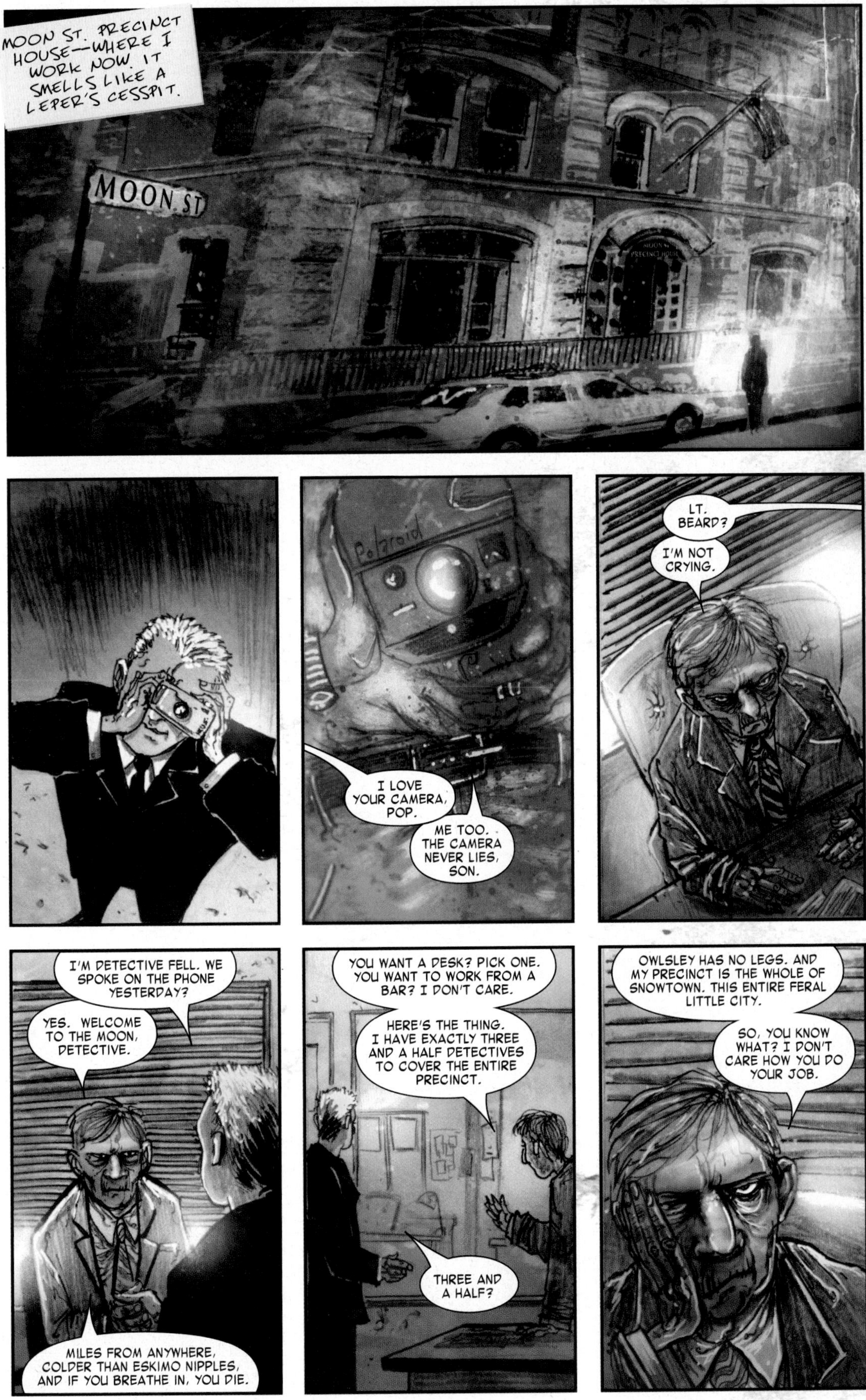
MOON ST. PRECINCT HOUSE—WHERE I WORK NOW. IT SMELLS LIKE A LEPER'S CESSPIT.
MOON ST
I LOVE YOUR CAMERA, POP.
ME TOO. THE CAMERA NEVER LIES, SON.
LT. BEARD?
I'M NOT CRYING.
I'M DETECTIVE FELL. WE SPOKE ON THE PHONE YESTERDAY?
YES. WELCOME TO THE MOON, DETECTIVE.
MILES FROM ANYWHERE, COLDER THAN ESKIMO NIPPLES, AND IF YOU BREATHE IN, YOU DIE.
YOU WANT A DESK? PICK ONE. YOU WANT TO WORK FROM A BAR? I DON'T CARE.
HERE'S THE THING. I HAVE EXACTLY THREE AND A HALF DETECTIVES TO COVER THE ENTIRE PRECINCT.
THREE AND A HALF?
OWLSLEY HAS NO LEGS. AND MY PRECINCT IS THE WHOLE OF SNOWTOWN. THIS ENTIRE FERAL LITTLE CITY.
SO, YOU KNOW WHAT? I DON'T CARE HOW YOU DO YOUR JOB.

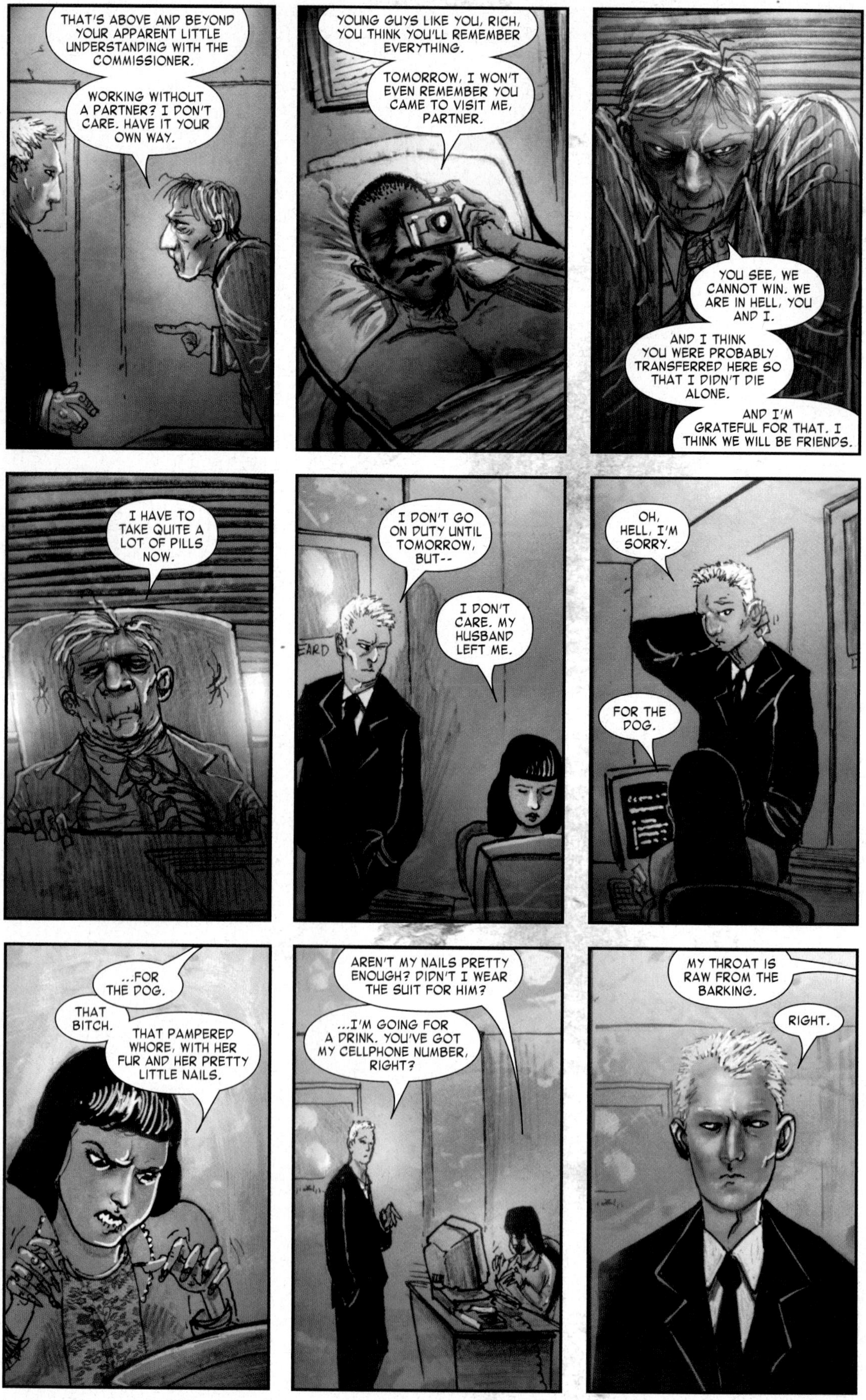
THAT'S ABOVE AND BEYOND YOUR APPARENT LITTLE UNDERSTANDING WITH THE COMMISSIONER.
WORKING WITHOUT A PARTNER? I DON'T CARE. HAVE IT YOUR OWN WAY.
YOUNG GUYS LIKE YOU, RICH, YOU THINK YOU'LL REMEMBER EVERYTHING.
TOMORROW, I WON'T EVEN REMEMBER YOU CAME TO VISIT ME, PARTNER.
YOU SEE, WE CANNOT WIN. WE ARE IN HELL, YOU AND I.
AND I THINK YOU WERE PROBABLY TRANSFERRED HERE SO THAT I DIDN'T DIE ALONE.
AND I'M GRATEFUL FOR THAT. I THINK WE WILL BE FRIENDS.
I HAVE TO TAKE QUITE A LOT OF PILLS NOW.
I DON'T GO ON DUTY UNTIL TOMORROW, BUT--
I DON'T CARE. MY HUSBAND LEFT ME.
OH, HELL, I'M SORRY.
FOR THE DOG.
...FOR THE DOG.
THAT BITCH.
THAT PAMPERED WHORE, WITH HER FUR AND HER PRETTY LITTLE NAILS.
AREN'T MY NAILS PRETTY ENOUGH? DIDN'T I WEAR THE SUIT FOR HIM?
...I'M GOING FOR A DRINK. YOU'VE GOT MY CELLPHONE NUMBER, RIGHT?
MY THROAT IS RAW FROM THE BARKING.
RIGHT.

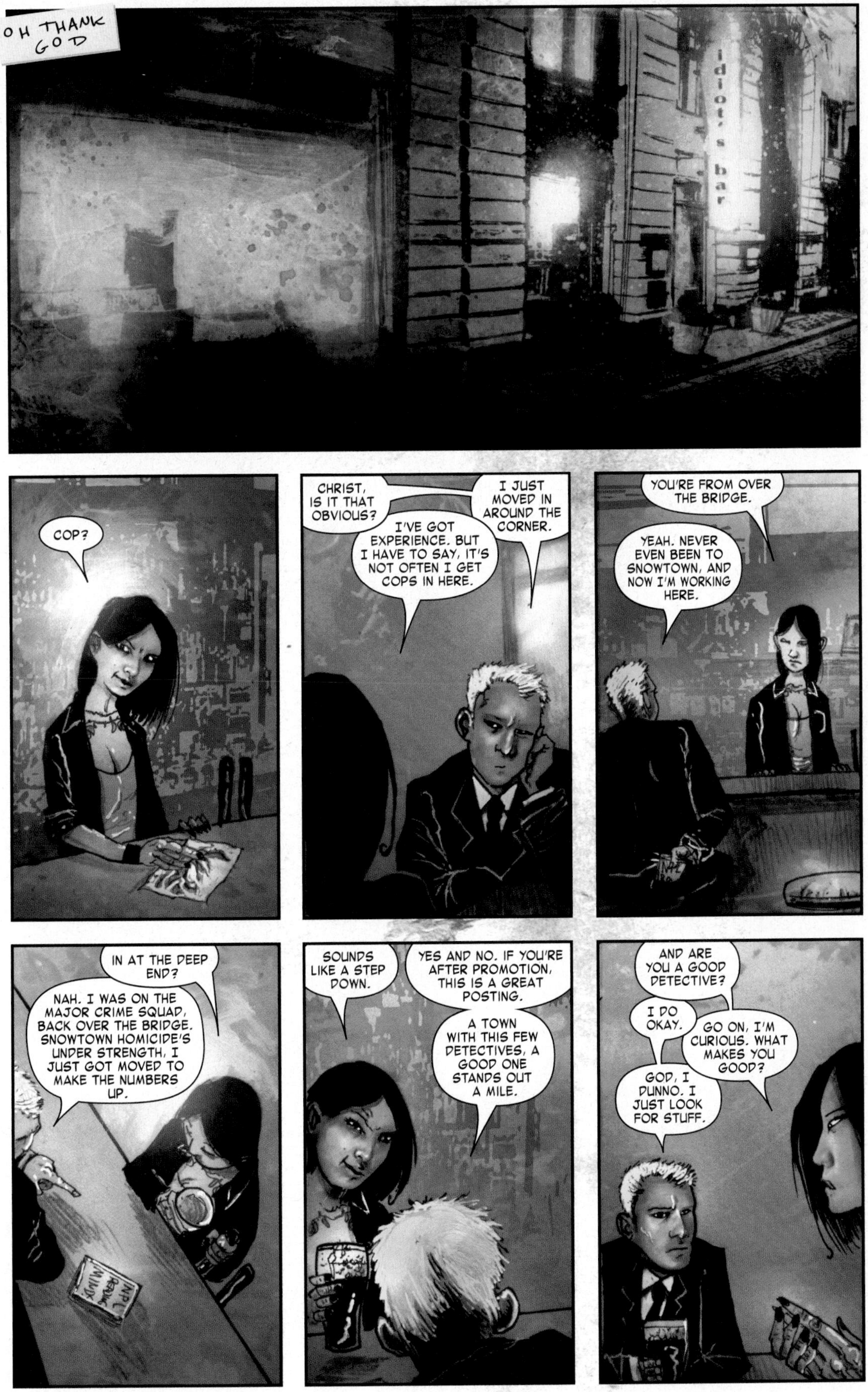
OH THANK GOD
idiot's bar
COP?
CHRIST, IS IT THAT OBVIOUS?
I'VE GOT EXPERIENCE. BUT I HAVE TO SAY, IT'S NOT OFTEN I GET COPS IN HERE.
I JUST MOVED IN AROUND THE CORNER.
YOU'RE FROM OVER THE BRIDGE.
YEAH. NEVER EVEN BEEN TO SNOWTOWN, AND NOW I'M WORKING HERE.
IN AT THE DEEP END?
NAH. I WAS ON THE MAJOR CRIME SQUAD, BACK OVER THE BRIDGE. SNOWTOWN HOMICIDE'S UNDER STRENGTH, I JUST GOT MOVED TO MAKE THE NUMBERS UP.
SOUNDS LIKE A STEP DOWN.
YES AND NO. IF YOU'RE AFTER PROMOTION, THIS IS A GREAT POSTING.
A TOWN WITH THIS FEW DETECTIVES, A GOOD ONE STANDS OUT A MILE.
AND ARE YOU A GOOD DETECTIVE?
I DO OKAY.
GO ON, I'M CURIOUS. WHAT MAKES YOU GOOD?
GOD, I DUNNO. I JUST LOOK FOR STUFF.

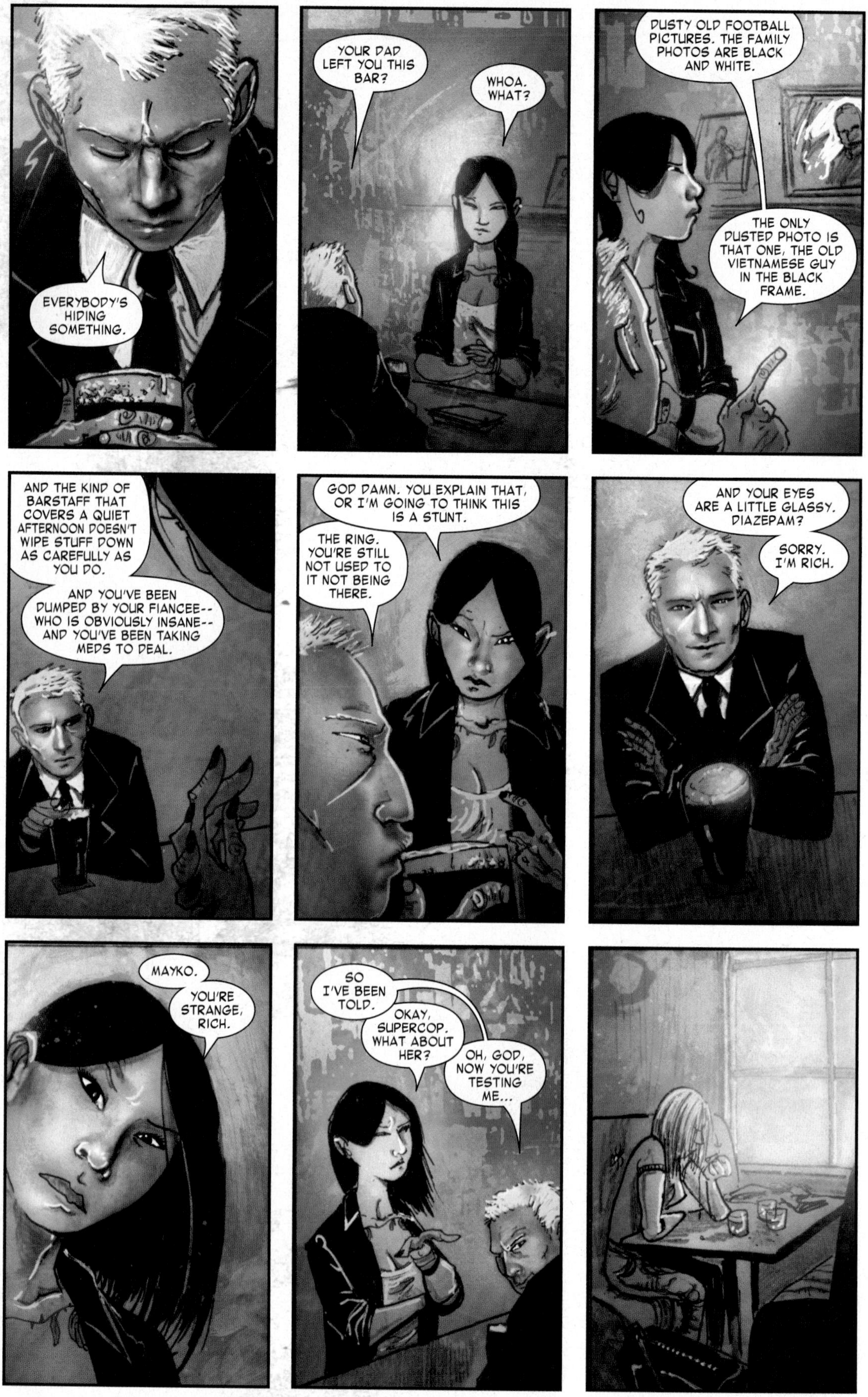
EVERYBODY'S HIDING SOMETHING.
YOUR DAD LEFT YOU THIS BAR?
WHOA. WHAT?
DUSTY OLD FOOTBALL PICTURES. THE FAMILY PHOTOS ARE BLACK AND WHITE.
THE ONLY DUSTED PHOTO IS THAT ONE, THE OLD VIETNAMESE GUY IN THE BLACK FRAME.
AND THE KIND OF BARSTAFF THAT COVERS A QUIET AFTERNOON DOESN'T WIPE STUFF DOWN AS CAREFULLY AS YOU DO.
AND YOU'VE BEEN DUMPED BY YOUR FIANCEE--WHO IS OBVIOUSLY INSANE--AND YOU'VE BEEN TAKING MEDS TO DEAL.
GOD DAMN. YOU EXPLAIN THAT, OR I'M GOING TO THINK THIS IS A STUNT.
THE RING. YOU'RE STILL NOT USED TO IT NOT BEING THERE.
AND YOUR EYES ARE A LITTLE GLASSY. DIAZEPAM?
SORRY. I'M RICH.
MAYKO.
YOU'RE STRANGE, RICH.
SO I'VE BEEN TOLD.
OKAY, SUPERCOP. WHAT ABOUT HER?
OH, GOD, NOW YOU'RE TESTING ME...

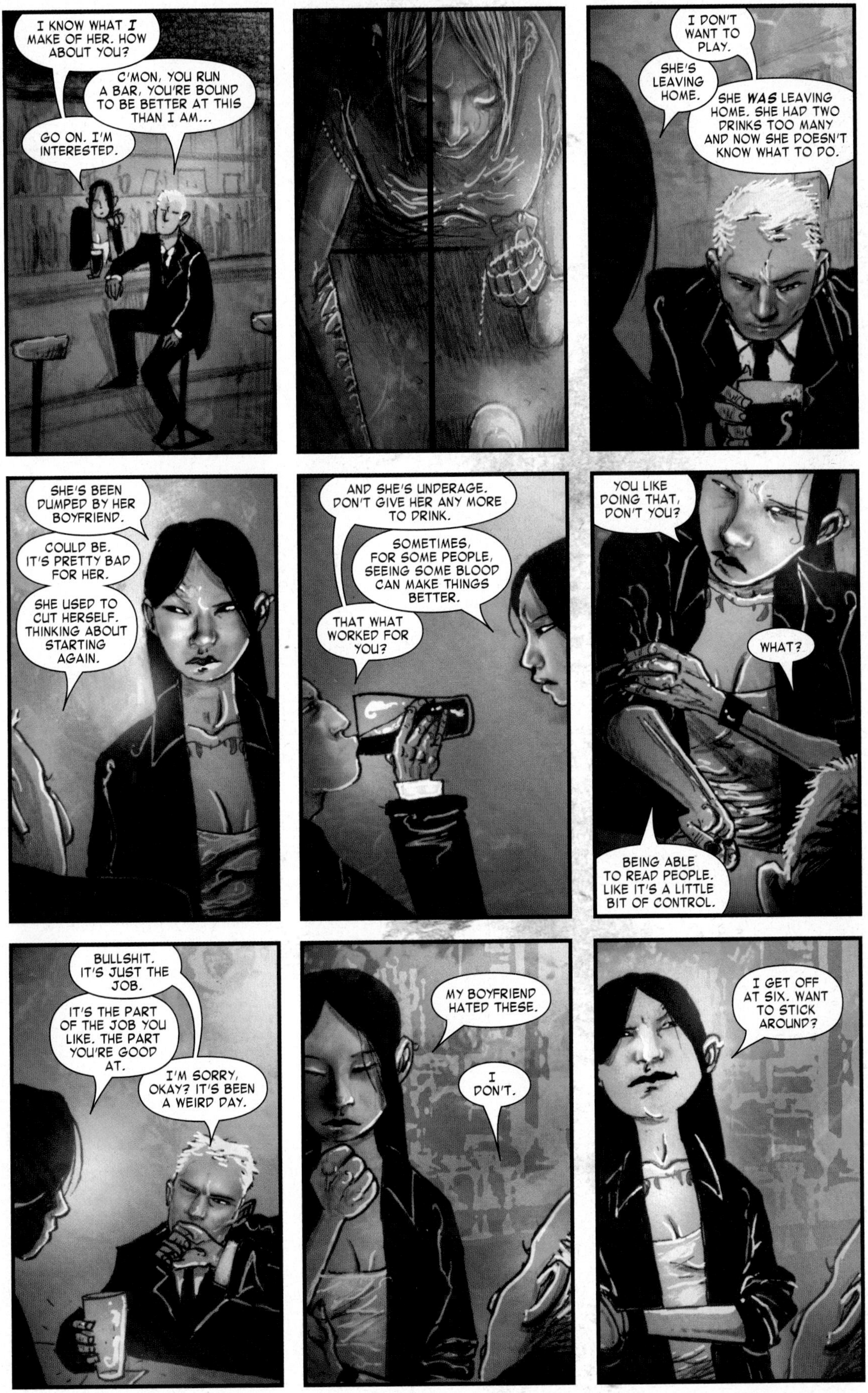
I KNOW WHAT I MAKE OF HER. HOW ABOUT YOU?
C'MON, YOU RUN A BAR, YOU'RE BOUND TO BE BETTER AT THIS THAN I AM...
GO ON. I'M INTERESTED.
I DON'T WANT TO PLAY.
SHE'S LEAVING HOME.
SHE WAS LEAVING HOME. SHE HAD TWO DRINKS TOO MANY AND NOW SHE DOESN'T KNOW WHAT TO DO.
SHE'S BEEN DUMPED BY HER BOYFRIEND.
COULD BE. IT'S PRETTY BAD FOR HER.
SHE USED TO CUT HERSELF. THINKING ABOUT STARTING AGAIN.
AND SHE'S UNDERAGE. DON'T GIVE HER ANY MORE TO DRINK.
SOMETIMES, FOR SOME PEOPLE, SEEING SOME BLOOD CAN MAKE THINGS BETTER.
THAT WHAT WORKED FOR YOU?
YOU LIKE DOING THAT, DON'T YOU?
WHAT?
BEING ABLE TO READ PEOPLE. LIKE IT'S A LITTLE BIT OF CONTROL.
BULLSHIT. IT'S JUST THE JOB.
IT'S THE PART OF THE JOB YOU LIKE. THE PART YOU'RE GOOD AT.
I'M SORRY, OKAY? IT'S BEEN A WEIRD DAY.
MY BOYFRIEND HATED THESE.
I DON'T.
I GET OFF AT SIX. WANT TO STICK AROUND?

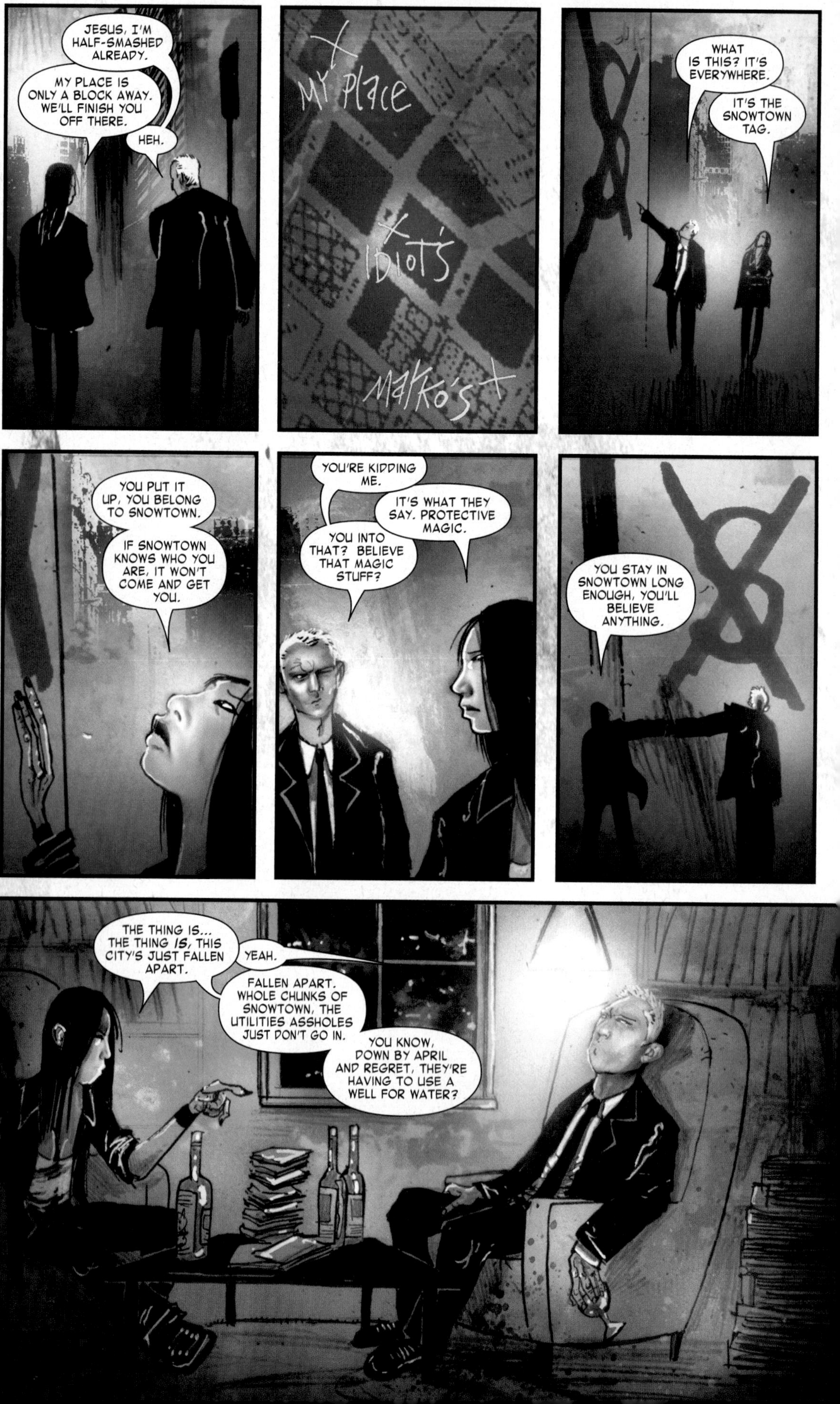

JESUS, I'M HALF-SMASHED ALREADY.
MY PLACE IS ONLY A BLOCK AWAY. WE'LL FINISH YOU OFF THERE.
HEH.
MY PLACE
IDIOT'S
MARKO'S
WHAT IS THIS? IT'S EVERYWHERE.
IT'S THE SNOWTOWN TAG.
YOU PUT IT UP, YOU BELONG TO SNOWTOWN.
IF SNOWTOWN KNOWS WHO YOU ARE, IT WON'T COME AND GET YOU.
YOU'RE KIDDING ME.
IT'S WHAT THEY SAY. PROTECTIVE MAGIC.
YOU INTO THAT? BELIEVE THAT MAGIC STUFF?
YOU STAY IN SNOWTOWN LONG ENOUGH, YOU'LL BELIEVE ANYTHING.
THE THING IS... THE THING *IS*, THIS CITY'S JUST FALLEN APART.
YEAH.
FALLEN APART. WHOLE CHUNKS OF SNOWTOWN, THE UTILITIES ASSHOLES JUST DON'T GO IN.
YOU KNOW, DOWN BY APRIL AND REGRET, THEY'RE HAVING TO USE A WELL FOR WATER?

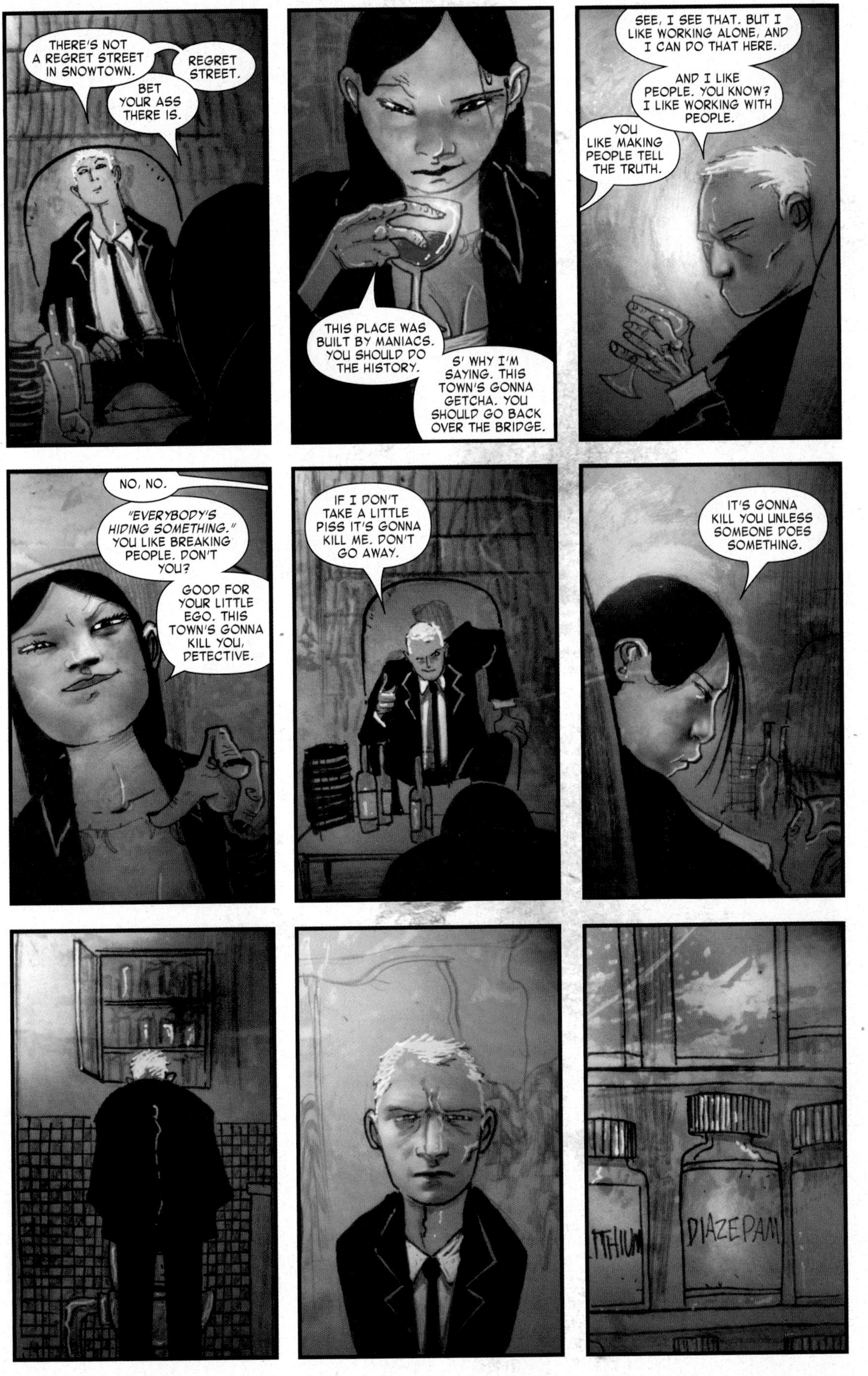
THERE'S NOT A REGRET STREET IN SNOWTOWN.
REGRET STREET.
BET YOUR ASS THERE IS.
THIS PLACE WAS BUILT BY MANIACS. YOU SHOULD DO THE HISTORY.
S' WHY I'M SAYING. THIS TOWN'S GONNA GETCHA. YOU SHOULD GO BACK OVER THE BRIDGE.
SEE, I SEE THAT. BUT I LIKE WORKING ALONE, AND I CAN DO THAT HERE.
AND I LIKE PEOPLE. YOU KNOW? I LIKE WORKING WITH PEOPLE.
YOU LIKE MAKING PEOPLE TELL THE TRUTH.
NO, NO.
"EVERYBODY'S HIDING SOMETHING." YOU LIKE BREAKING PEOPLE. DON'T YOU?
GOOD FOR YOUR LITTLE EGO. THIS TOWN'S GONNA KILL YOU, DETECTIVE.
IF I DON'T TAKE A LITTLE PISS IT'S GONNA KILL ME. DON'T GO AWAY.
IT'S GONNA KILL YOU UNLESS SOMEONE DOES SOMETHING.
LITHIUM
DIAZEPAM

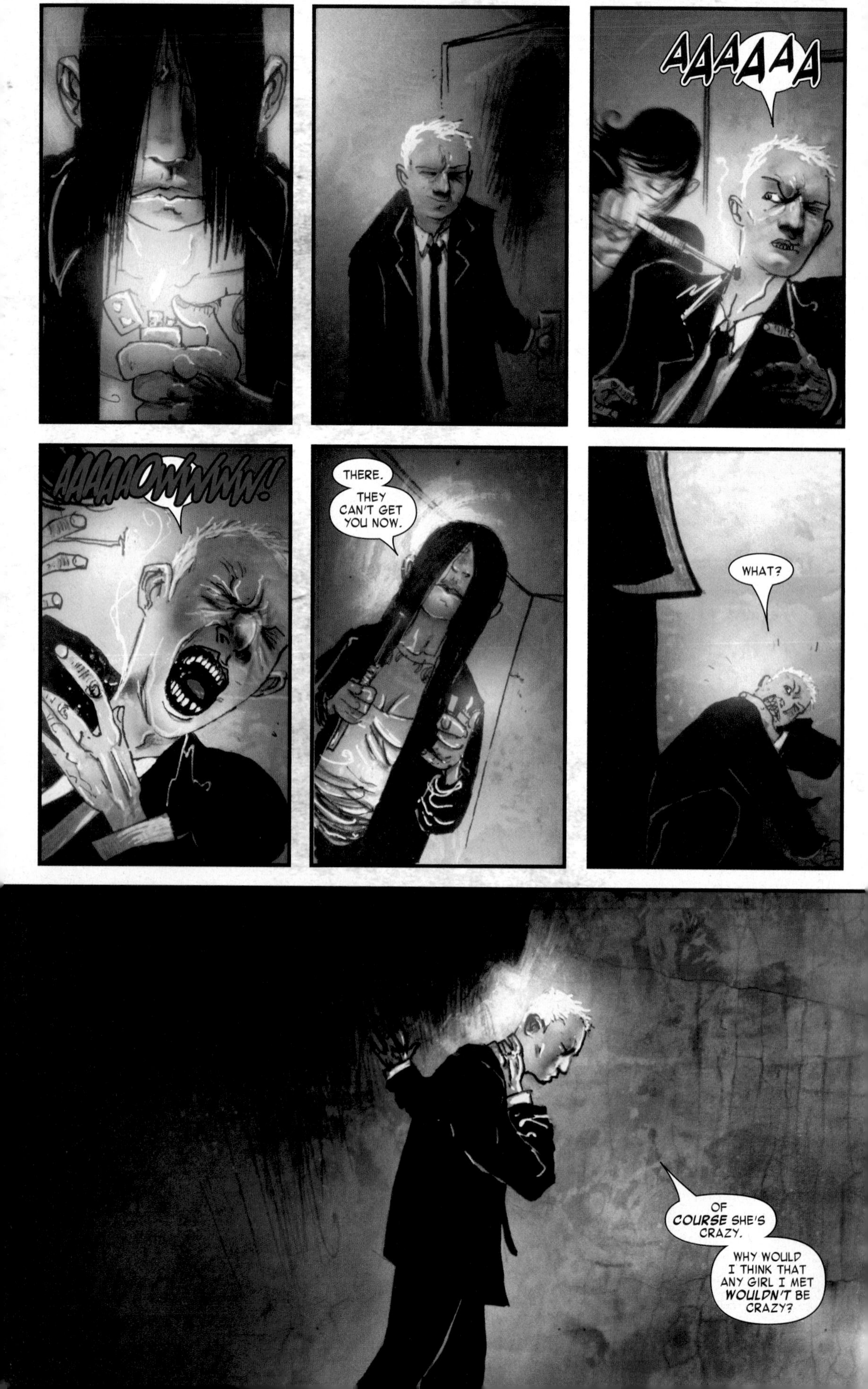
AAAAA
AAAAAOWWWW!
THERE. THEY CAN'T GET YOU NOW.
WHAT?
OF COURSE SHE'S CRAZY.
WHY WOULD I THINK THAT ANY GIRL I MET WOULDN'T BE CRAZY?

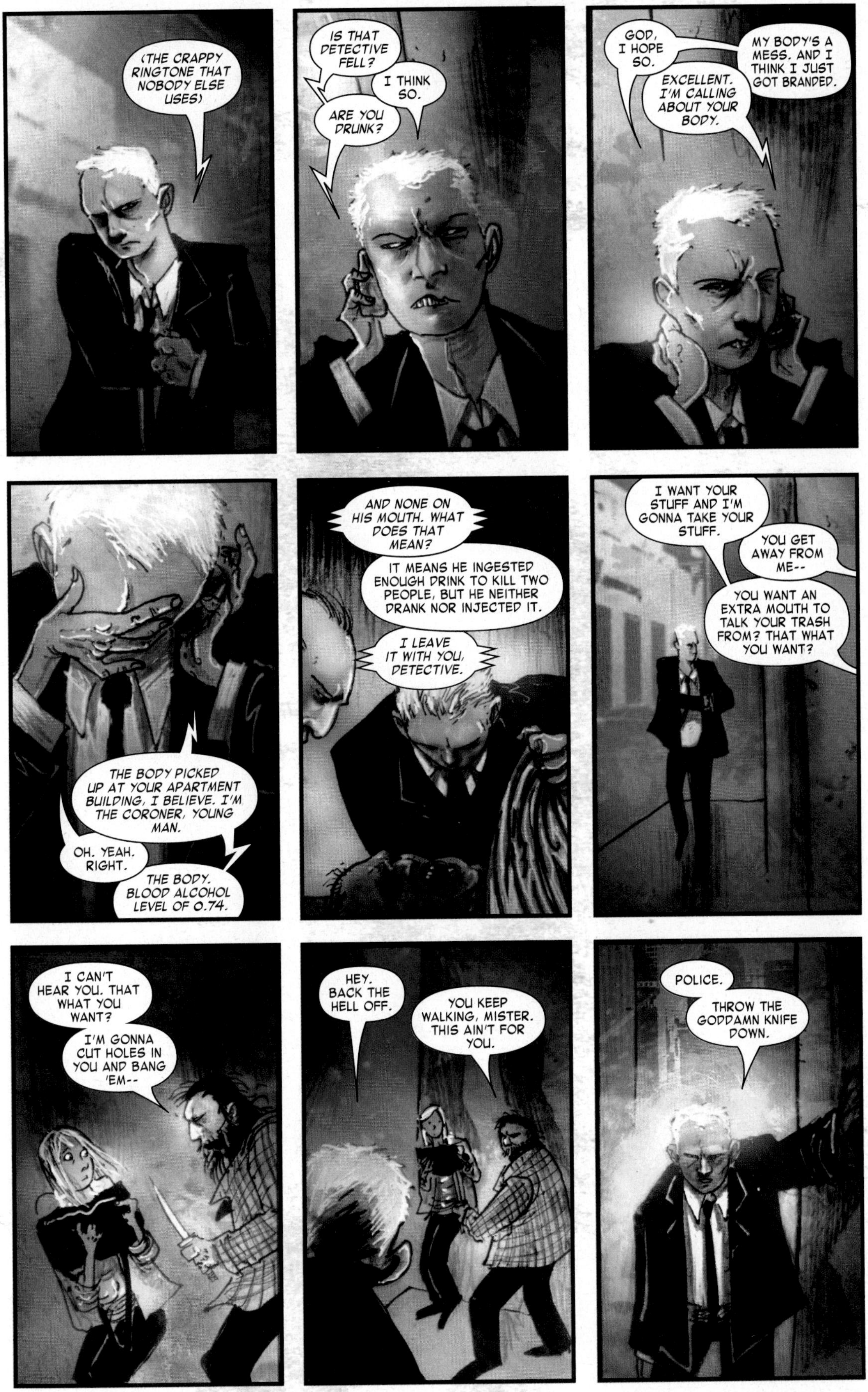
(THE CRAPPY RINGTONE THAT NOBODY ELSE USES)
IS THAT DETECTIVE FELL?
I THINK SO.
ARE YOU DRUNK?
GOD, I HOPE SO.
EXCELLENT. I'M CALLING ABOUT YOUR BODY.
MY BODY'S A MESS. AND I THINK I JUST GOT BRANDED.
THE BODY PICKED UP AT YOUR APARTMENT BUILDING, I BELIEVE. I'M THE CORONER, YOUNG MAN.
OH. YEAH. RIGHT.
THE BODY. BLOOD ALCOHOL LEVEL OF 0.74.
AND NONE ON HIS MOUTH. WHAT DOES THAT MEAN?
IT MEANS HE INGESTED ENOUGH DRINK TO KILL TWO PEOPLE, BUT HE NEITHER DRANK NOR INJECTED IT.
I LEAVE IT WITH YOU, DETECTIVE.
I WANT YOUR STUFF AND I'M GONNA TAKE YOUR STUFF.
YOU GET AWAY FROM ME--
YOU WANT AN EXTRA MOUTH TO TALK YOUR TRASH FROM? THAT WHAT YOU WANT?
I CAN'T HEAR YOU. THAT WHAT YOU WANT?
I'M GONNA CUT HOLES IN YOU AND BANG 'EM--
HEY. BACK THE HELL OFF.
YOU KEEP WALKING, MISTER. THIS AIN'T FOR YOU.
POLICE.
THROW THE GODDAMN KNIFE DOWN.

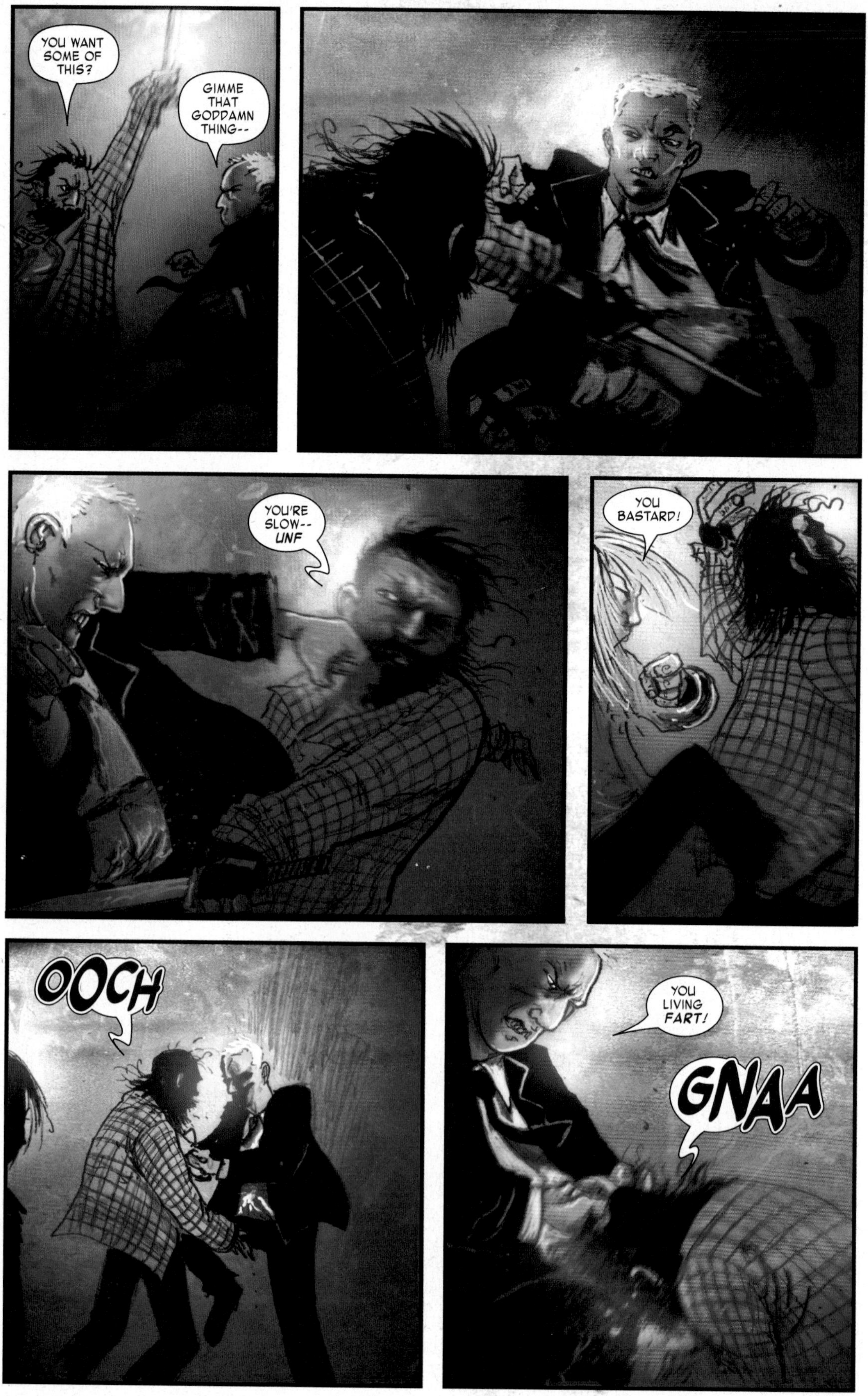
YOU WANT SOME OF THIS?
GIMME THAT GODDAMN THING--
YOU'RE SLOW-- *UNF*
YOU BASTARD!
OOCH
YOU LIVING *FART!*
GNAA

I SEE YOU AGAIN AND I'LL SHOVE THIS UP YOUR ASS SO HARD IT'LL HIT YOU IN THE BACK OF THE TEETH!

JESUS.

I COULD LEARN TO HATE THIS TOWN.

AND WHAT THE HELL ARE YOU DOING HANGING AROUND IN ALLEYWAYS?

I CAN'T GO HOME.

MY DAD'S DEAD.

AH, HELL.

WHAT HAPPENED?

HE DIED THIS MORNING. DRINK.

HE WAS A SCUMBAG, BUT HE WAS MY DAD, YOU KNOW?

MY MOM NEVER LAID A FINGER ON ME LIKE HE DID, BUT SHE'S LIKE A HUNDRED TIMES WORSE.

HE MADE THIS FOR ME LAST BIRTHDAY. SHE FORGOT IT.

DRANK HIMSELF TO DEATH?

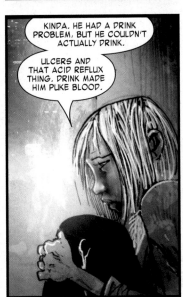

KINDA. HE HAD A DRINK PROBLEM, BUT HE COULDN'T ACTUALLY DRINK.

ULCERS AND THAT ACID REFLUX THING. DRINK MADE HIM PUKE BLOOD.

HE DOES--DID--THIS THING WITH BAGS AND PIPES? TO GET THE DRINK INTO HIM? JUST WINE, NOTHING STRONG.

I SAW HIM DO IT WHEN I WAS A KID, BUT THE LAST FEW YEARS, HE WOULDN'T LET ME SEE. I DON'T REMEMBER IT TOO WELL.

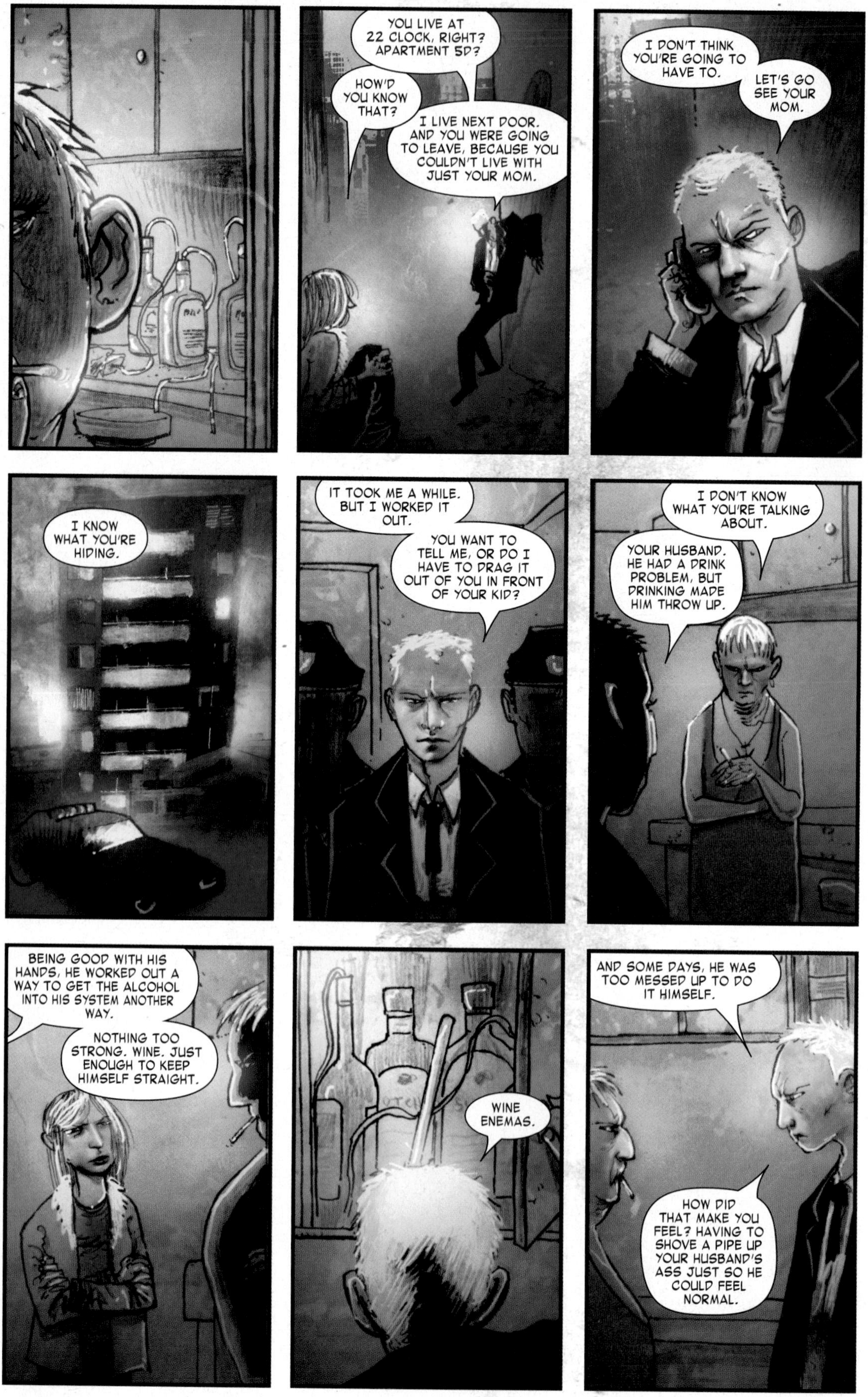

YOU LIVE AT 22 CLOCK, RIGHT? APARTMENT 5D?
HOW'D YOU KNOW THAT?
I LIVE NEXT DOOR. AND YOU WERE GOING TO LEAVE, BECAUSE YOU COULDN'T LIVE WITH JUST YOUR MOM.
I DON'T THINK YOU'RE GOING TO HAVE TO.
LET'S GO SEE YOUR MOM.
I KNOW WHAT YOU'RE HIDING.
IT TOOK ME A WHILE. BUT I WORKED IT OUT.
YOU WANT TO TELL ME, OR DO I HAVE TO DRAG IT OUT OF YOU IN FRONT OF YOUR KID?
I DON'T KNOW WHAT YOU'RE TALKING ABOUT.
YOUR HUSBAND. HE HAD A DRINK PROBLEM, BUT DRINKING MADE HIM THROW UP.
BEING GOOD WITH HIS HANDS, HE WORKED OUT A WAY TO GET THE ALCOHOL INTO HIS SYSTEM ANOTHER WAY.
NOTHING TOO STRONG. WINE. JUST ENOUGH TO KEEP HIMSELF STRAIGHT.
WINE ENEMAS.
AND SOME DAYS, HE WAS TOO MESSED UP TO DO IT HIMSELF.
HOW DID THAT MAKE YOU FEEL? HAVING TO SHOVE A PIPE UP YOUR HUSBAND'S ASS JUST SO HE COULD FEEL NORMAL.

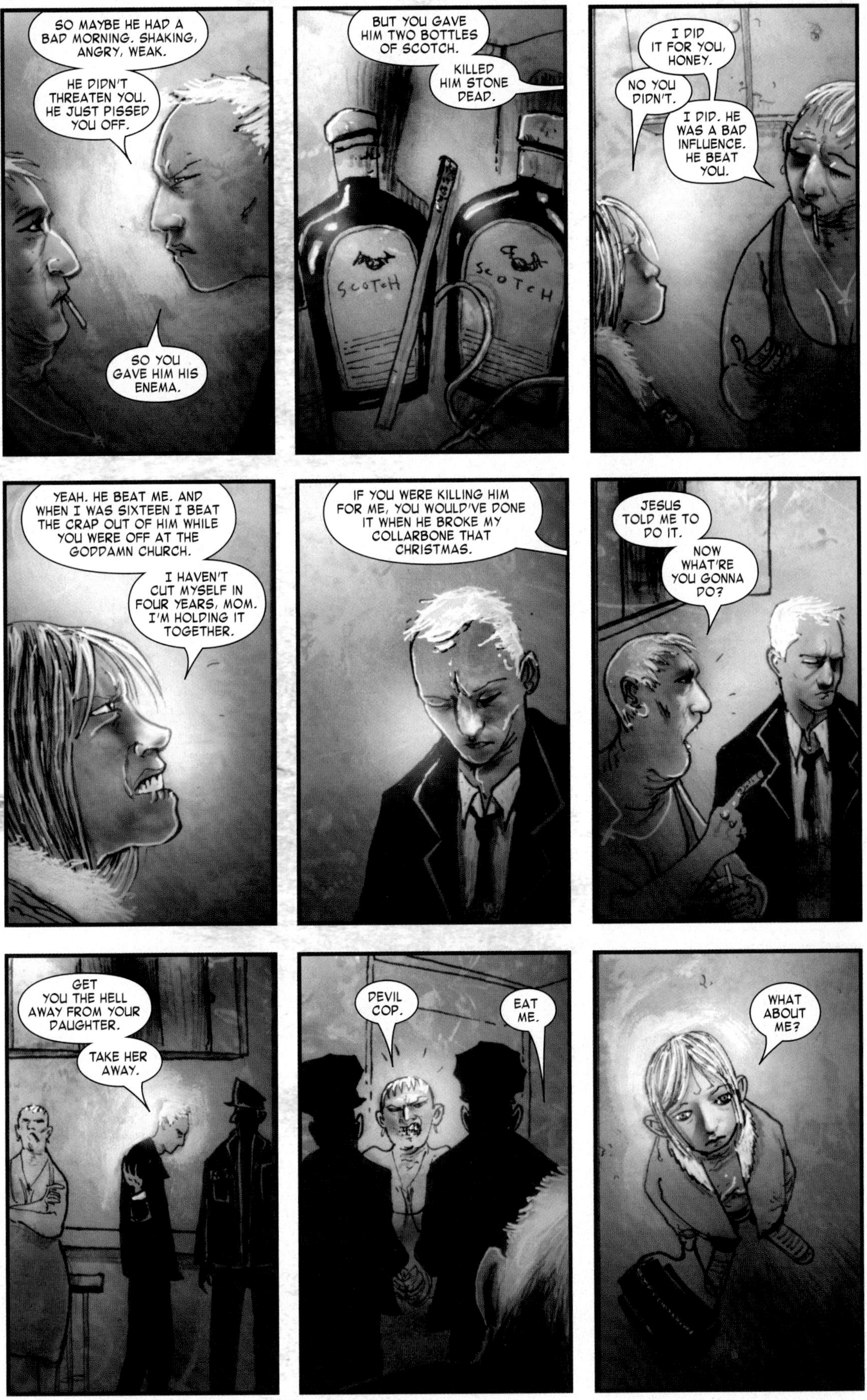
SO MAYBE HE HAD A BAD MORNING. SHAKING, ANGRY, WEAK.
HE DIDN'T THREATEN YOU. HE JUST PISSED YOU OFF.
SO YOU GAVE HIM HIS ENEMA.
BUT YOU GAVE HIM TWO BOTTLES OF SCOTCH.
KILLED HIM STONE DEAD.
SCOTCH
SCOTCH
I DID IT FOR YOU, HONEY.
NO YOU DIDN'T.
I DID. HE WAS A BAD INFLUENCE. HE BEAT YOU.
YEAH. HE BEAT ME. AND WHEN I WAS SIXTEEN I BEAT THE CRAP OUT OF HIM WHILE YOU WERE OFF AT THE GODDAMN CHURCH.
I HAVEN'T CUT MYSELF IN FOUR YEARS, MOM. I'M HOLDING IT TOGETHER.
IF YOU WERE KILLING HIM FOR ME, YOU WOULD'VE DONE IT WHEN HE BROKE MY COLLARBONE THAT CHRISTMAS.
JESUS TOLD ME TO DO IT.
NOW WHAT'RE YOU GONNA DO?
GET YOU THE HELL AWAY FROM YOUR DAUGHTER.
TAKE HER AWAY.
DEVIL COP.
EAT ME.
WHAT ABOUT ME?

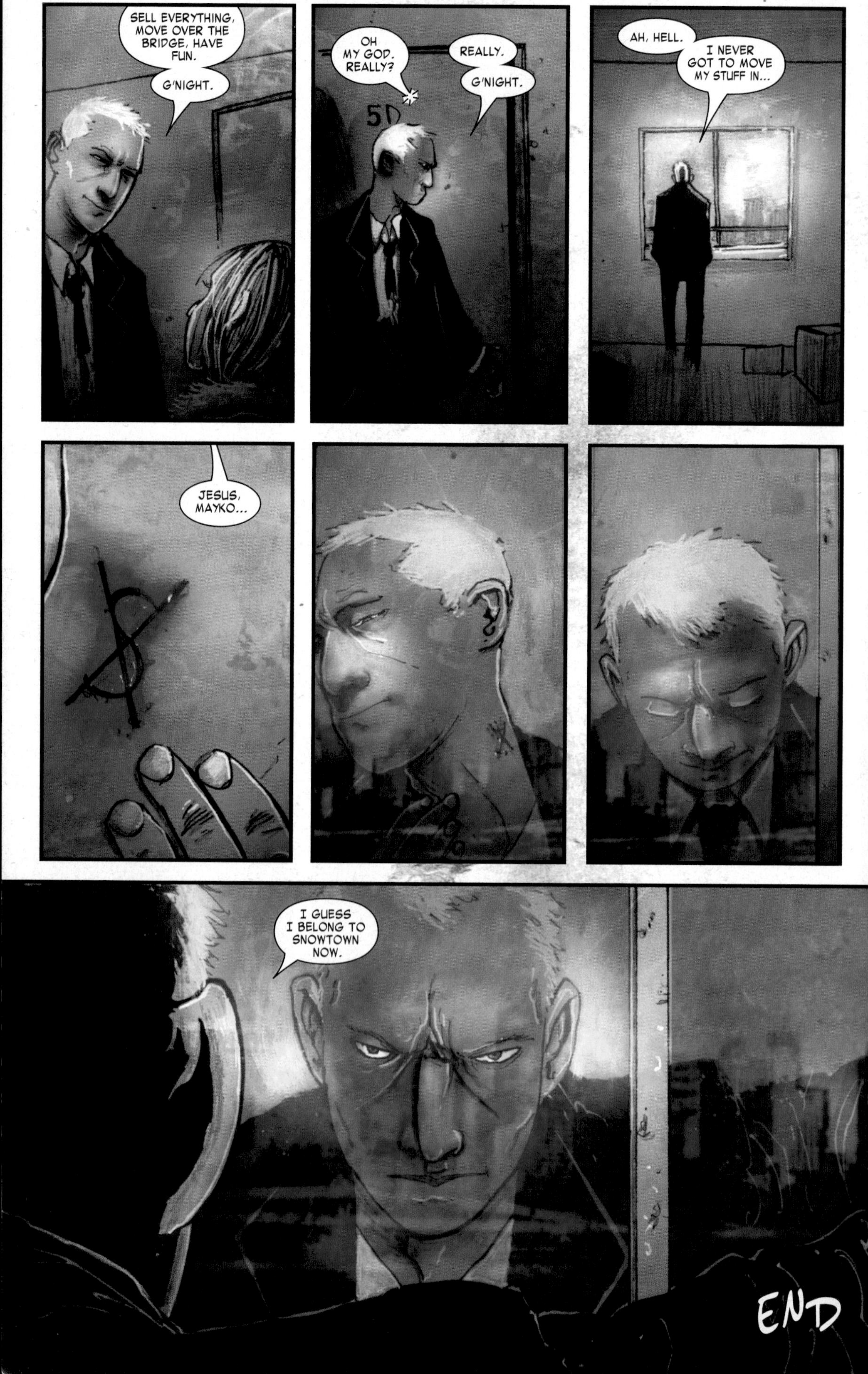
SELL EVERYTHING, MOVE OVER THE BRIDGE, HAVE FUN.
G'NIGHT.
OH MY GOD. REALLY?
REALLY.
G'NIGHT.
5D
AH, HELL.
I NEVER GOT TO MOVE MY STUFF IN...
JESUS, MAYKO...
I GUESS I BELONG TO SNOWTOWN NOW.
END

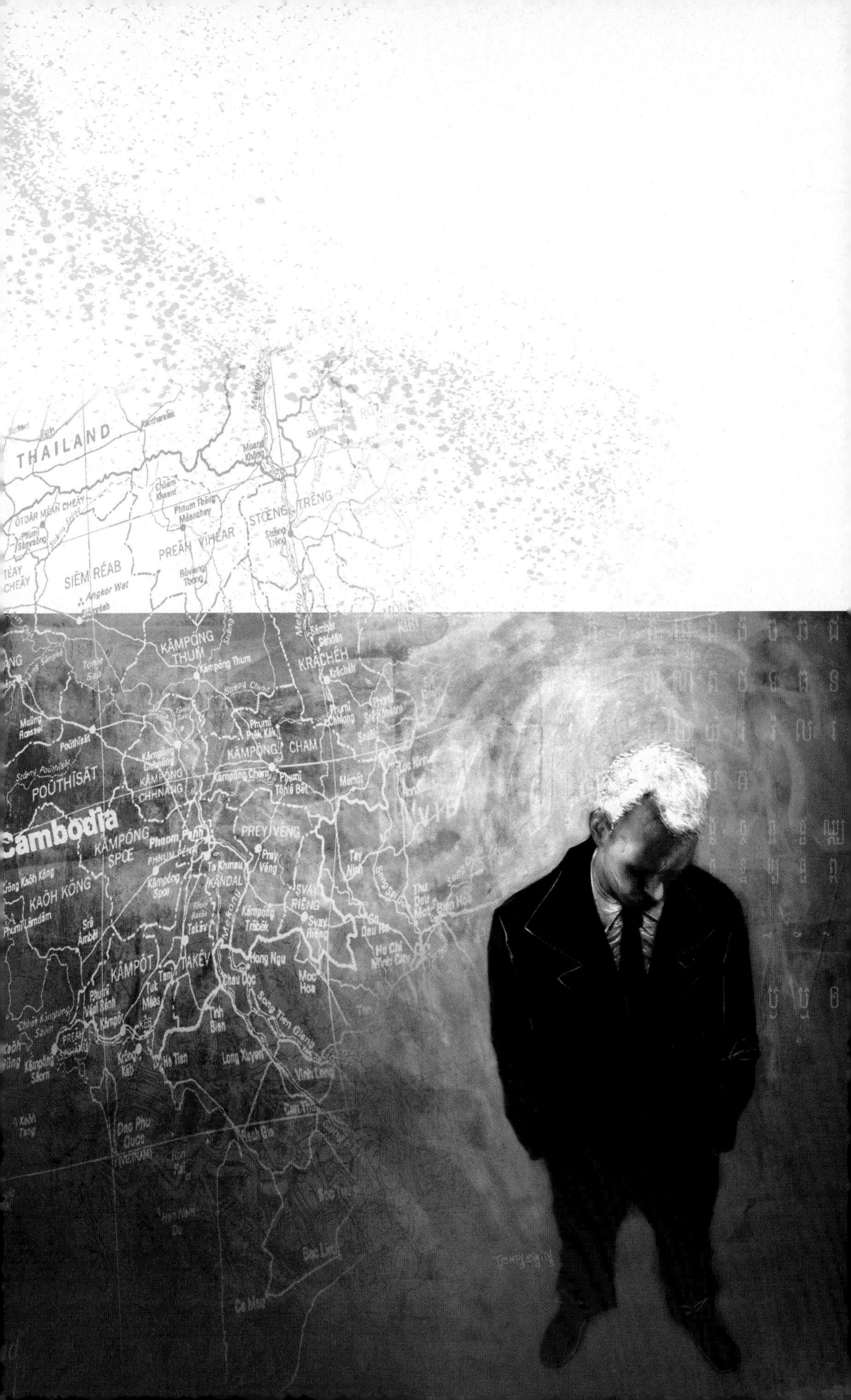
THAILAND
SIĔM RÉAB
PREĂH VIHEAR
STŒNG TRĔNG
Angkor Wat
KĂMPONG THUM
KRACHÉH
KĂMPONG CHAM
POŬTHĬSĂT
KĂMPONG CHHNANG
Cambodia
KĂMPONG SPŒ
Phnom Penh
PREY VENG
SVAY RIĔNG
KAŎH KONG
KÂNDAL
KĂMPOT
TAKĔV
Mekong
Hong Ngu
Chau Doc
Long Xuyen
Ha Tien
Templesmith

# F E L L .

CHAPTER

## 2

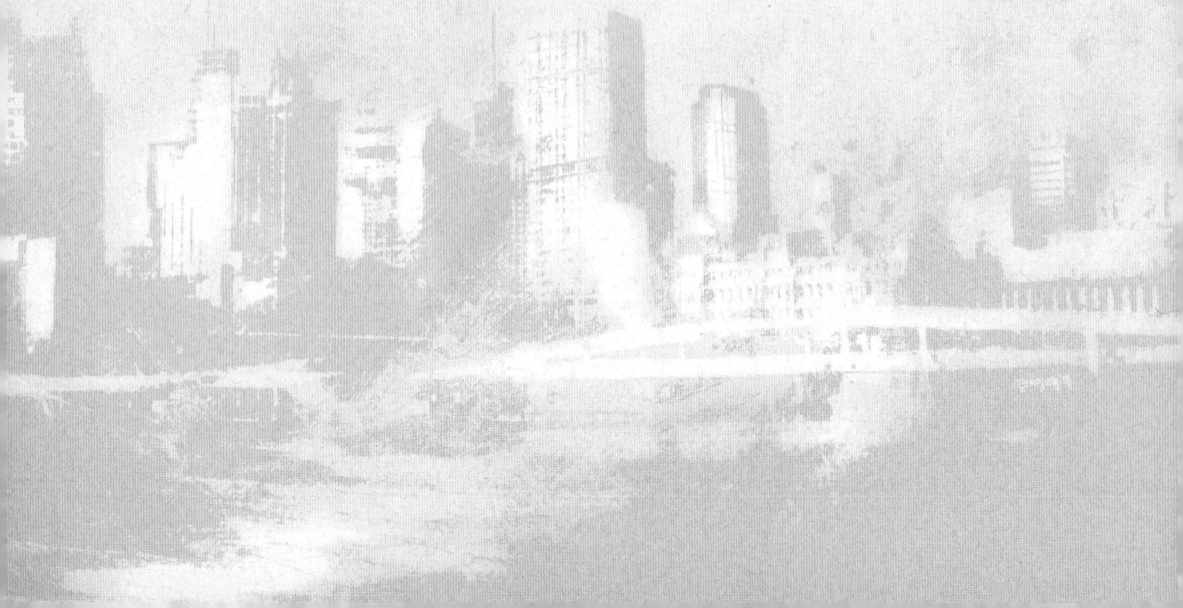

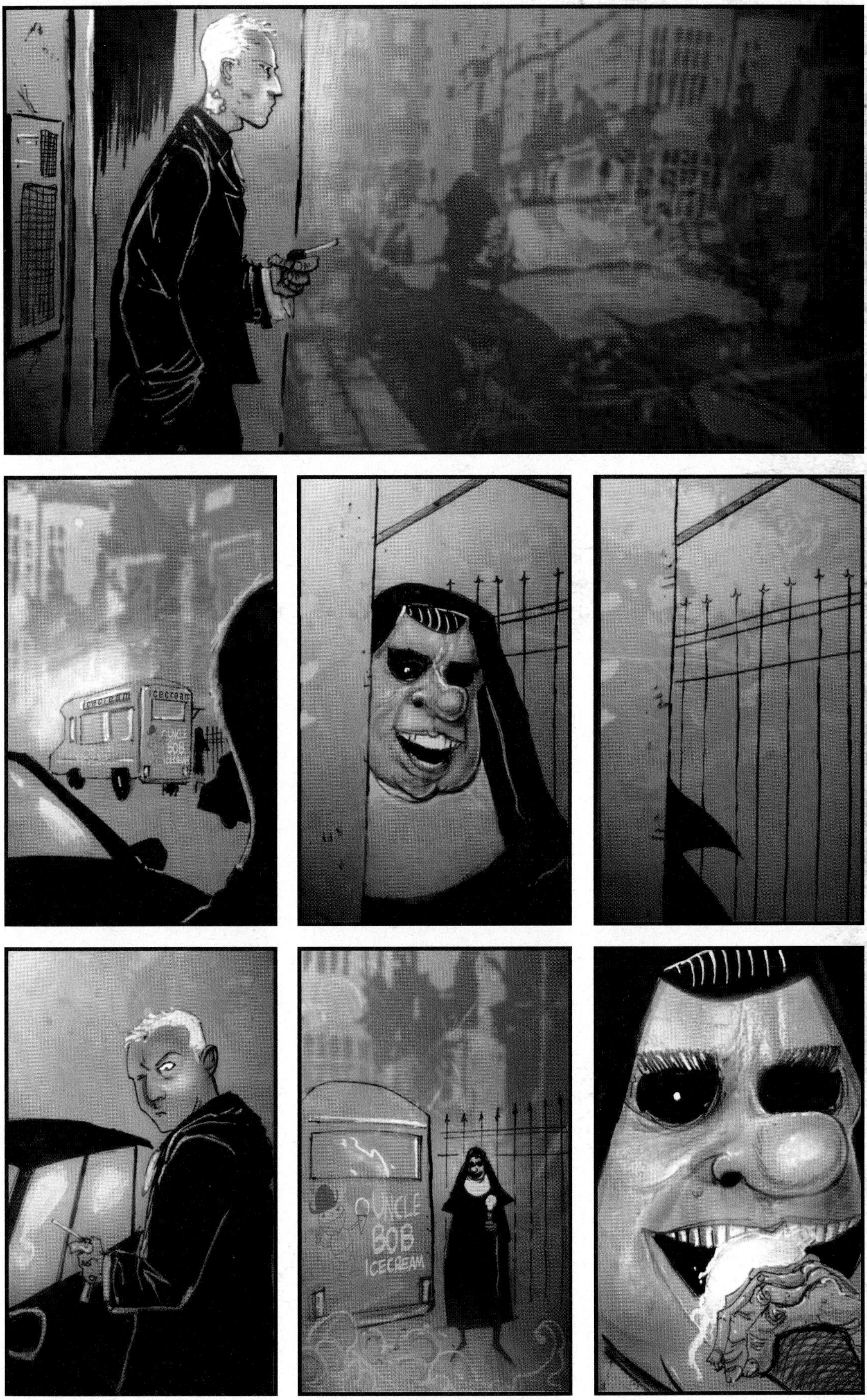
icecream
icecream
UNCLE
BOB
ICECREAM
UNCLE
BOB
ICECREAM

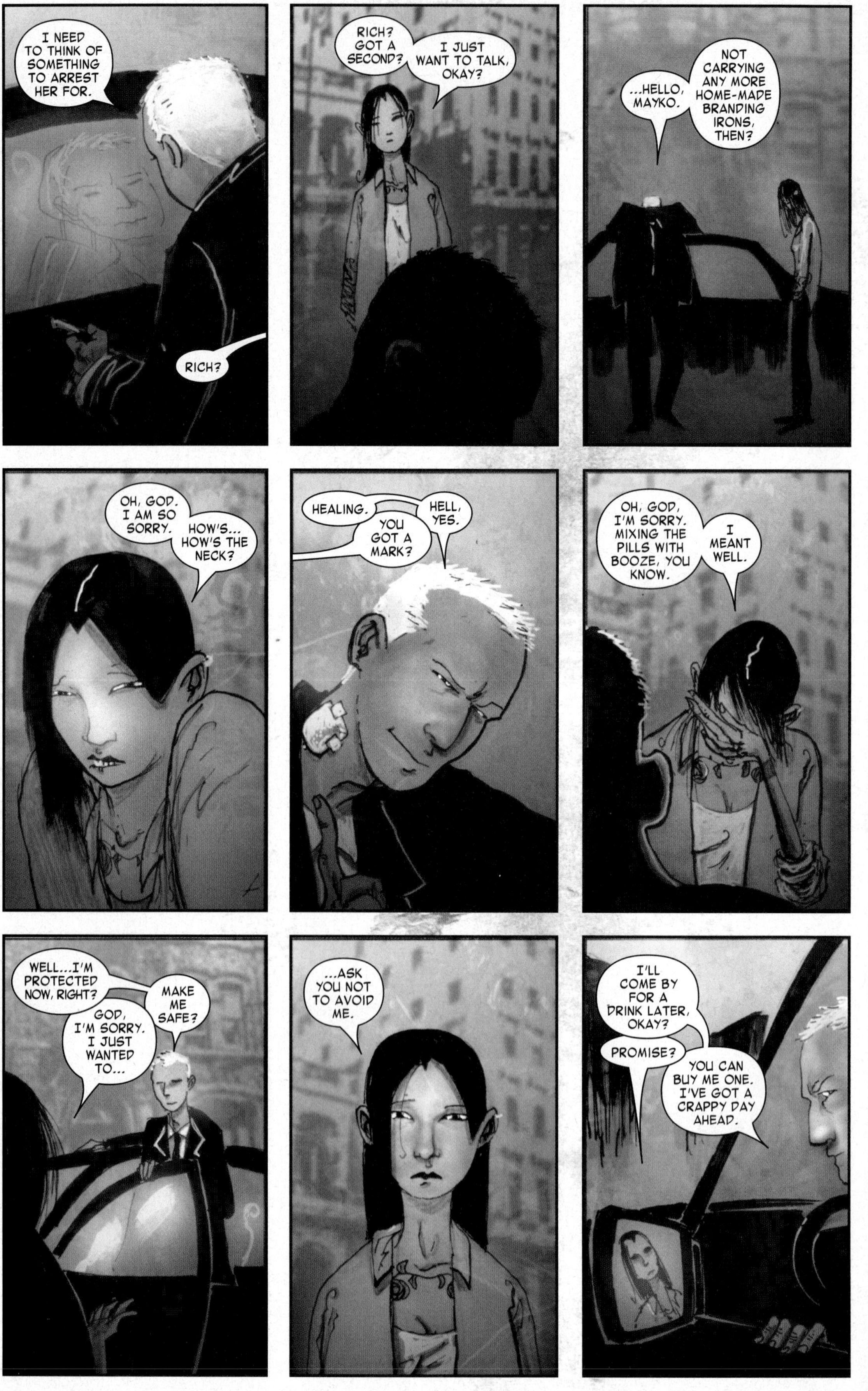

I NEED TO THINK OF SOMETHING TO ARREST HER FOR.
RICH?
RICH? GOT A SECOND?
I JUST WANT TO TALK, OKAY?
...HELLO, MAYKO.
NOT CARRYING ANY MORE HOME-MADE BRANDING IRONS, THEN?
OH, GOD. I AM SO SORRY.
HOW'S... HOW'S THE NECK?
HEALING.
YOU GOT A MARK?
HELL, YES.
OH, GOD, I'M SORRY. MIXING THE PILLS WITH BOOZE, YOU KNOW.
I MEANT WELL.
WELL...I'M PROTECTED NOW, RIGHT?
MAKE ME SAFE?
GOD, I'M SORRY. I JUST WANTED TO...
...ASK YOU NOT TO AVOID ME.
I'LL COME BY FOR A DRINK LATER, OKAY?
PROMISE?
YOU CAN BUY ME ONE. I'VE GOT A CRAPPY DAY AHEAD.

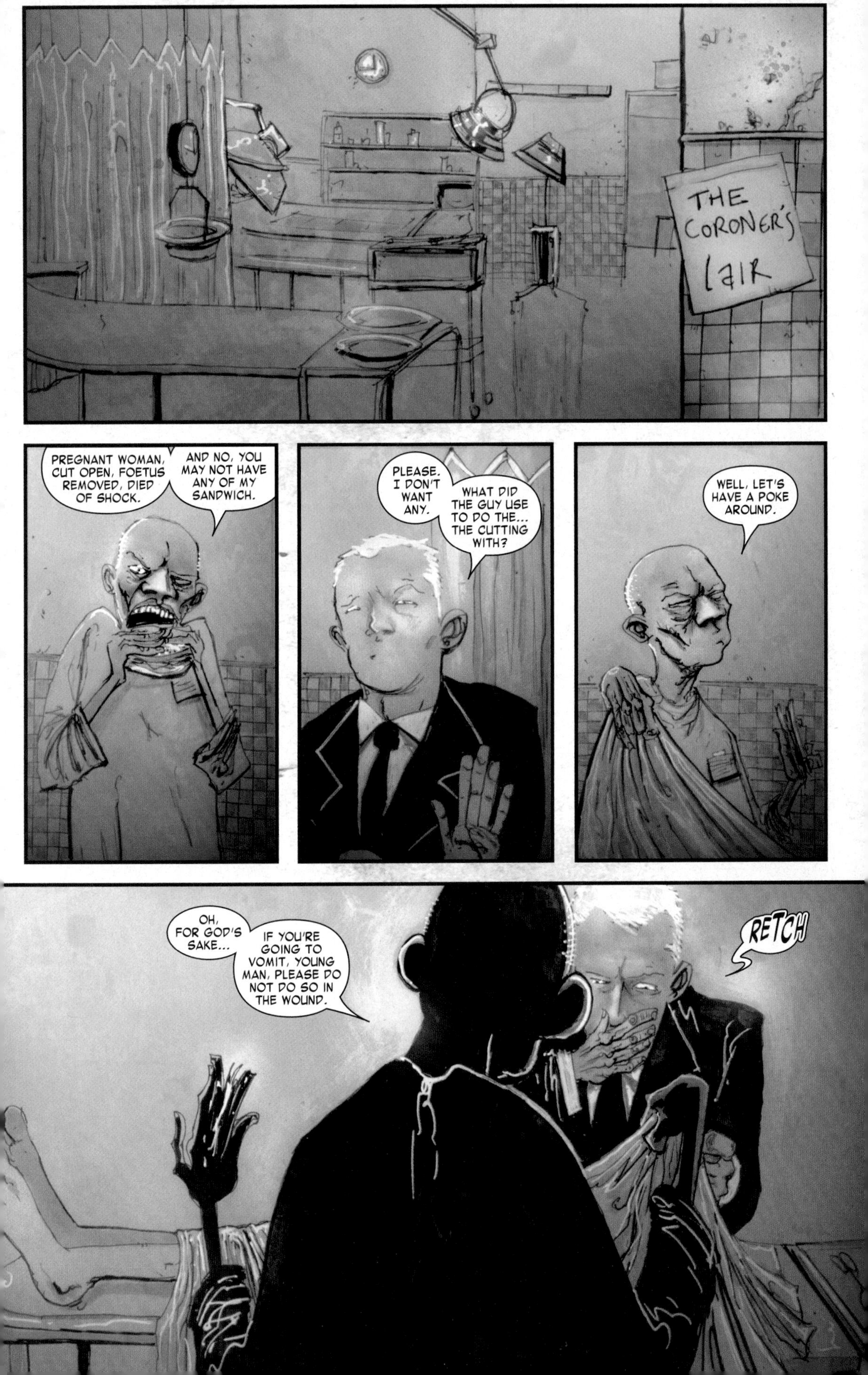
THE CORONER'S lair
PREGNANT WOMAN, CUT OPEN, FOETUS REMOVED, DIED OF SHOCK.
AND NO, YOU MAY NOT HAVE ANY OF MY SANDWICH.
PLEASE. I DON'T WANT ANY.
WHAT DID THE GUY USE TO DO THE... THE CUTTING WITH?
WELL, LET'S HAVE A POKE AROUND.
OH, FOR GOD'S SAKE...
IF YOU'RE GOING TO VOMIT, YOUNG MAN, PLEASE DO NOT DO SO IN THE WOUND.
RETCH

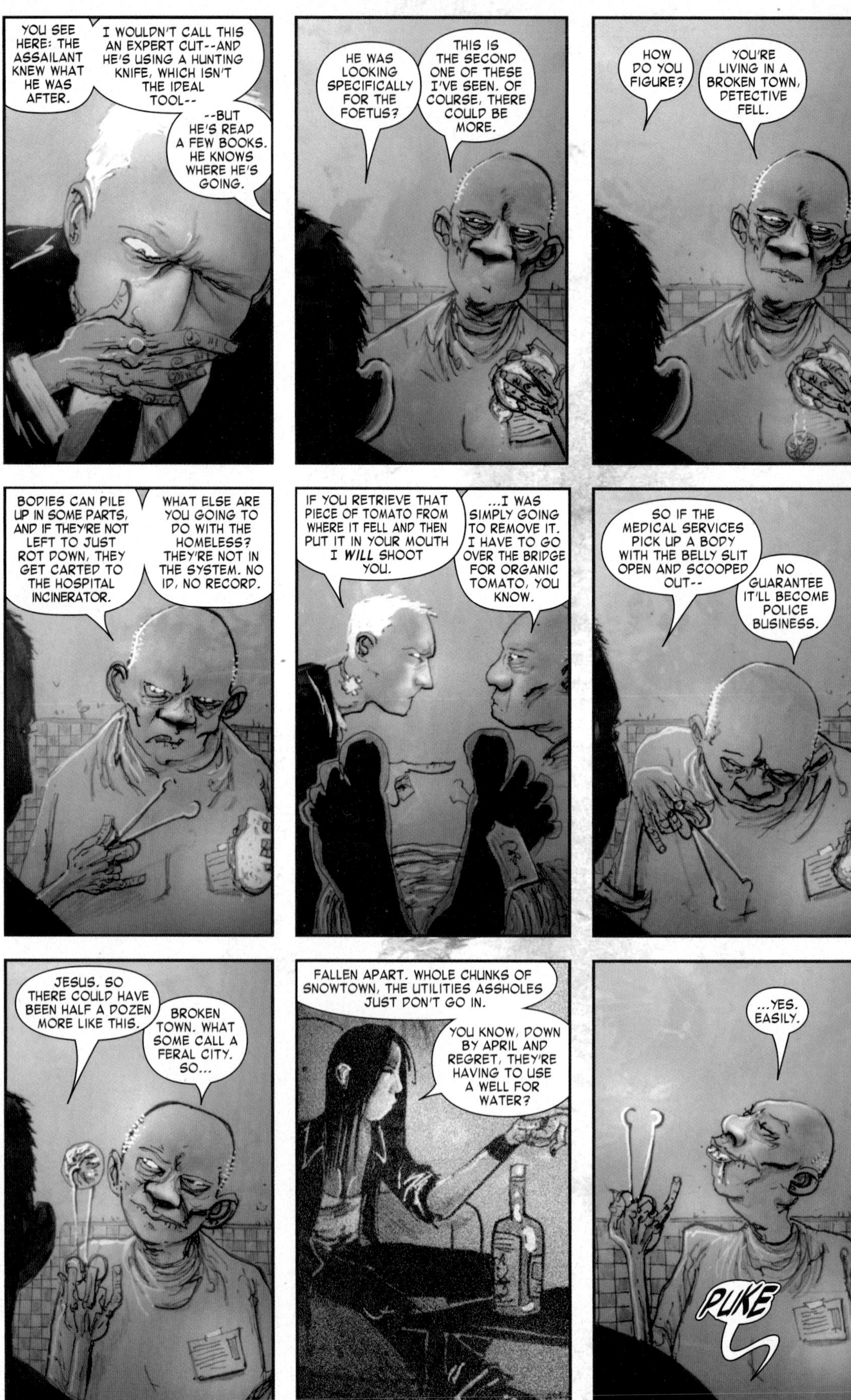
YOU SEE HERE: THE ASSAILANT KNEW WHAT HE WAS AFTER.
I WOULDN'T CALL THIS AN EXPERT CUT--AND HE'S USING A HUNTING KNIFE, WHICH ISN'T THE IDEAL TOOL--
--BUT HE'S READ A FEW BOOKS. HE KNOWS WHERE HE'S GOING.
HE WAS LOOKING SPECIFICALLY FOR THE FOETUS?
THIS IS THE SECOND ONE OF THESE I'VE SEEN. OF COURSE, THERE COULD BE MORE.
HOW DO YOU FIGURE?
YOU'RE LIVING IN A BROKEN TOWN, DETECTIVE FELL.
BODIES CAN PILE UP IN SOME PARTS, AND IF THEY'RE NOT LEFT TO JUST ROT DOWN, THEY GET CARTED TO THE HOSPITAL INCINERATOR.
WHAT ELSE ARE YOU GOING TO DO WITH THE HOMELESS? THEY'RE NOT IN THE SYSTEM. NO ID, NO RECORD.
IF YOU RETRIEVE THAT PIECE OF TOMATO FROM WHERE IT FELL AND THEN PUT IT IN YOUR MOUTH I *WILL* SHOOT YOU.
...I WAS SIMPLY GOING TO REMOVE IT. I HAVE TO GO OVER THE BRIDGE FOR ORGANIC TOMATO, YOU KNOW.
SO IF THE MEDICAL SERVICES PICK UP A BODY WITH THE BELLY SLIT OPEN AND SCOOPED OUT--
NO GUARANTEE IT'LL BECOME POLICE BUSINESS.
JESUS. SO THERE COULD HAVE BEEN HALF A DOZEN MORE LIKE THIS.
BROKEN TOWN. WHAT SOME CALL A FERAL CITY. SO...
FALLEN APART. WHOLE CHUNKS OF SNOWTOWN, THE UTILITIES ASSHOLES JUST DON'T GO IN.
YOU KNOW, DOWN BY APRIL AND REGRET, THEY'RE HAVING TO USE A WELL FOR WATER?
...YES. EASILY.
PUKE

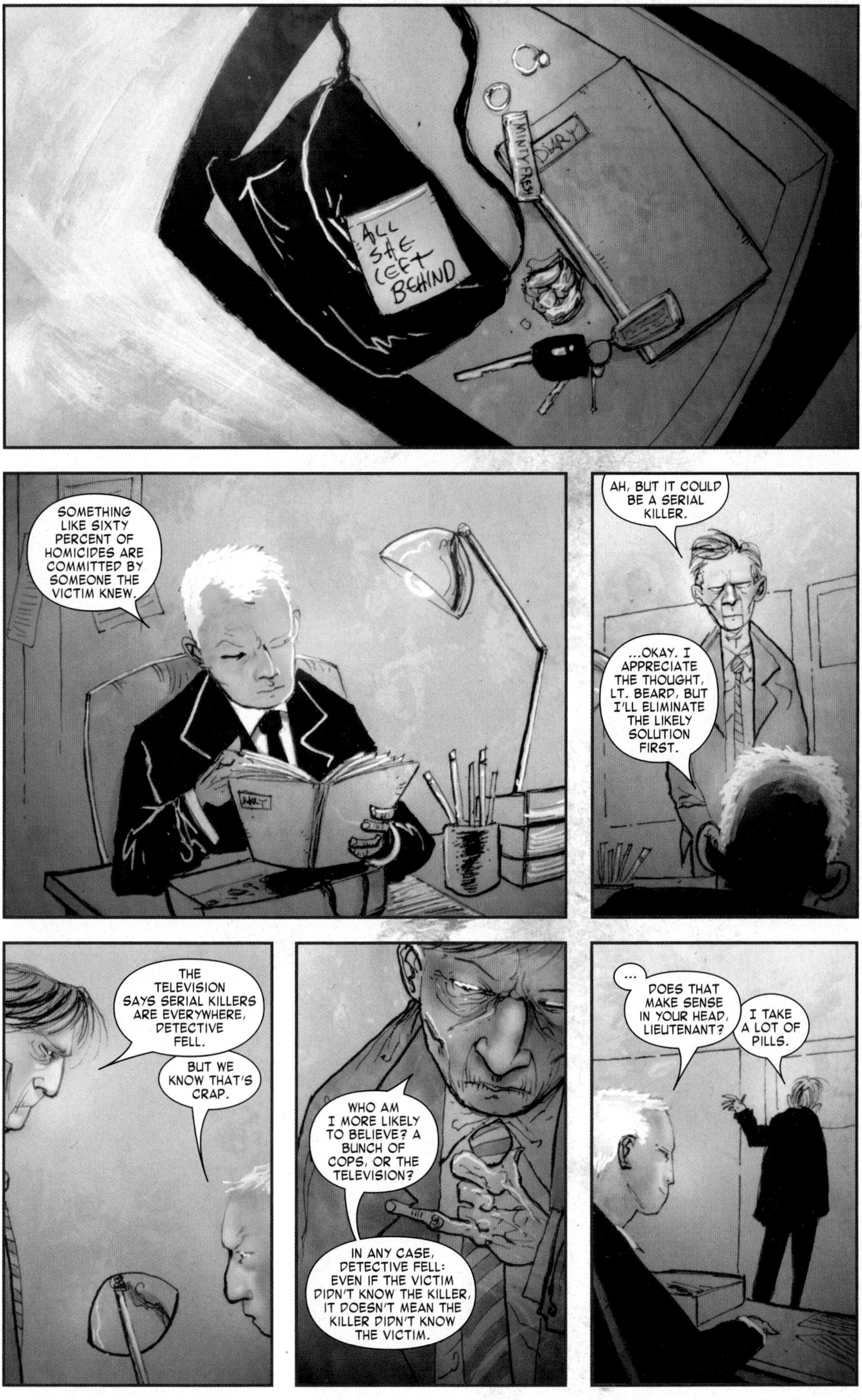
ALL SHE LEFT BEHIND
MINTY FRESH
DIARY
SOMETHING LIKE SIXTY PERCENT OF HOMICIDES ARE COMMITTED BY SOMEONE THE VICTIM KNEW.
AH, BUT IT COULD BE A SERIAL KILLER.
...OKAY. I APPRECIATE THE THOUGHT, LT. BEARD, BUT I'LL ELIMINATE THE LIKELY SOLUTION FIRST.
THE TELEVISION SAYS SERIAL KILLERS ARE EVERYWHERE, DETECTIVE FELL.
BUT WE KNOW THAT'S CRAP.
WHO AM I MORE LIKELY TO BELIEVE? A BUNCH OF COPS, OR THE TELEVISION?
IN ANY CASE, DETECTIVE FELL: EVEN IF THE VICTIM DIDN'T KNOW THE KILLER, IT DOESN'T MEAN THE KILLER DIDN'T KNOW THE VICTIM.
...
DOES THAT MAKE SENSE IN YOUR HEAD, LIEUTENANT?
I TAKE A LOT OF PILLS.

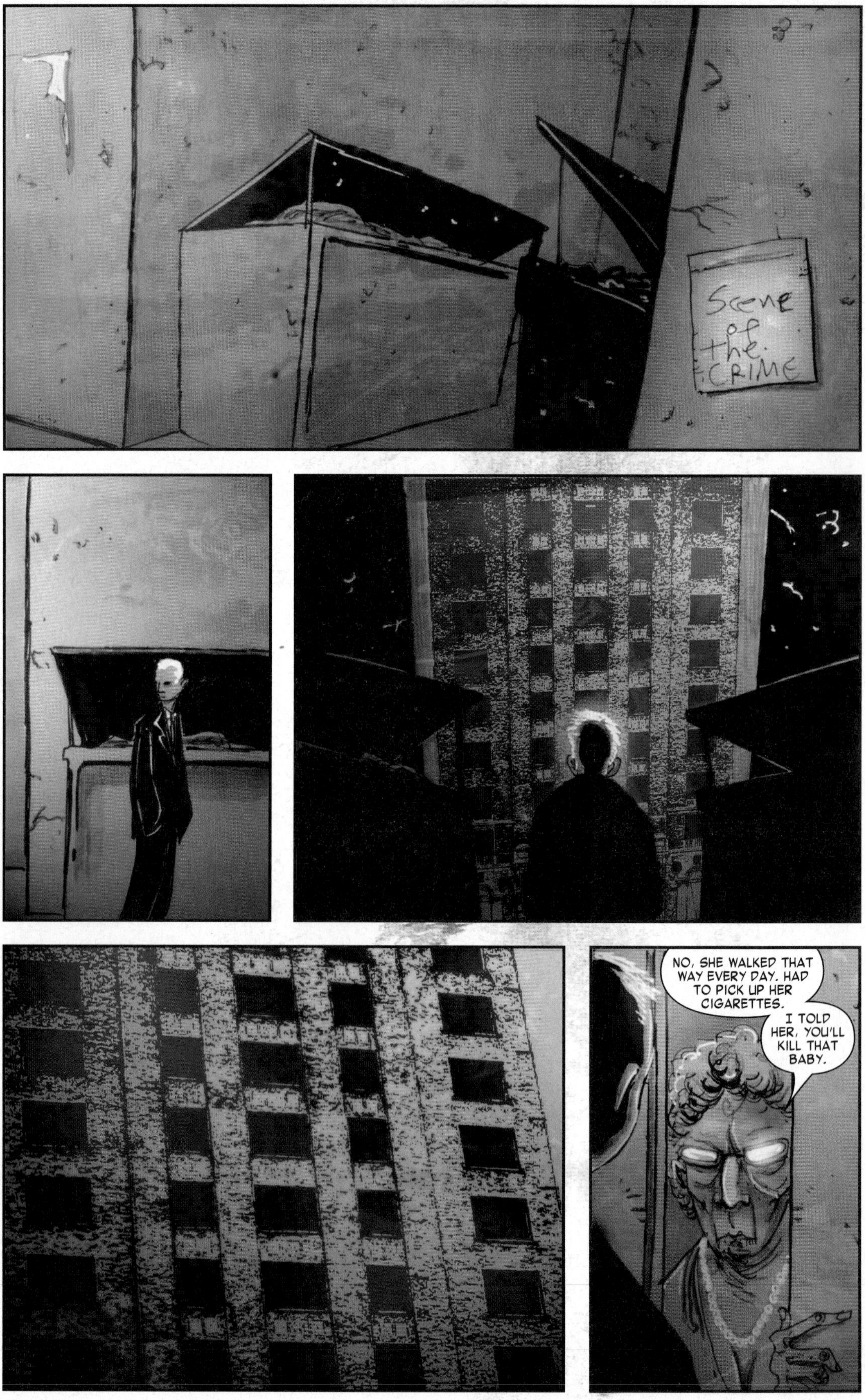
Scene of the CRIME
NO, SHE WALKED THAT WAY EVERY DAY. HAD TO PICK UP HER CIGARETTES.
I TOLD HER, YOU'LL KILL THAT BABY.

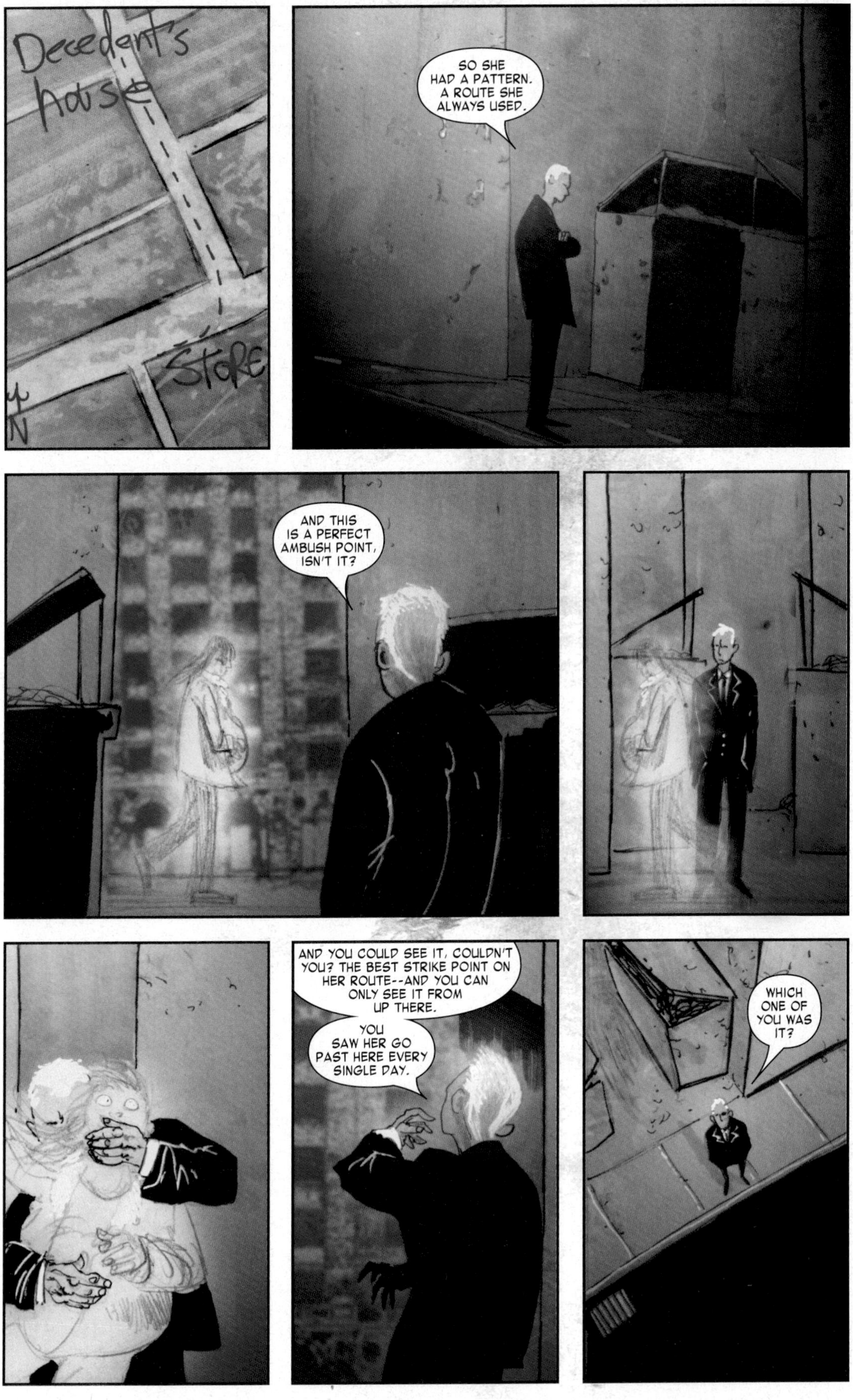
Decedent's house
STORE
SO SHE HAD A PATTERN. A ROUTE SHE ALWAYS USED.
AND THIS IS A PERFECT AMBUSH POINT, ISN'T IT?
AND YOU COULD SEE IT, COULDN'T YOU? THE BEST STRIKE POINT ON HER ROUTE--AND YOU CAN ONLY SEE IT FROM UP THERE.
YOU SAW HER GO PAST HERE EVERY SINGLE DAY.
WHICH ONE OF YOU WAS IT?

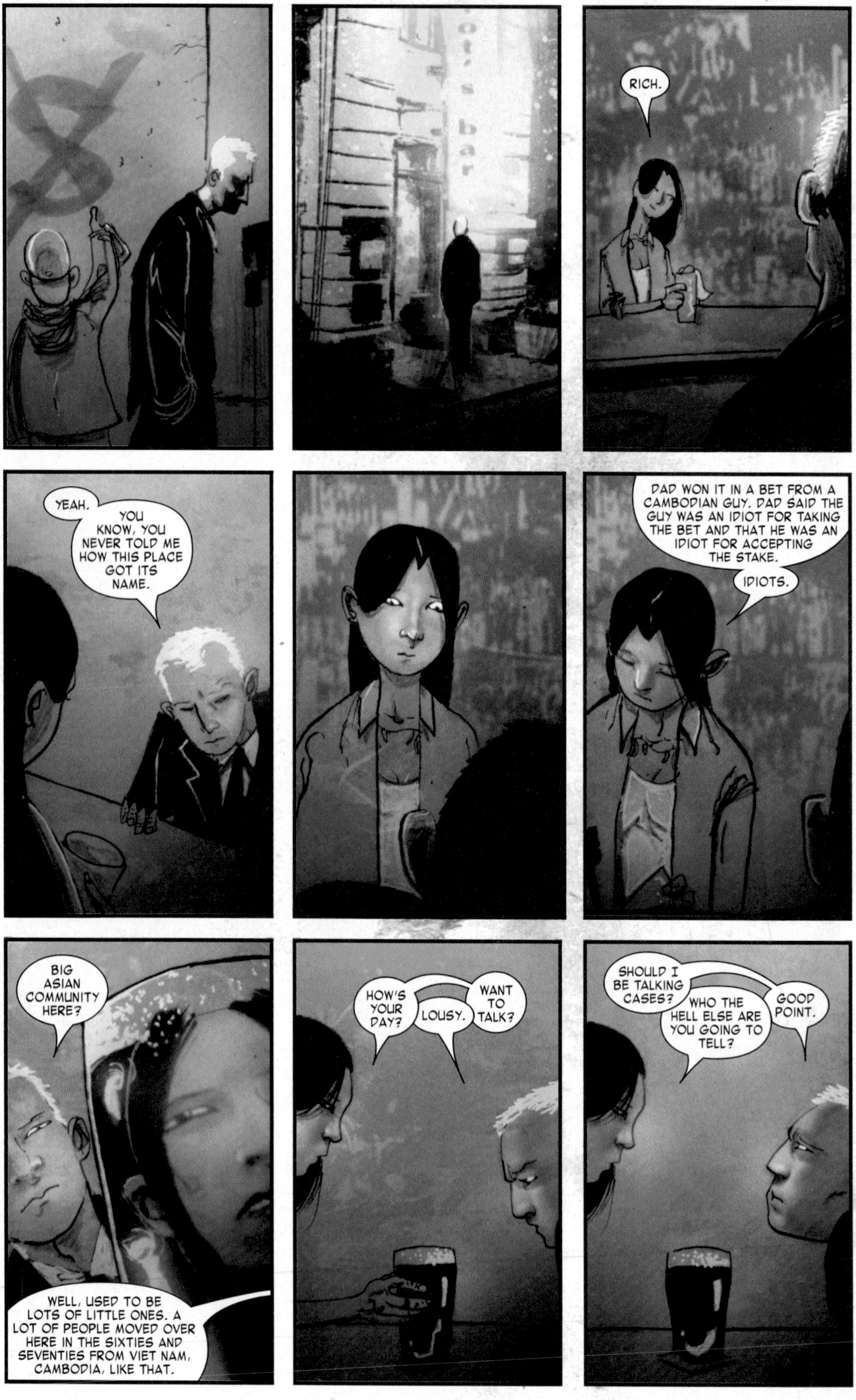

RICH.
YEAH.
YOU KNOW, YOU NEVER TOLD ME HOW THIS PLACE GOT ITS NAME.
DAD WON IT IN A BET FROM A CAMBODIAN GUY. DAD SAID THE GUY WAS AN IDIOT FOR TAKING THE BET AND THAT HE WAS AN IDIOT FOR ACCEPTING THE STAKE.
IDIOTS.
BIG ASIAN COMMUNITY HERE?
WELL, USED TO BE LOTS OF LITTLE ONES. A LOT OF PEOPLE MOVED OVER HERE IN THE SIXTIES AND SEVENTIES FROM VIET NAM, CAMBODIA, LIKE THAT.
HOW'S YOUR DAY?
LOUSY.
WANT TO TALK?
SHOULD I BE TALKING CASES?
WHO THE HELL ELSE ARE YOU GOING TO TELL?
GOOD POINT.

SOMEONE KILLED A PREGNANT WOMAN AND TOOK THE FOETUS OUT.

JESUS.

COULD HAVE HAPPENED MORE THAN ONCE, TOO. THIS SCREWED-UP TOWN, I SWEAR...

...TOOK THE FOETUS?

YEAH.

THE ONE I KNOW ABOUT WAS A REGULAR SMOKER.

THIS COULD BE A REAL NUTBAG, THE KIND OF GUY WHO THINKS HE'S SAVING AN UNBORN BABY FROM A DERELICT MOTHER.

REMINDS ME OF A STORY MY DAD TOLD ME.

GIVE.

WELL, ONE OF THE CAMBODIAN GUYS HE KNEW GOT OUT OF THE COUNTRY DURING THE WHOLE KHMER ROUGE THING. POL POT?

I DIMLY REMEMBER.

"CRAZY BASTARD" ABOUT COVERS IT. TRIED TO TAKE THE COUNTRY BACK TO THE STONE AGE, BASICALLY.

HE HAD THIS LIKE PEASANT ARMY ROAMING THE COUNTRYSIDE FOR HIM--AND, WELL, THEY DID STUFF.

THE VIETNAMESE ARMY WENT INTO CAMBODIA, IN THE END. THAT'S HOW MY DAD'S BROTHER MET THIS GUY, AND...ANYWAY.

CAMBODIA WAS KIND OF SURREAL AT THE TIME. ALMOST MEDIEVAL. OLD BELIEFS, YOU KNOW? MAGIC AND GHOSTS.

I MEAN, BEFORE POL POT TOOK POWER? THE PREVIOUS GUYS HAD A LINE OF COLORED SAND DRAWN AROUND THEIR CAPITOL TO PROTECT IT. MAGICALLY.

SOME PEOPLE SAY THE SNOWTOWN TAG CAME FROM ALL THAT.

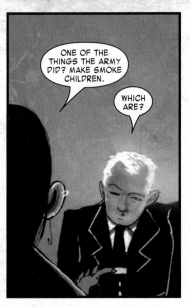

ONE OF THE THINGS THE ARMY DID? MAKE SMOKE CHILDREN.

WHICH ARE?

THEY'D CUT THE FOETUSES OUT OF PREGNANT WOMEN AND DRY THEM, THEN USE THEM AS TALISMANS TO WARD OFF EVIL.

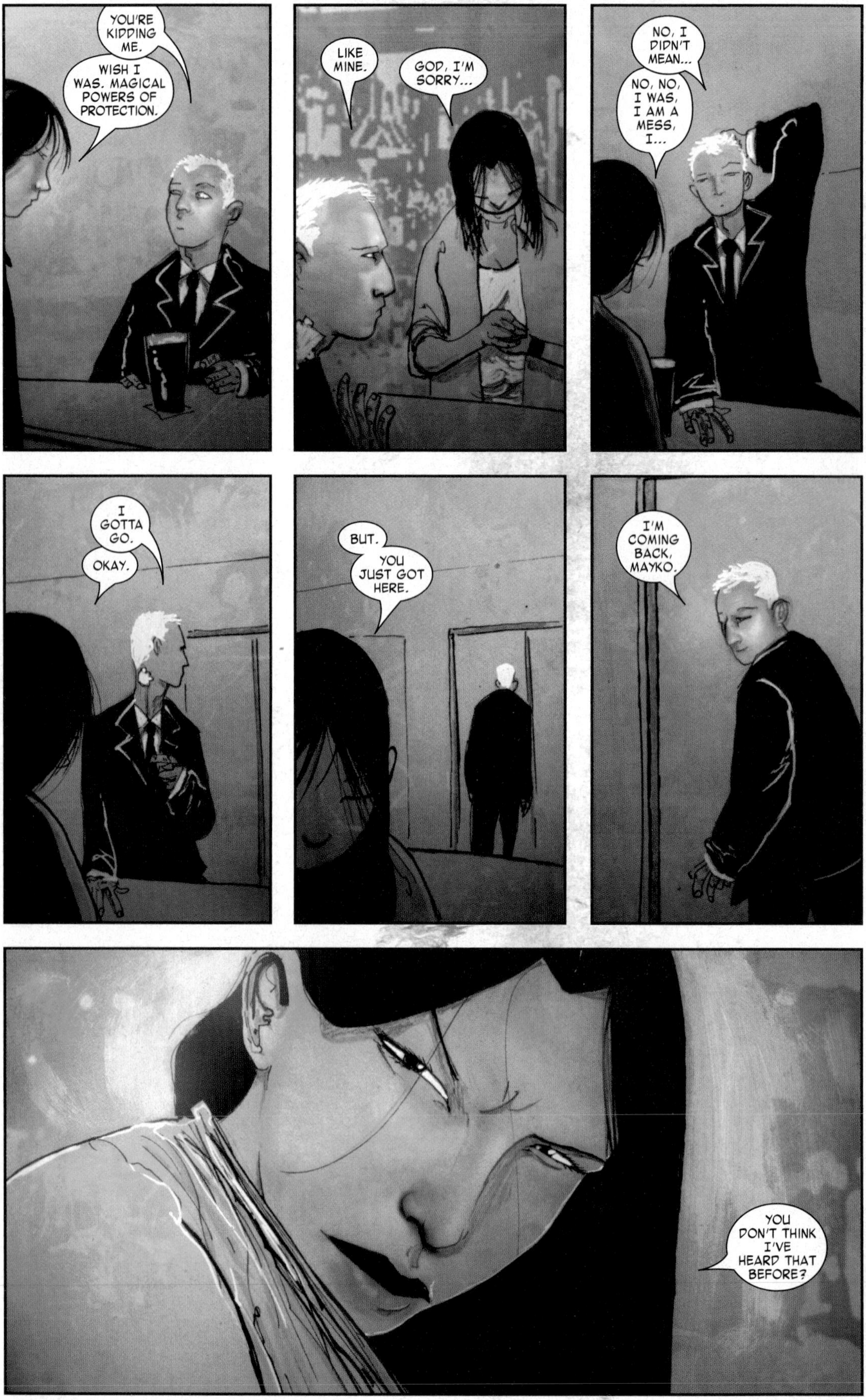
YOU'RE KIDDING ME.
WISH I WAS. MAGICAL POWERS OF PROTECTION.
LIKE MINE.
GOD, I'M SORRY...
NO, I DIDN'T MEAN...
NO, NO, I WAS, I AM A MESS, I...
I GOTTA GO.
OKAY.
BUT.
YOU JUST GOT HERE.
I'M COMING BACK, MAYKO.
YOU DON'T THINK I'VE HEARD THAT BEFORE?

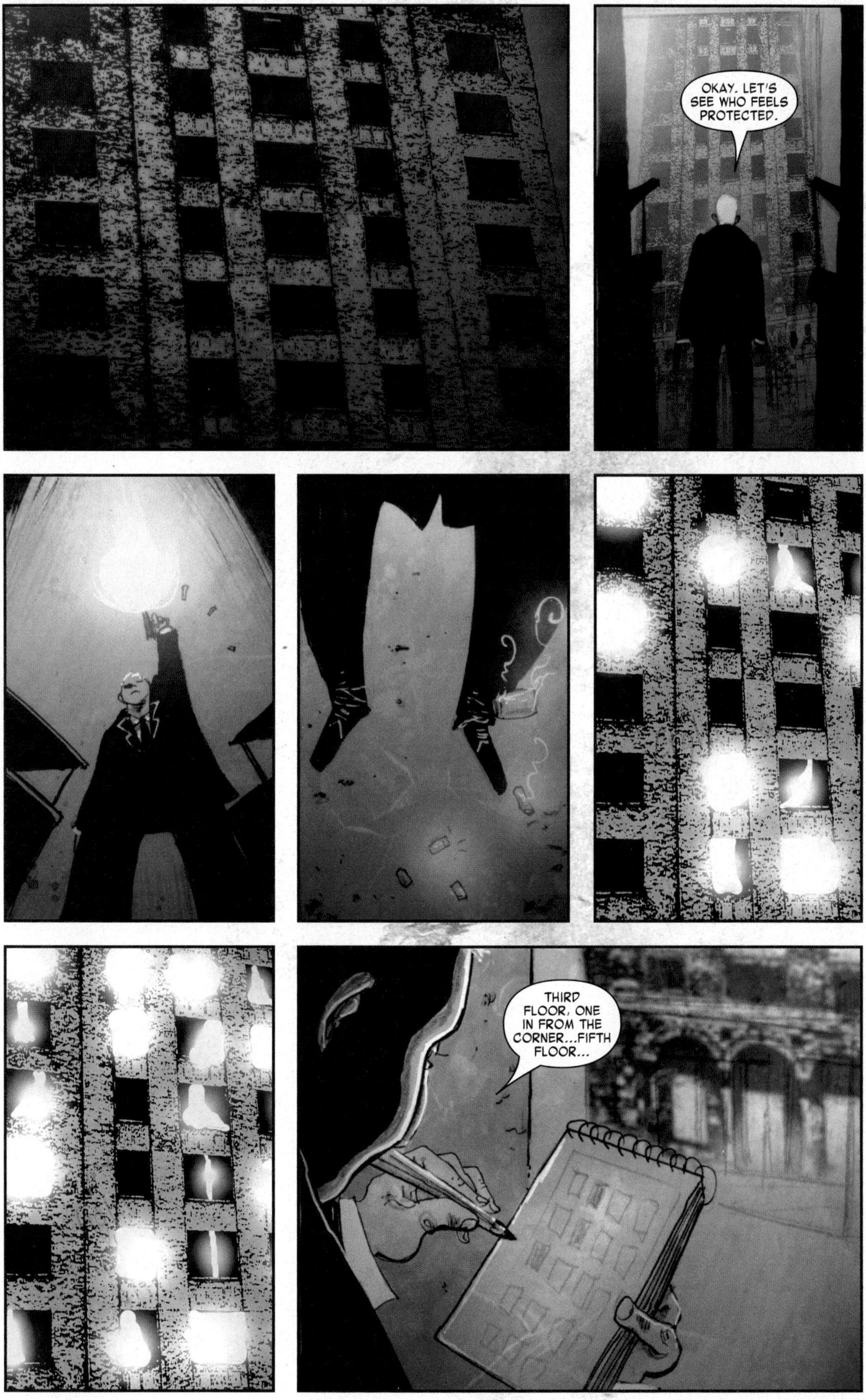
OKAY. LET'S SEE WHO FEELS PROTECTED.
THIRD FLOOR, ONE IN FROM THE CORNER...FIFTH FLOOR...

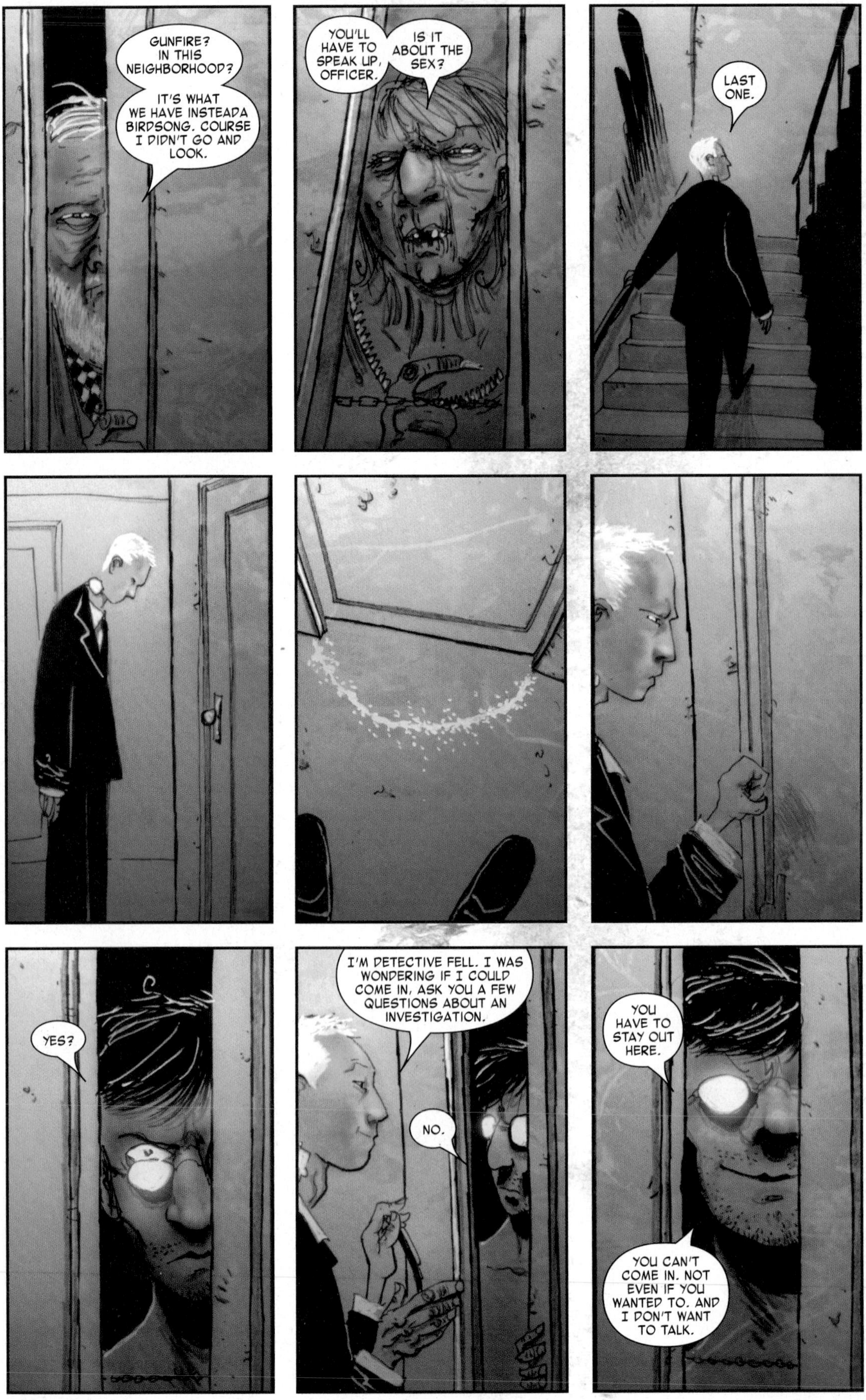

GUNFIRE? IN THIS NEIGHBORHOOD?
IT'S WHAT WE HAVE INSTEADA BIRDSONG. COURSE I DIDN'T GO AND LOOK.
YOU'LL HAVE TO SPEAK UP, OFFICER.
IS IT ABOUT THE SEX?
LAST ONE.
YES?
I'M DETECTIVE FELL. I WAS WONDERING IF I COULD COME IN, ASK YOU A FEW QUESTIONS ABOUT AN INVESTIGATION.
NO.
YOU HAVE TO STAY OUT HERE.
YOU CAN'T COME IN. NOT EVEN IF YOU WANTED TO. AND I DON'T WANT TO TALK.

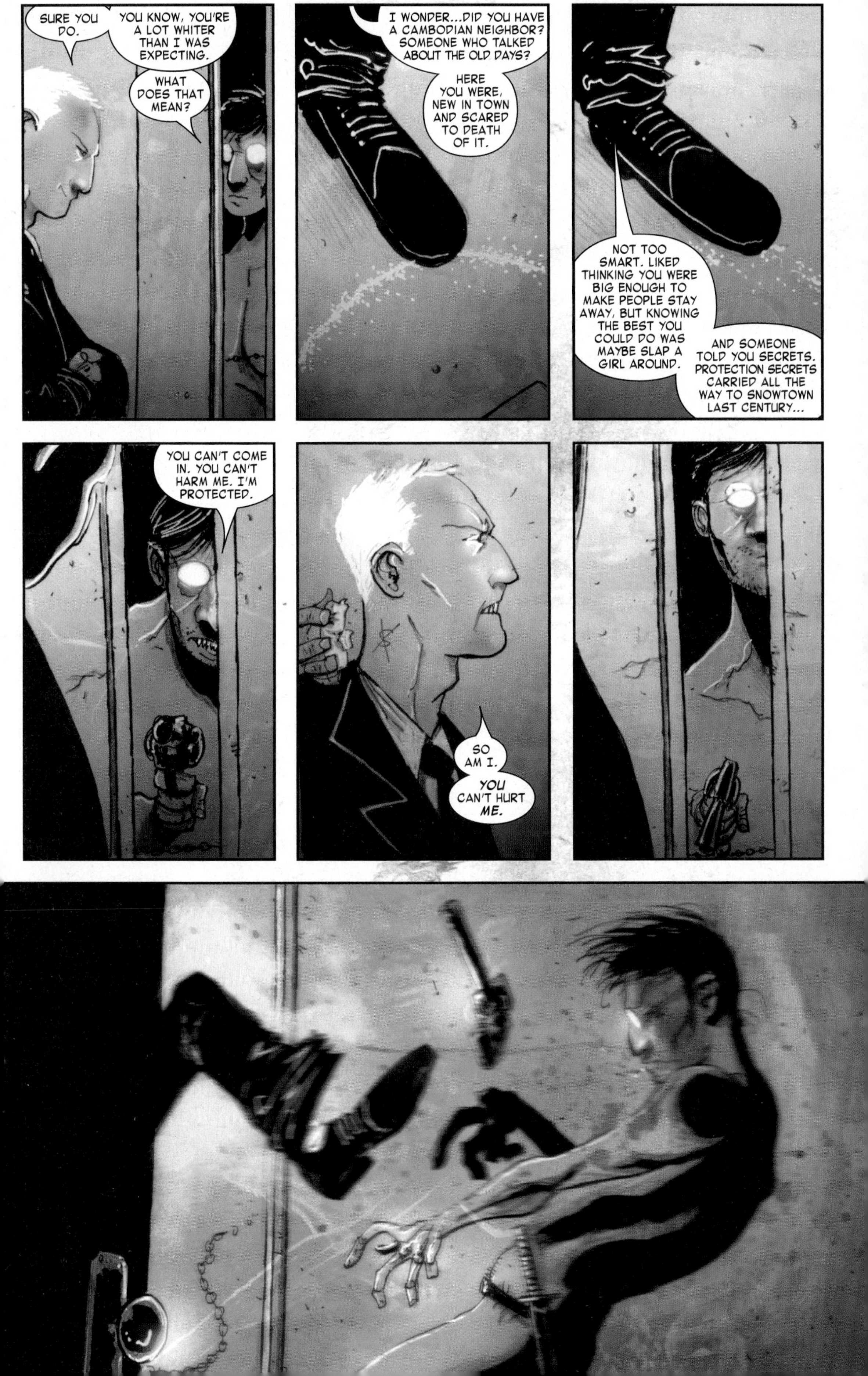
SURE YOU DO.
YOU KNOW, YOU'RE A LOT WHITER THAN I WAS EXPECTING.
WHAT DOES THAT MEAN?
I WONDER...DID YOU HAVE A CAMBODIAN NEIGHBOR? SOMEONE WHO TALKED ABOUT THE OLD DAYS?
HERE YOU WERE, NEW IN TOWN AND SCARED TO DEATH OF IT.
NOT TOO SMART. LIKED THINKING YOU WERE BIG ENOUGH TO MAKE PEOPLE STAY AWAY, BUT KNOWING THE BEST YOU COULD DO WAS MAYBE SLAP A GIRL AROUND.
AND SOMEONE TOLD YOU SECRETS. PROTECTION SECRETS CARRIED ALL THE WAY TO SNOWTOWN LAST CENTURY...
YOU CAN'T COME IN. YOU CAN'T HARM ME. I'M PROTECTED.
SO AM I.
*YOU* CAN'T HURT *ME.*

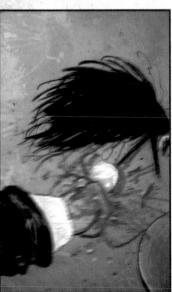

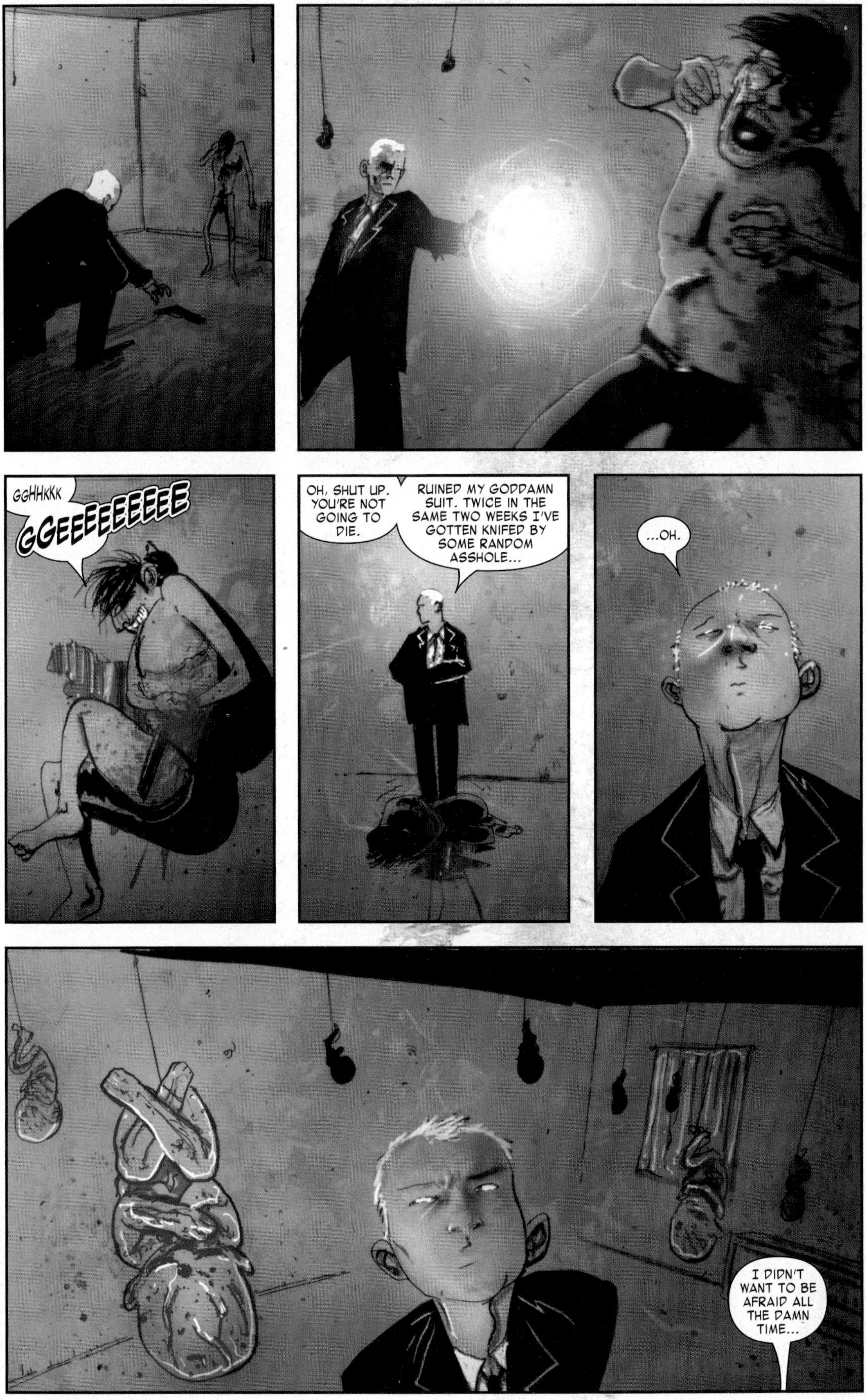
GGHHKKK
GGEEEEEEEEEE
OH, SHUT UP. YOU'RE NOT GOING TO DIE.
RUINED MY GODDAMN SUIT. TWICE IN THE SAME TWO WEEKS I'VE GOTTEN KNIFED BY SOME RANDOM ASSHOLE...
...OH.
I DIDN'T WANT TO BE AFRAID ALL THE DAMN TIME...

SEE THIS?

I MIGHT'VE GOTTEN KILLED WITHOUT IT, TONIGHT.

SO THANKS.

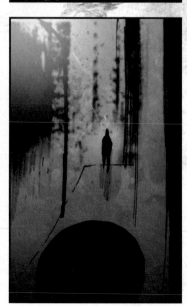

END

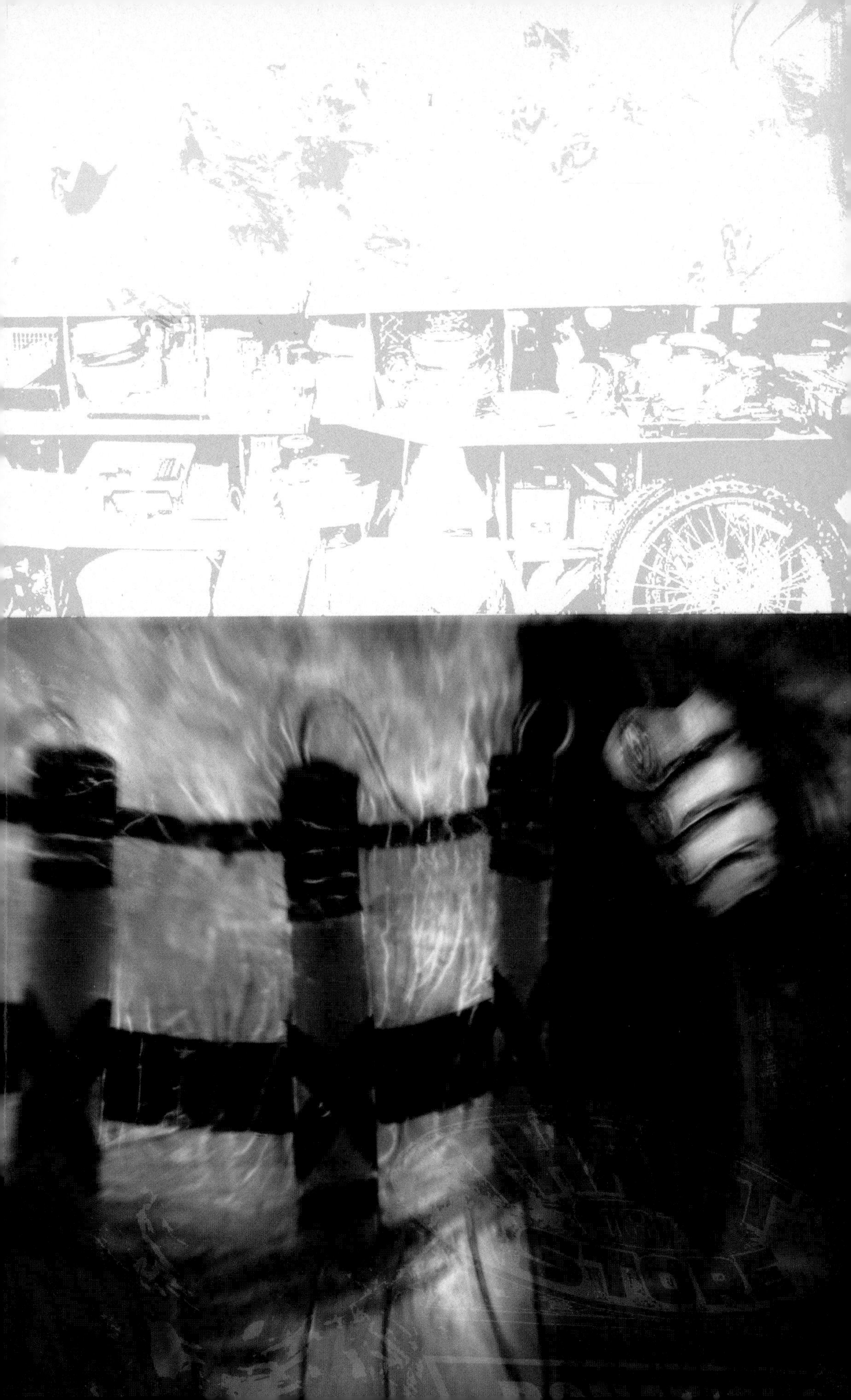

# FELL.

## CHAPTER 3

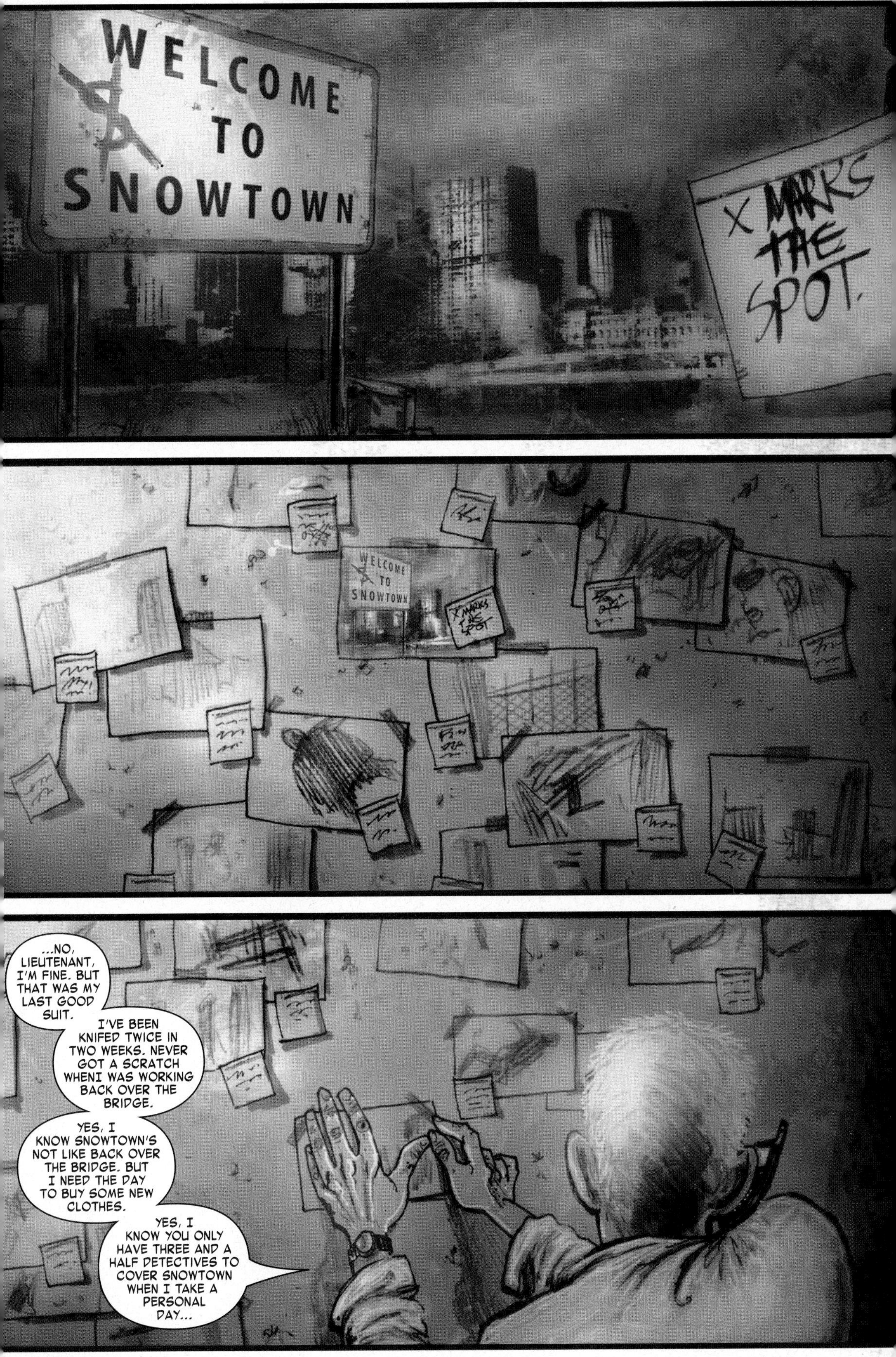
WELCOME TO SNOWTOWN
X MARKS THE SPOT.
WELCOME TO SNOWTOWN
X MARKS THE SPOT
...NO, LIEUTENANT, I'M FINE. BUT THAT WAS MY LAST GOOD SUIT.
I'VE BEEN KNIFED TWICE IN TWO WEEKS. NEVER GOT A SCRATCH WHENI WAS WORKING BACK OVER THE BRIDGE.
YES, I KNOW SNOWTOWN'S NOT LIKE BACK OVER THE BRIDGE. BUT I NEED THE DAY TO BUY SOME NEW CLOTHES.
YES, I KNOW YOU ONLY HAVE THREE AND A HALF DETECTIVES TO COVER SNOWTOWN WHEN I TAKE A PERSONAL DAY...

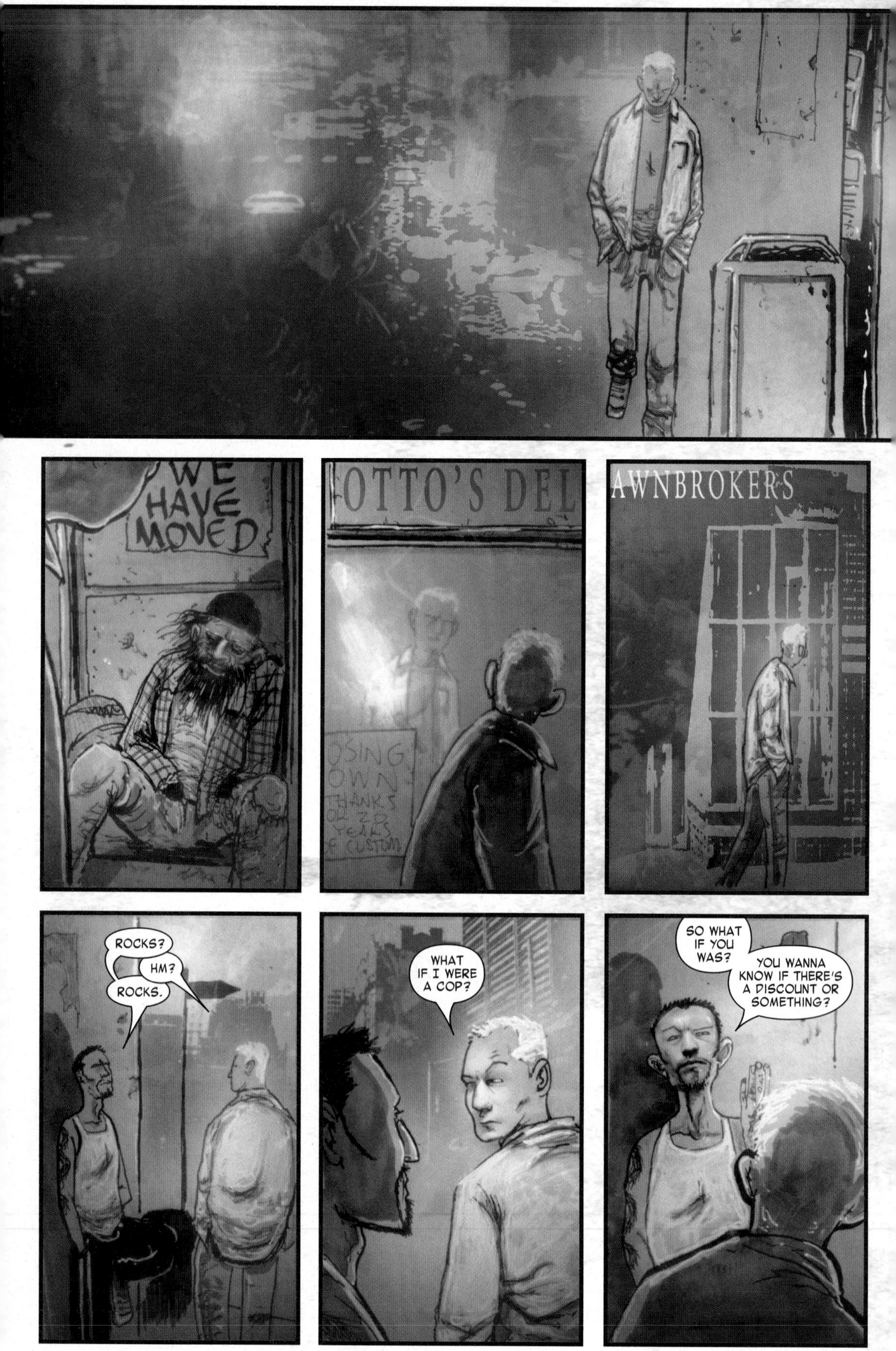

WE HAVE MOVED
OTTO'S DEL
OSING OWN THANKS OR 20 YEARS F CUSTOM
AWNBROKERS
ROCKS?
HM?
ROCKS.
WHAT IF I WERE A COP?
SO WHAT IF YOU WAS?
YOU WANNA KNOW IF THERE'S A DISCOUNT OR SOMETHING?

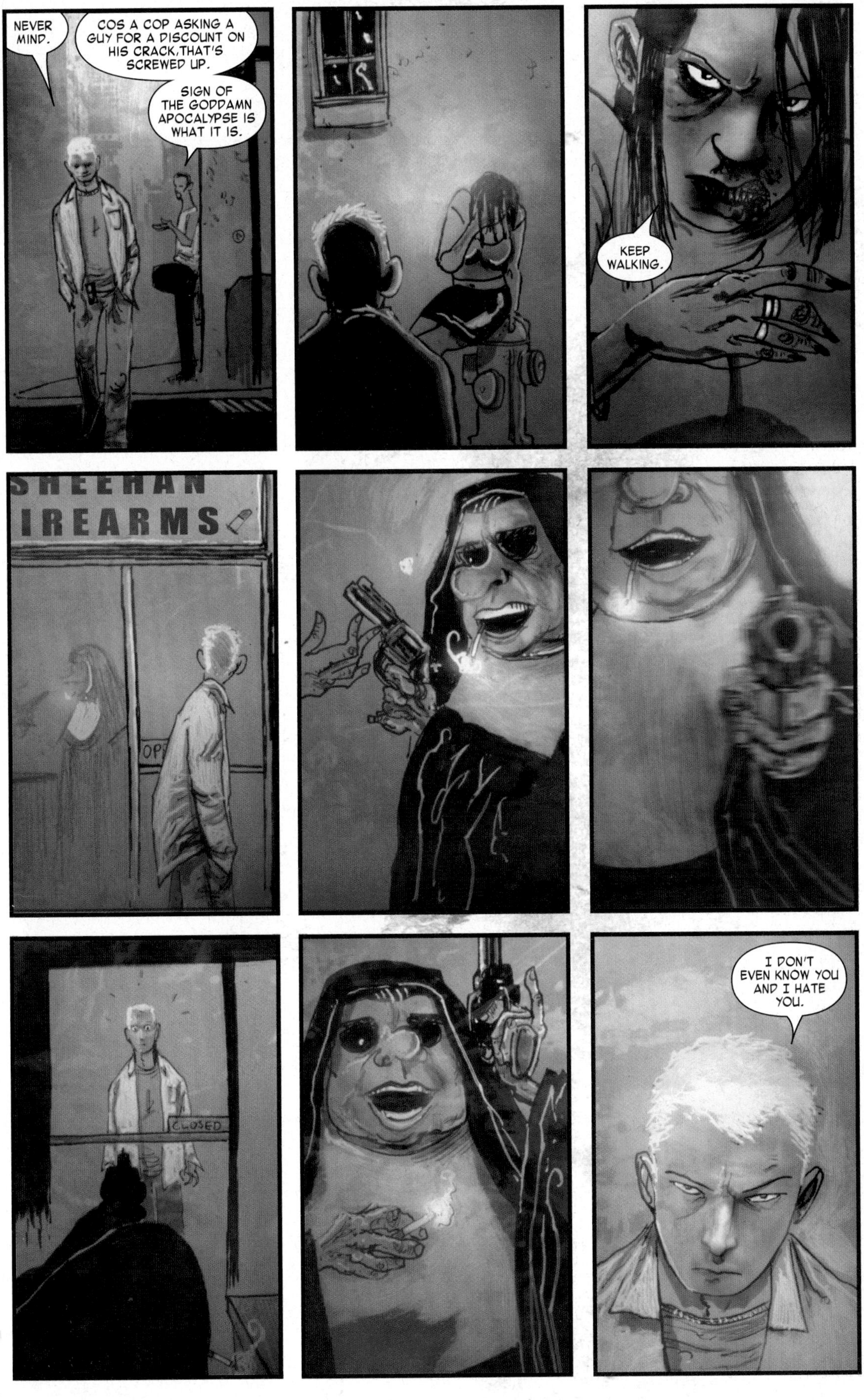
NEVER MIND.
COS A COP ASKING A GUY FOR A DISCOUNT ON HIS CRACK, THAT'S SCREWED UP.
SIGN OF THE GODDAMN APOCALYPSE IS WHAT IT IS.
KEEP WALKING.
SHEEHAN FIREARMS
OPE
CLOSED
I DON'T EVEN KNOW YOU AND I HATE YOU.

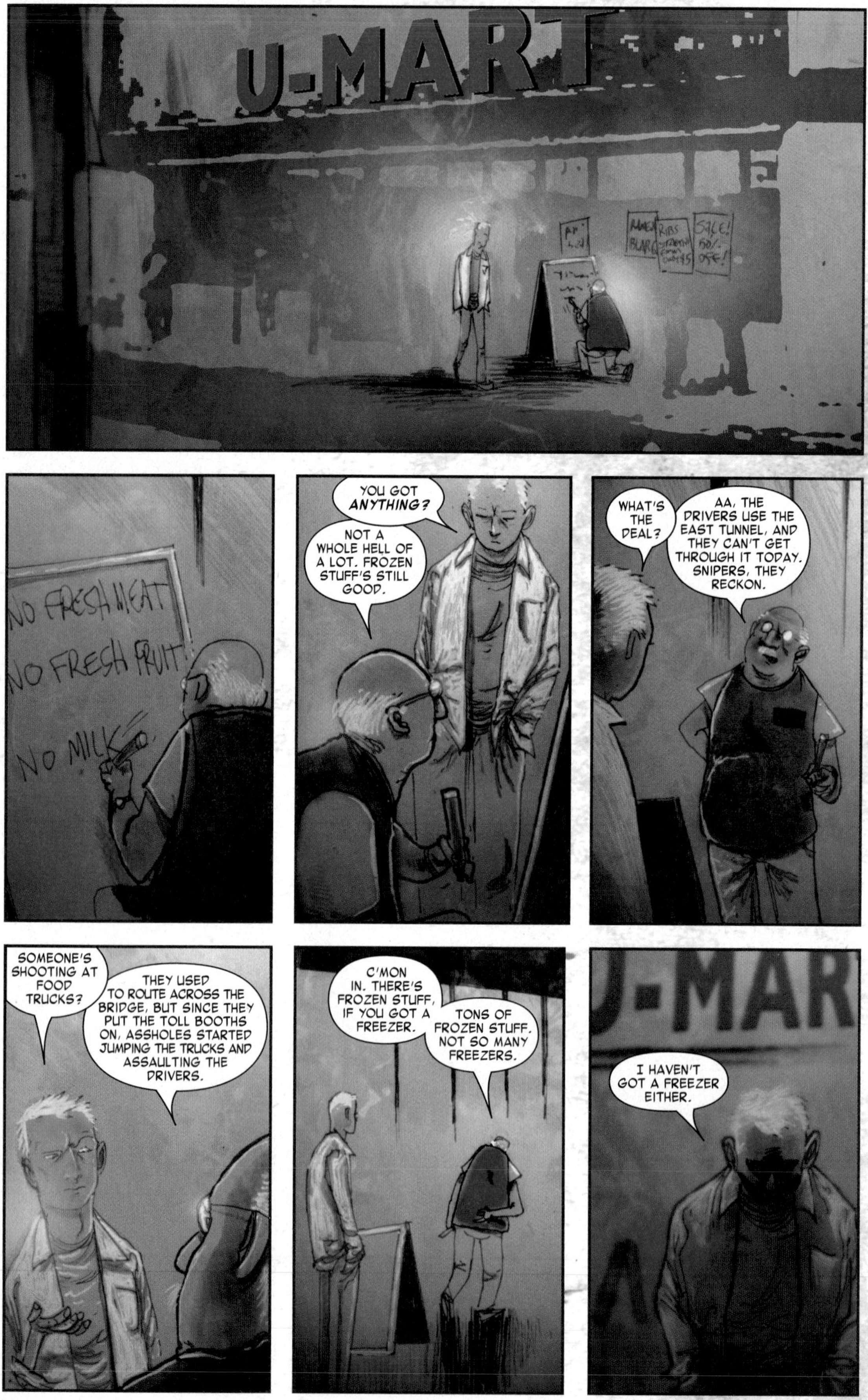
U-MART
SALE! 50% OFF!
NO FRESH MEAT
NO FRESH FRUIT
NO MILK
YOU GOT *ANYTHING?*
NOT A WHOLE HELL OF A LOT. FROZEN STUFF'S STILL GOOD.
WHAT'S THE DEAL?
AA, THE DRIVERS USE THE EAST TUNNEL, AND THEY CAN'T GET THROUGH IT TODAY. SNIPERS, THEY RECKON.
SOMEONE'S SHOOTING AT FOOD TRUCKS?
THEY USED TO ROUTE ACROSS THE BRIDGE, BUT SINCE THEY PUT THE TOLL BOOTHS ON, ASSHOLES STARTED JUMPING THE TRUCKS AND ASSAULTING THE DRIVERS.
C'MON IN. THERE'S FROZEN STUFF, IF YOU GOT A FREEZER.
TONS OF FROZEN STUFF. NOT SO MANY FREEZERS.
U-MAR
I HAVEN'T GOT A FREEZER EITHER.

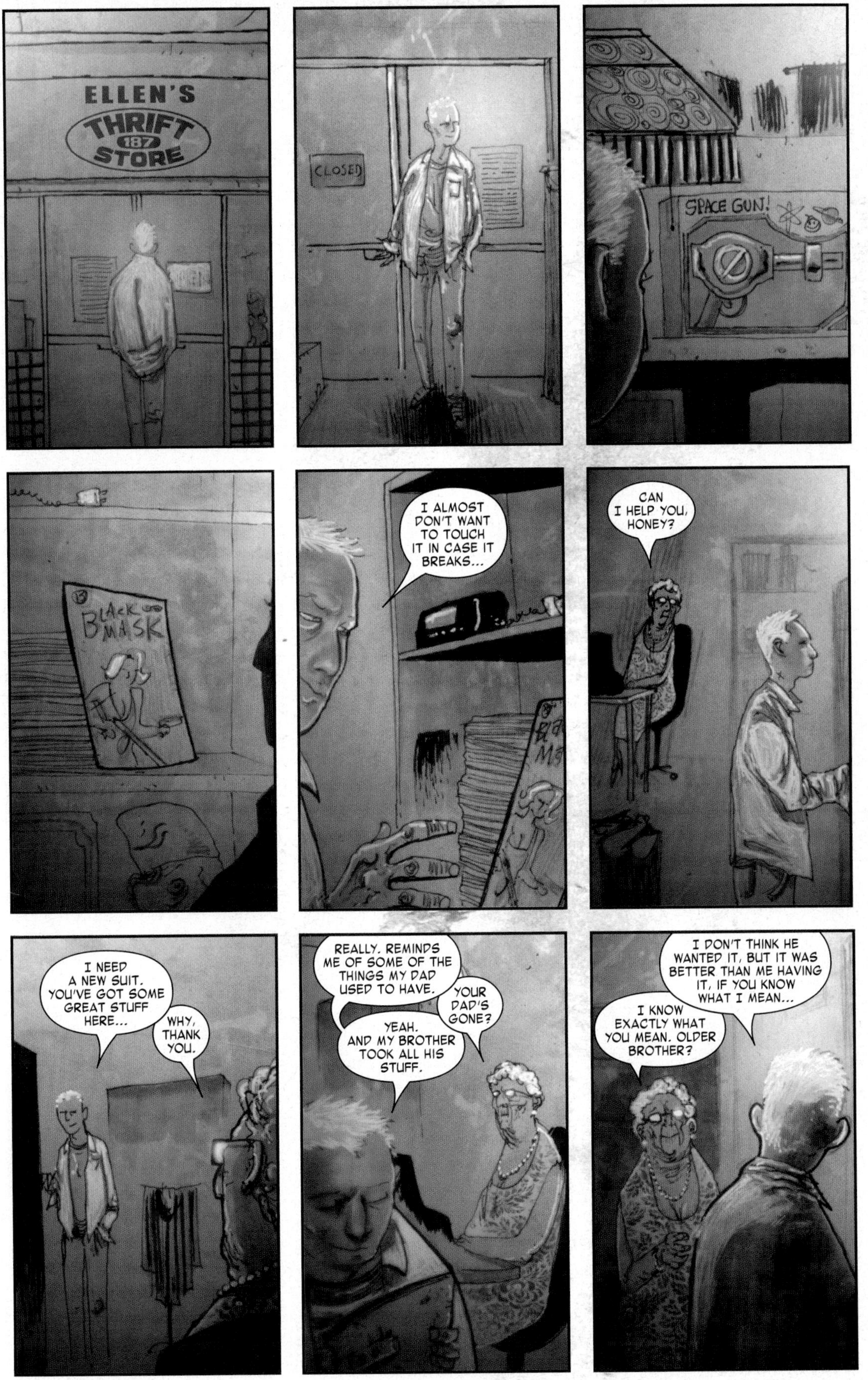
ELLEN'S
THRIFT
187
STORE
CLOSED
SPACE GUN!
BLACK MASK
I ALMOST DON'T WANT TO TOUCH IT IN CASE IT BREAKS...
CAN I HELP YOU, HONEY?
I NEED A NEW SUIT. YOU'VE GOT SOME GREAT STUFF HERE...
WHY, THANK YOU.
REALLY. REMINDS ME OF SOME OF THE THINGS MY DAD USED TO HAVE.
YOUR DAD'S GONE?
YEAH. AND MY BROTHER TOOK ALL HIS STUFF.
I DON'T THINK HE WANTED IT, BUT IT WAS BETTER THAN ME HAVING IT, IF YOU KNOW WHAT I MEAN...
I KNOW EXACTLY WHAT YOU MEAN. OLDER BROTHER?

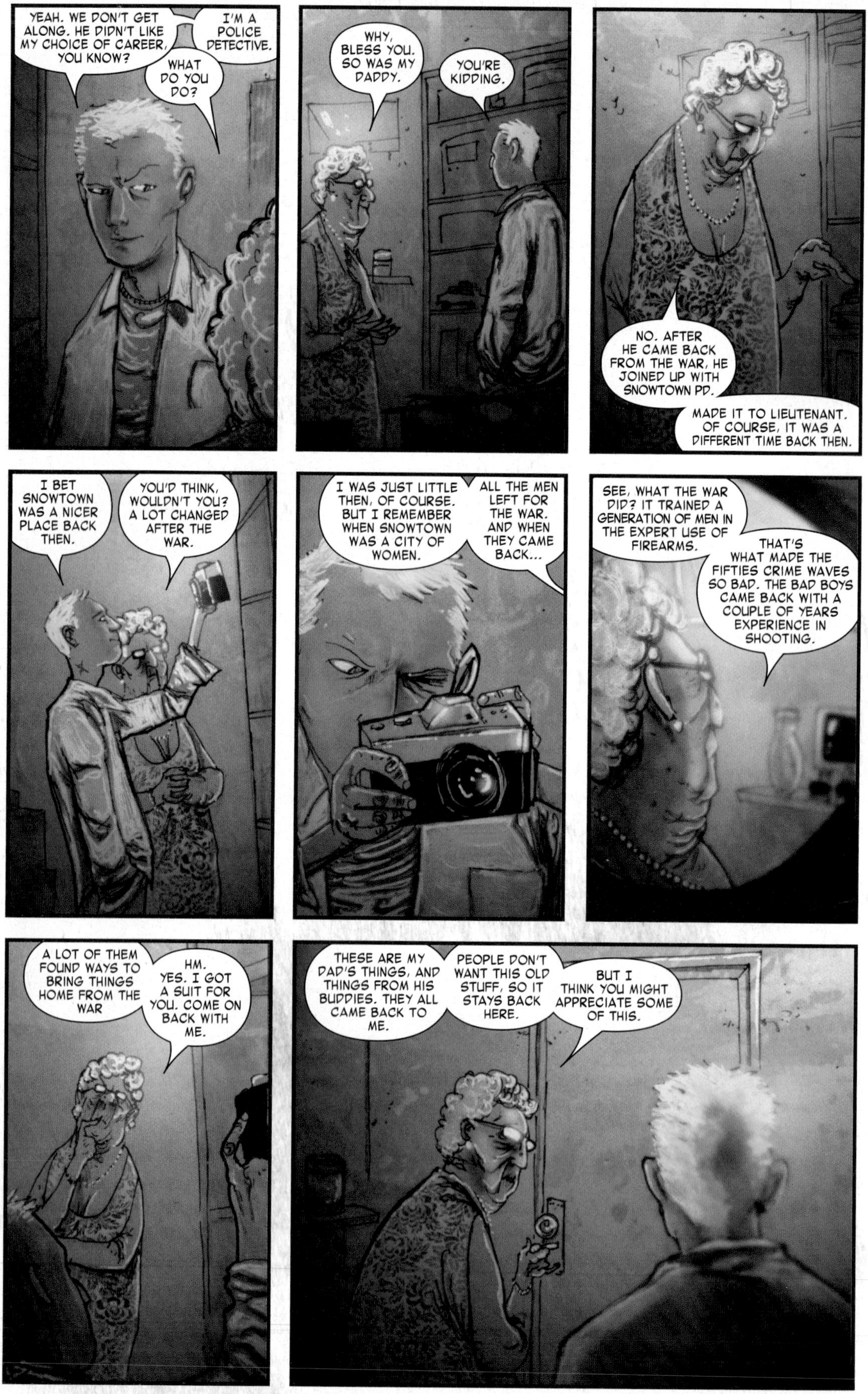
YEAH. WE DON'T GET ALONG. HE DIDN'T LIKE MY CHOICE OF CAREER, YOU KNOW?
WHAT DO YOU DO?
I'M A POLICE DETECTIVE.
WHY, BLESS YOU. SO WAS MY DADDY.
YOU'RE KIDDING.
NO. AFTER HE CAME BACK FROM THE WAR, HE JOINED UP WITH SNOWTOWN PD.
MADE IT TO LIEUTENANT. OF COURSE, IT WAS A DIFFERENT TIME BACK THEN.
I BET SNOWTOWN WAS A NICER PLACE BACK THEN.
YOU'D THINK, WOULDN'T YOU? A LOT CHANGED AFTER THE WAR.
I WAS JUST LITTLE THEN, OF COURSE. BUT I REMEMBER WHEN SNOWTOWN WAS A CITY OF WOMEN.
ALL THE MEN LEFT FOR THE WAR. AND WHEN THEY CAME BACK...
SEE, WHAT THE WAR DID? IT TRAINED A GENERATION OF MEN IN THE EXPERT USE OF FIREARMS.
THAT'S WHAT MADE THE FIFTIES CRIME WAVES SO BAD. THE BAD BOYS CAME BACK WITH A COUPLE OF YEARS EXPERIENCE IN SHOOTING.
A LOT OF THEM FOUND WAYS TO BRING THINGS HOME FROM THE WAR
HM. YES. I GOT A SUIT FOR YOU. COME ON BACK WITH ME.
THESE ARE MY DAD'S THINGS, AND THINGS FROM HIS BUDDIES. THEY ALL CAME BACK TO ME.
PEOPLE DON'T WANT THIS OLD STUFF, SO IT STAYS BACK HERE.
BUT I THINK YOU MIGHT APPRECIATE SOME OF THIS.

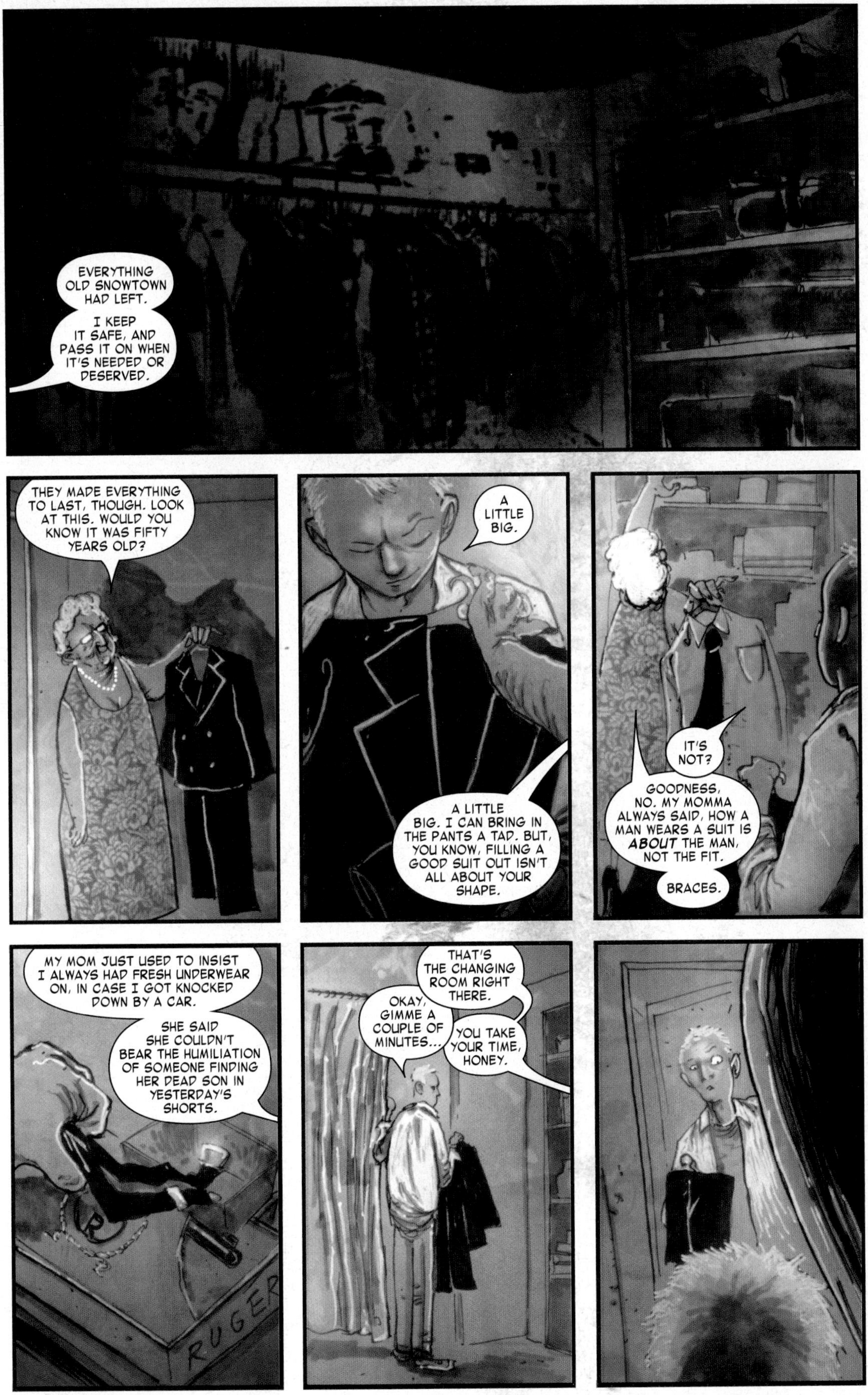
EVERYTHING OLD SNOWTOWN HAD LEFT.
I KEEP IT SAFE, AND PASS IT ON WHEN IT'S NEEDED OR DESERVED.
THEY MADE EVERYTHING TO LAST, THOUGH. LOOK AT THIS. WOULD YOU KNOW IT WAS FIFTY YEARS OLD?
A LITTLE BIG.
A LITTLE BIG. I CAN BRING IN THE PANTS A TAD. BUT, YOU KNOW, FILLING A GOOD SUIT OUT ISN'T ALL ABOUT YOUR SHAPE.
IT'S NOT?
GOODNESS, NO. MY MOMMA ALWAYS SAID, HOW A MAN WEARS A SUIT IS ABOUT THE MAN, NOT THE FIT.
BRACES.
MY MOM JUST USED TO INSIST I ALWAYS HAD FRESH UNDERWEAR ON, IN CASE I GOT KNOCKED DOWN BY A CAR.
SHE SAID SHE COULDN'T BEAR THE HUMILIATION OF SOMEONE FINDING HER DEAD SON IN YESTERDAY'S SHORTS.
RUGER
THAT'S THE CHANGING ROOM RIGHT THERE.
OKAY, GIMME A COUPLE OF MINUTES...
YOU TAKE YOUR TIME, HONEY.

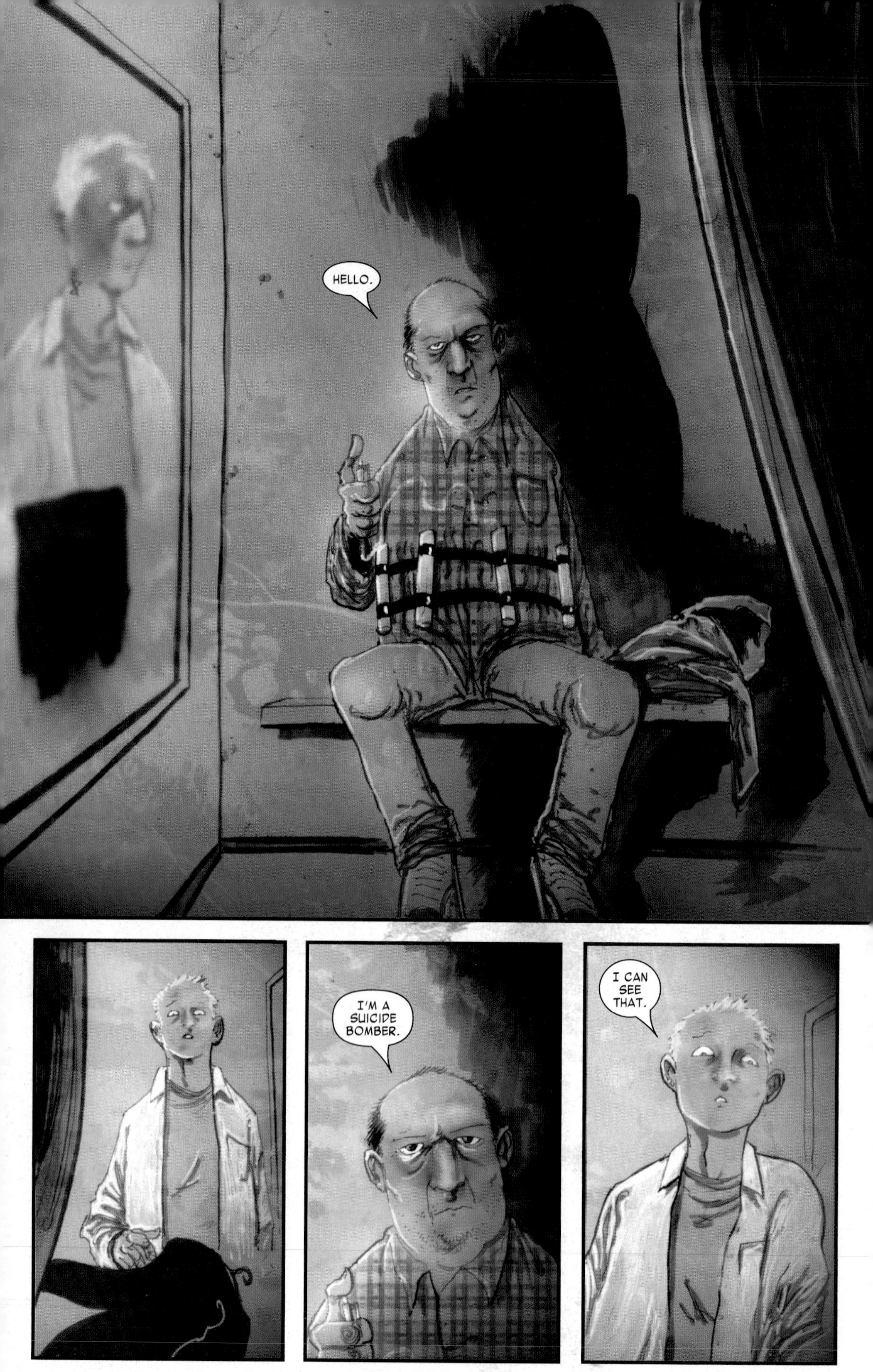
HELLO.
I'M A SUICIDE BOMBER.
I CAN SEE THAT.

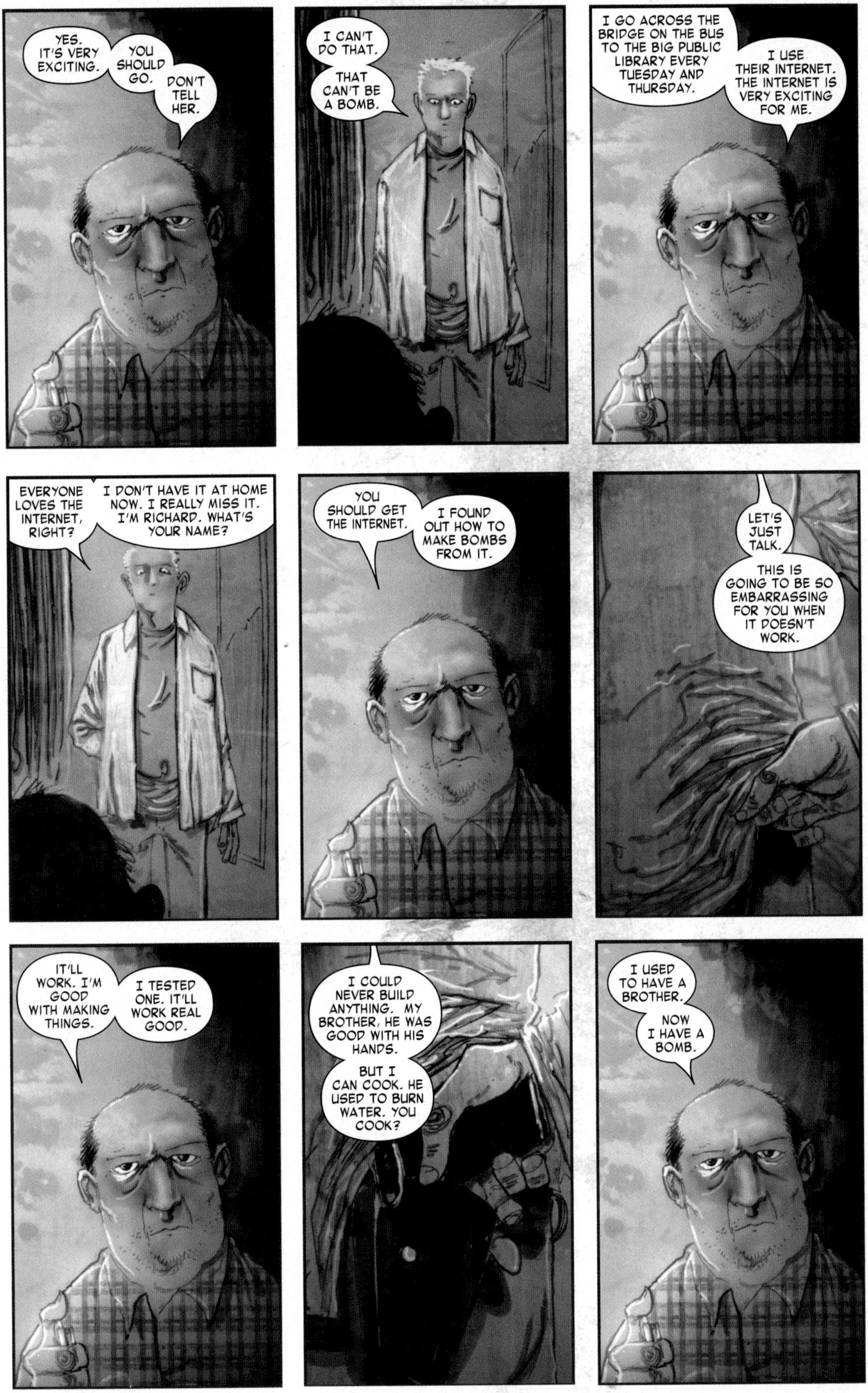

YES. IT'S VERY EXCITING.
YOU SHOULD GO.
DON'T TELL HER.
I CAN'T DO THAT.
THAT CAN'T BE A BOMB.
I GO ACROSS THE BRIDGE ON THE BUS TO THE BIG PUBLIC LIBRARY EVERY TUESDAY AND THURSDAY.
I USE THEIR INTERNET. THE INTERNET IS VERY EXCITING FOR ME.
EVERYONE LOVES THE INTERNET, RIGHT?
I DON'T HAVE IT AT HOME NOW. I REALLY MISS IT. I'M RICHARD. WHAT'S YOUR NAME?
YOU SHOULD GET THE INTERNET.
I FOUND OUT HOW TO MAKE BOMBS FROM IT.
LET'S JUST TALK.
THIS IS GOING TO BE SO EMBARRASSING FOR YOU WHEN IT DOESN'T WORK.
IT'LL WORK. I'M GOOD WITH MAKING THINGS.
I TESTED ONE. IT'LL WORK REAL GOOD.
I COULD NEVER BUILD ANYTHING. MY BROTHER, HE WAS GOOD WITH HIS HANDS.
BUT I CAN COOK. HE USED TO BURN WATER. YOU COOK?
I USED TO HAVE A BROTHER.
NOW I HAVE A BOMB.

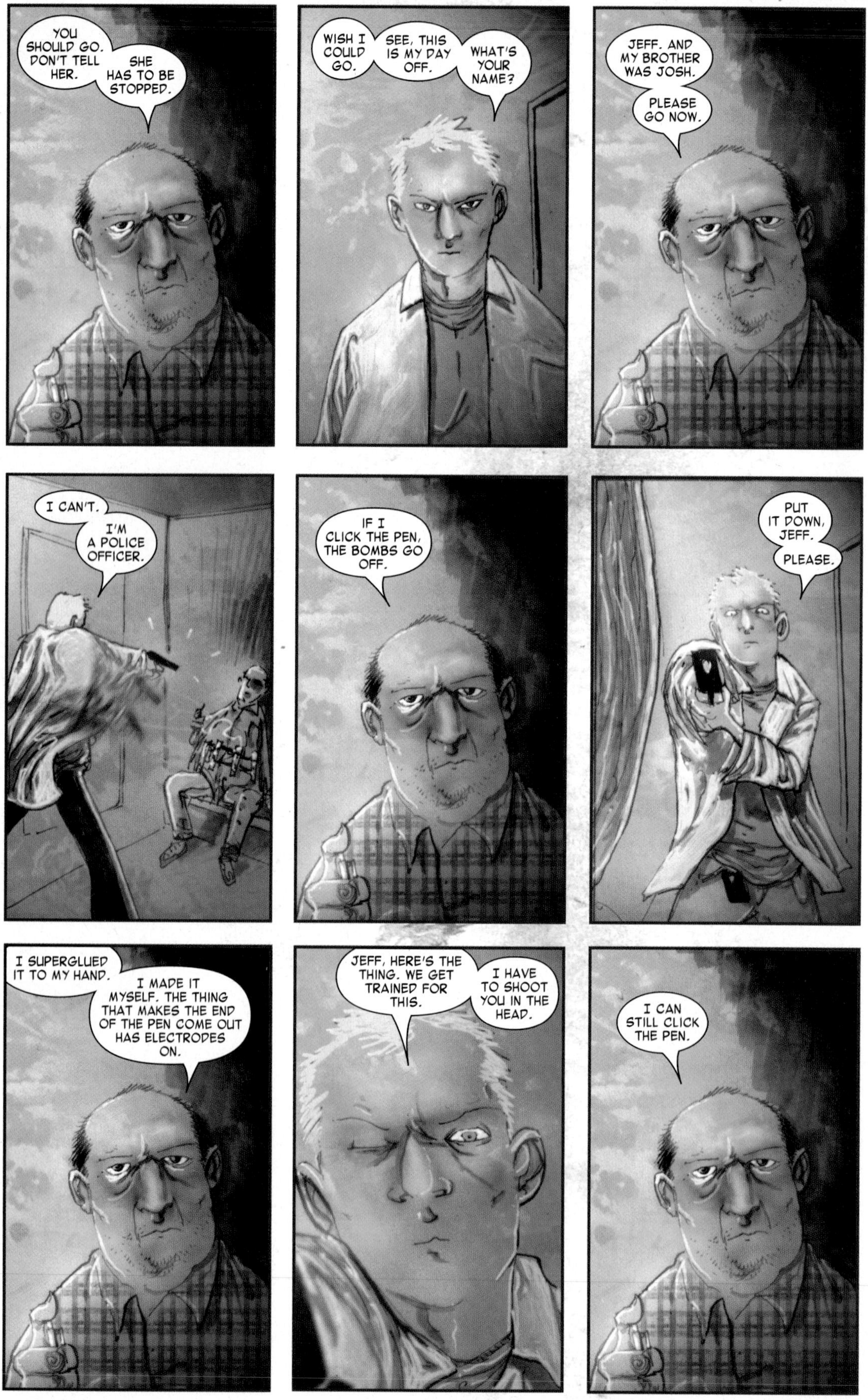
YOU SHOULD GO. DON'T TELL HER.
SHE HAS TO BE STOPPED.
WISH I COULD GO.
SEE, THIS IS MY DAY OFF.
WHAT'S YOUR NAME?
JEFF. AND MY BROTHER WAS JOSH.
PLEASE GO NOW.
I CAN'T.
I'M A POLICE OFFICER.
IF I CLICK THE PEN, THE BOMBS GO OFF.
PUT IT DOWN, JEFF.
PLEASE.
I SUPERGLUED IT TO MY HAND.
I MADE IT MYSELF. THE THING THAT MAKES THE END OF THE PEN COME OUT HAS ELECTRODES ON.
JEFF, HERE'S THE THING. WE GET TRAINED FOR THIS.
I HAVE TO SHOOT YOU IN THE HEAD.
I CAN STILL CLICK THE PEN.

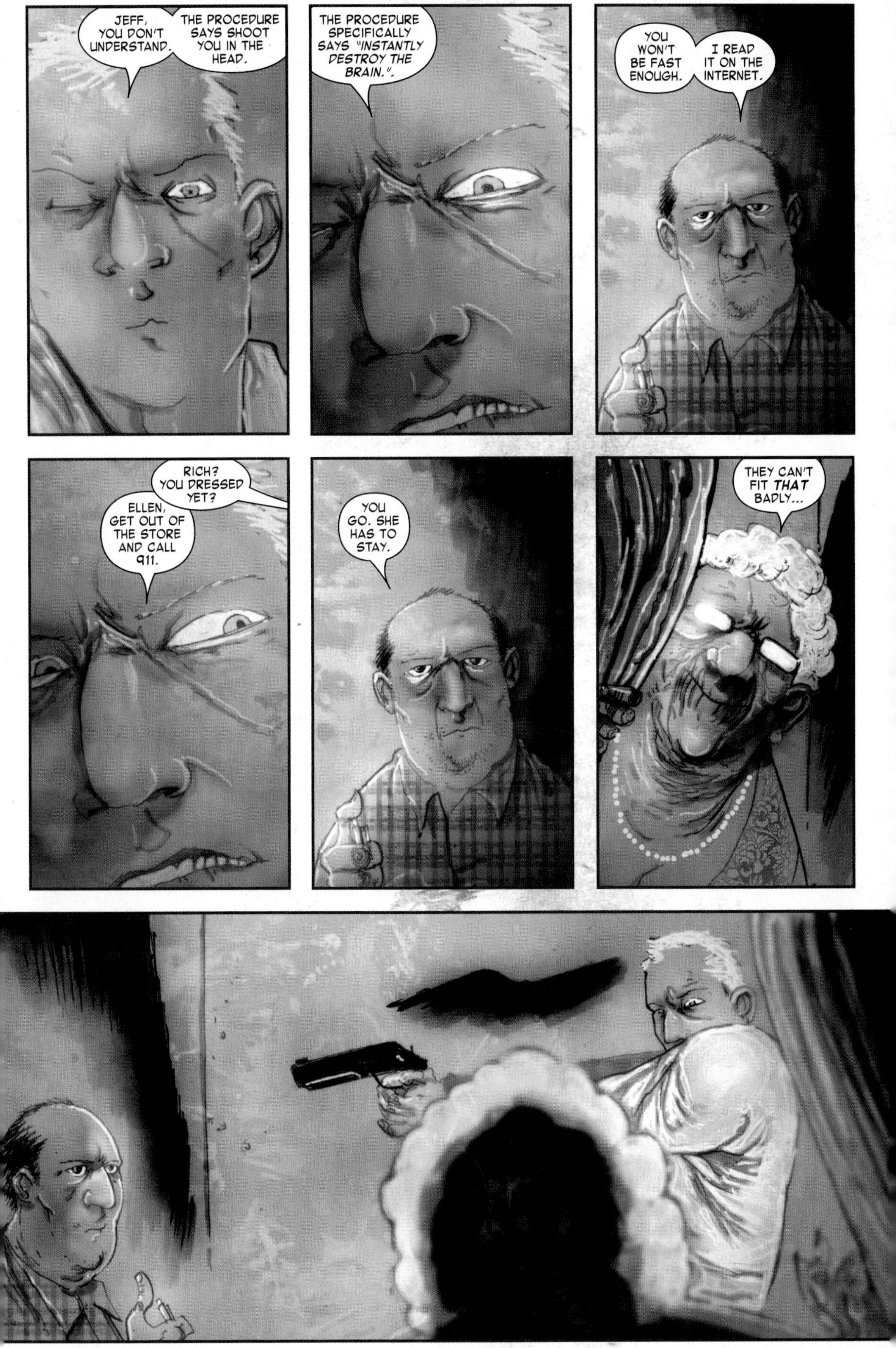

JEFF, YOU DON'T UNDERSTAND.
THE PROCEDURE SAYS SHOOT YOU IN THE HEAD.
THE PROCEDURE SPECIFICALLY SAYS "INSTANTLY DESTROY THE BRAIN.".
YOU WON'T BE FAST ENOUGH.
I READ IT ON THE INTERNET.
RICH? YOU DRESSED YET?
ELLEN, GET OUT OF THE STORE AND CALL 911.
YOU GO. SHE HAS TO STAY.
THEY CAN'T FIT *THAT* BADLY...

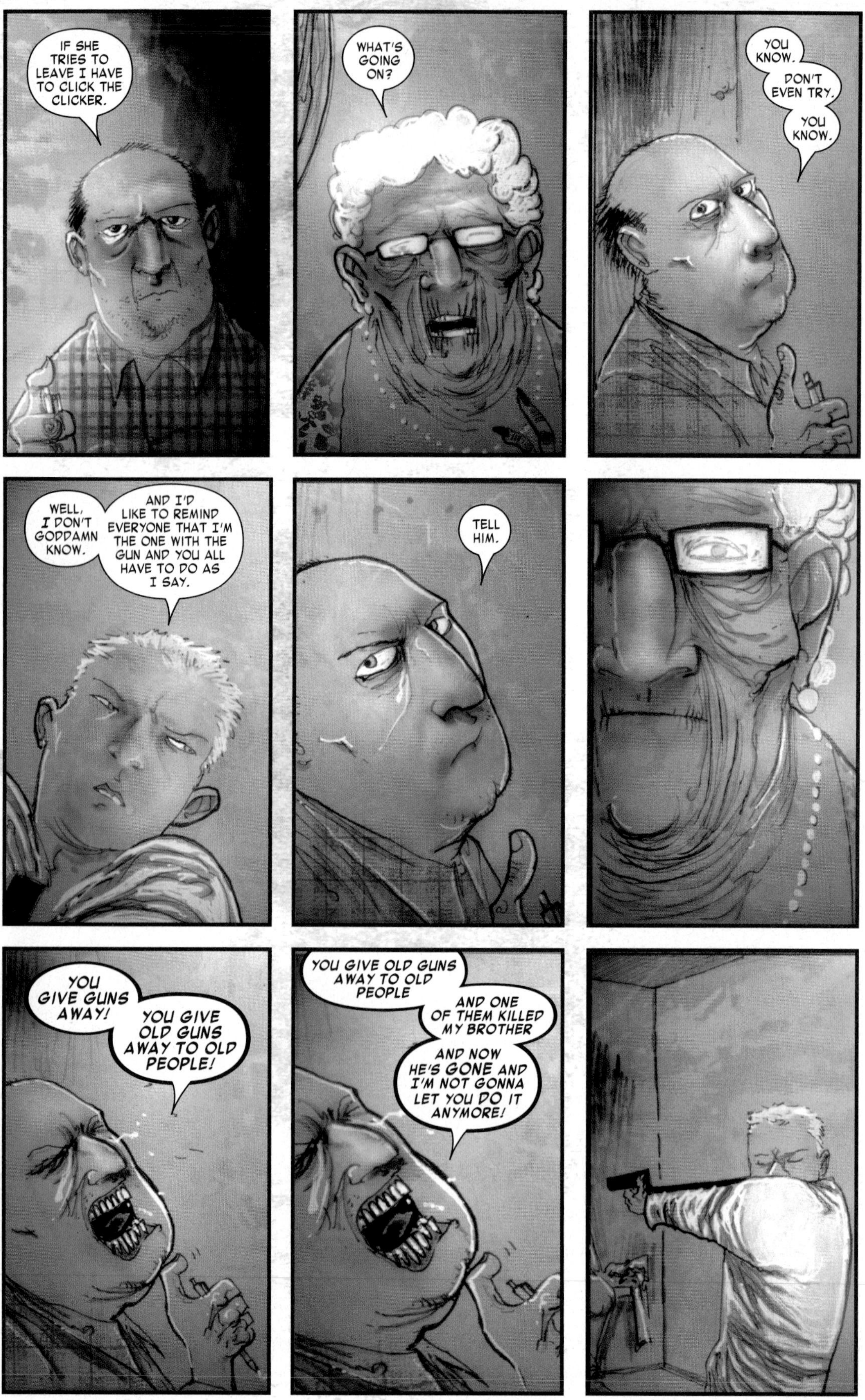
IF SHE TRIES TO LEAVE I HAVE TO CLICK THE CLICKER.
WHAT'S GOING ON?
YOU KNOW.
DON'T EVEN TRY.
YOU KNOW.
WELL, I DON'T GODDAMN KNOW.
AND I'D LIKE TO REMIND EVERYONE THAT I'M THE ONE WITH THE GUN AND YOU ALL HAVE TO DO AS I SAY.
TELL HIM.
YOU GIVE GUNS AWAY!
YOU GIVE OLD GUNS AWAY TO OLD PEOPLE!
YOU GIVE OLD GUNS AWAY TO OLD PEOPLE
AND ONE OF THEM KILLED MY BROTHER
AND NOW HE'S GONE AND I'M NOT GONNA LET YOU DO IT ANYMORE!

ELLEN?

IS ANYTHING HE'S SAYING TRUE?

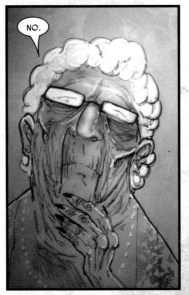

NO.

HAVE YOU EVER SHOT ANYONE YOURSELF, ELLEN?

GOODNESS, NO.

HAVE YOU GIVEN OLD GUNS TO PEOPLE?

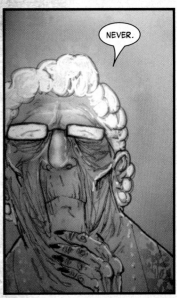

NEVER.

YOU'RE LYING TO ME, ELLEN. I CAN TELL.

I'M GUESSING THAT OLD THINGS CAME TO YOU FROM YOUR FAMILY, AND YOUR FAMILY'S FRIENDS.

GUNS BROUGHT BACK FROM WARS, OR RETAINED FROM THE POLICE DEPARTMENT.

YOU KEPT THEM SAFE, AND PASSED THEM ON WHEN THEY WERE NEEDED OR DESERVED.

TALK TO ME, ELLEN. TELL ME WHAT YOU'RE DOING.

THIS TOWN ISN'T *SAFE*... NOT FOR *OLD* PEOPLE...

MY DADDY WOULDN'T HAVE LET OLD PEOPLE BE SCARED ALL THE TIME...

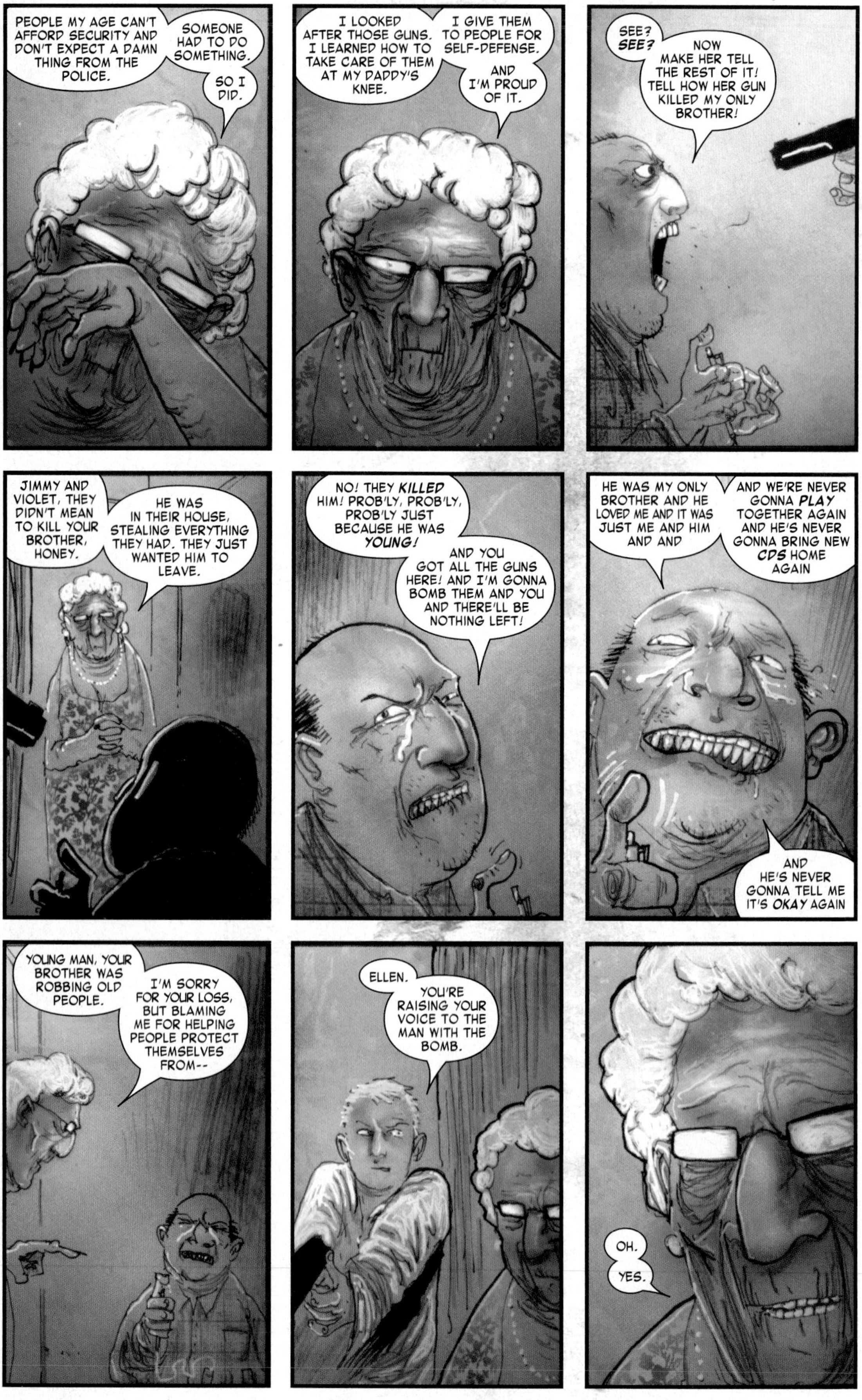
PEOPLE MY AGE CAN'T AFFORD SECURITY AND DON'T EXPECT A DAMN THING FROM THE POLICE.
SOMEONE HAD TO DO SOMETHING.
SO I DID.
I LOOKED AFTER THOSE GUNS. I LEARNED HOW TO TAKE CARE OF THEM AT MY DADDY'S KNEE.
I GIVE THEM TO PEOPLE FOR SELF-DEFENSE.
AND I'M PROUD OF IT.
SEE? SEE?
NOW MAKE HER TELL THE REST OF IT! TELL HOW HER GUN KILLED MY ONLY BROTHER!
JIMMY AND VIOLET, THEY DIDN'T MEAN TO KILL YOUR BROTHER, HONEY.
HE WAS IN THEIR HOUSE, STEALING EVERYTHING THEY HAD. THEY JUST WANTED HIM TO LEAVE.
NO! THEY KILLED HIM! PROB'LY, PROB'LY, PROB'LY JUST BECAUSE HE WAS YOUNG!
AND YOU GOT ALL THE GUNS HERE! AND I'M GONNA BOMB THEM AND YOU AND THERE'LL BE NOTHING LEFT!
HE WAS MY ONLY BROTHER AND HE LOVED ME AND IT WAS JUST ME AND HIM AND AND
AND WE'RE NEVER GONNA PLAY TOGETHER AGAIN AND HE'S NEVER GONNA BRING NEW CDS HOME AGAIN
AND HE'S NEVER GONNA TELL ME IT'S OKAY AGAIN
YOUNG MAN, YOUR BROTHER WAS ROBBING OLD PEOPLE.
I'M SORRY FOR YOUR LOSS, BUT BLAMING ME FOR HELPING PEOPLE PROTECT THEMSELVES FROM--
ELLEN.
YOU'RE RAISING YOUR VOICE TO THE MAN WITH THE BOMB.
OH.
YES.

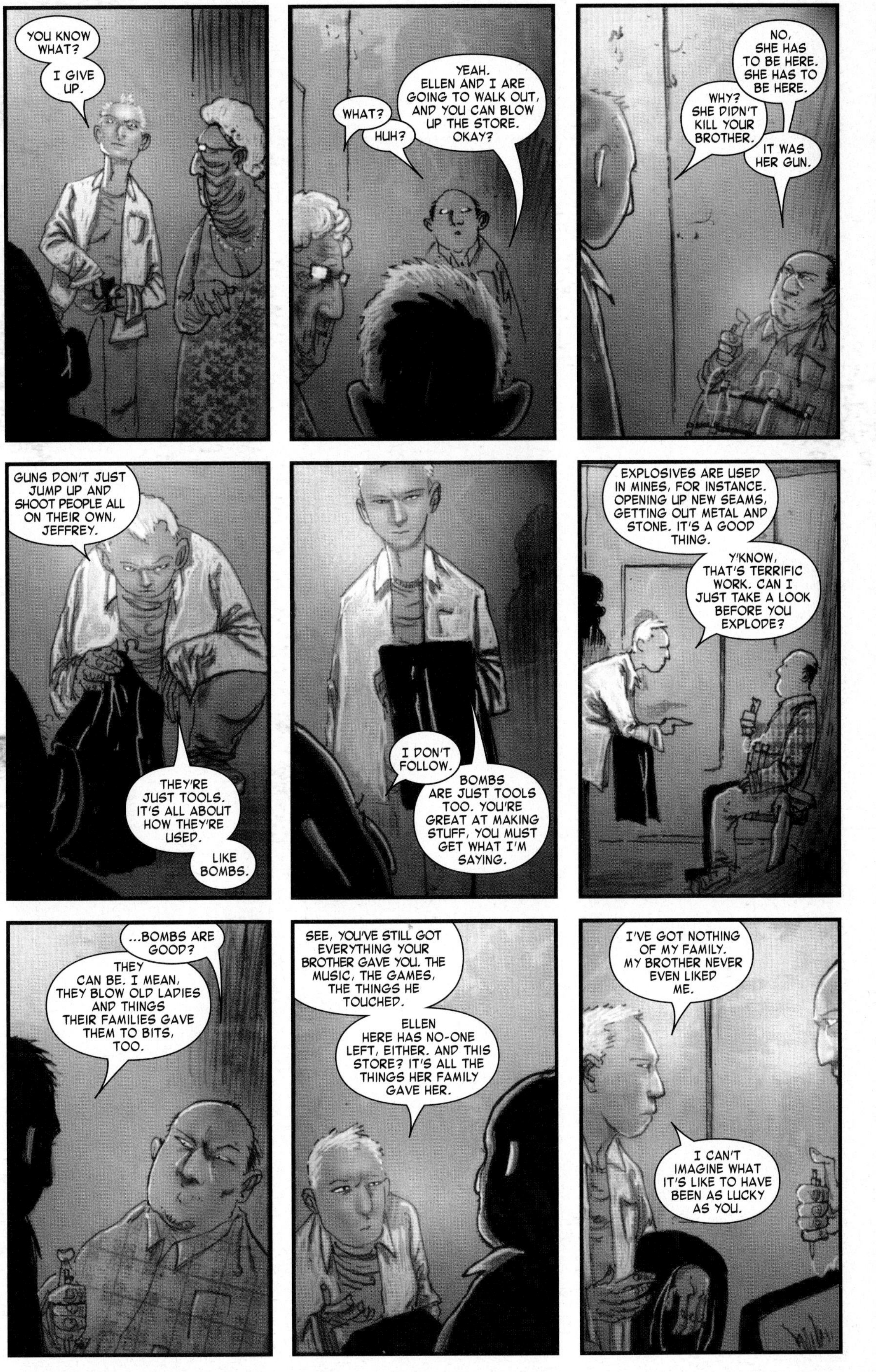
YOU KNOW WHAT?
I GIVE UP.
WHAT?
HUH?
YEAH. ELLEN AND I ARE GOING TO WALK OUT, AND YOU CAN BLOW UP THE STORE. OKAY?
NO, SHE HAS TO BE HERE. SHE HAS TO BE HERE.
WHY? SHE DIDN'T KILL YOUR BROTHER.
IT WAS HER GUN.
GUNS DON'T JUST JUMP UP AND SHOOT PEOPLE ALL ON THEIR OWN, JEFFREY.
THEY'RE JUST TOOLS. IT'S ALL ABOUT HOW THEY'RE USED.
LIKE BOMBS.
I DON'T FOLLOW.
BOMBS ARE JUST TOOLS TOO. YOU'RE GREAT AT MAKING STUFF, YOU MUST GET WHAT I'M SAYING.
EXPLOSIVES ARE USED IN MINES, FOR INSTANCE. OPENING UP NEW SEAMS, GETTING OUT METAL AND STONE. IT'S A GOOD THING.
Y'KNOW, THAT'S TERRIFIC WORK. CAN I JUST TAKE A LOOK BEFORE YOU EXPLODE?
...BOMBS ARE GOOD?
THEY CAN BE. I MEAN, THEY BLOW OLD LADIES AND THINGS THEIR FAMILIES GAVE THEM TO BITS, TOO.
SEE, YOU'VE STILL GOT EVERYTHING YOUR BROTHER GAVE YOU. THE MUSIC, THE GAMES, THE THINGS HE TOUCHED.
ELLEN HERE HAS NO-ONE LEFT, EITHER. AND THIS STORE? IT'S ALL THE THINGS HER FAMILY GAVE HER.
I'VE GOT NOTHING OF MY FAMILY. MY BROTHER NEVER EVEN LIKED ME.
I CAN'T IMAGINE WHAT IT'S LIKE TO HAVE BEEN AS LUCKY AS YOU.

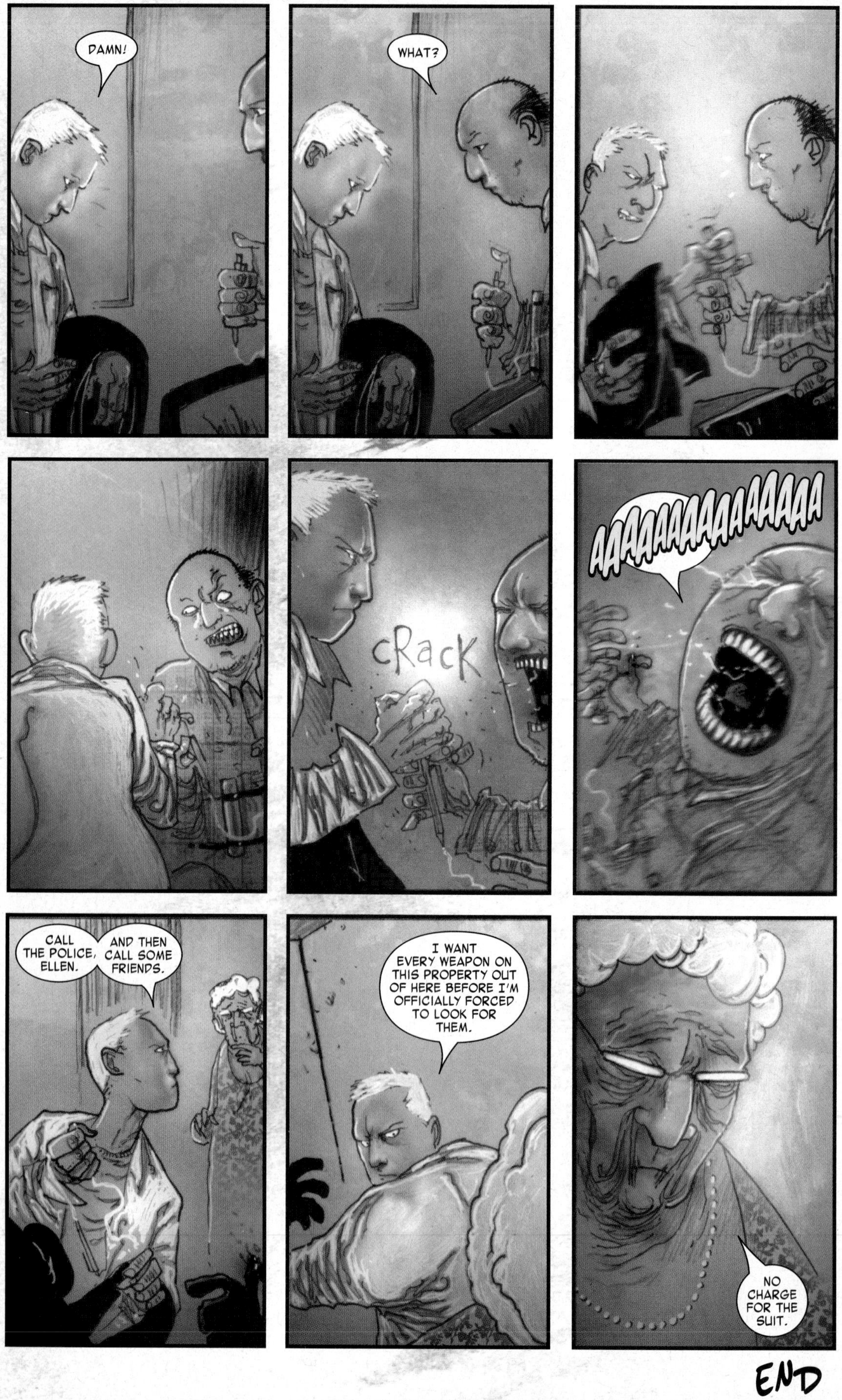
DAMN!
WHAT?
cRack
AAAAAAAAAAAAAA
CALL THE POLICE, ELLEN.
AND THEN CALL SOME FRIENDS.
I WANT EVERY WEAPON ON THIS PROPERTY OUT OF HERE BEFORE I'M OFFICIALLY FORCED TO LOOK FOR THEM.
NO CHARGE FOR THE SUIT.
END

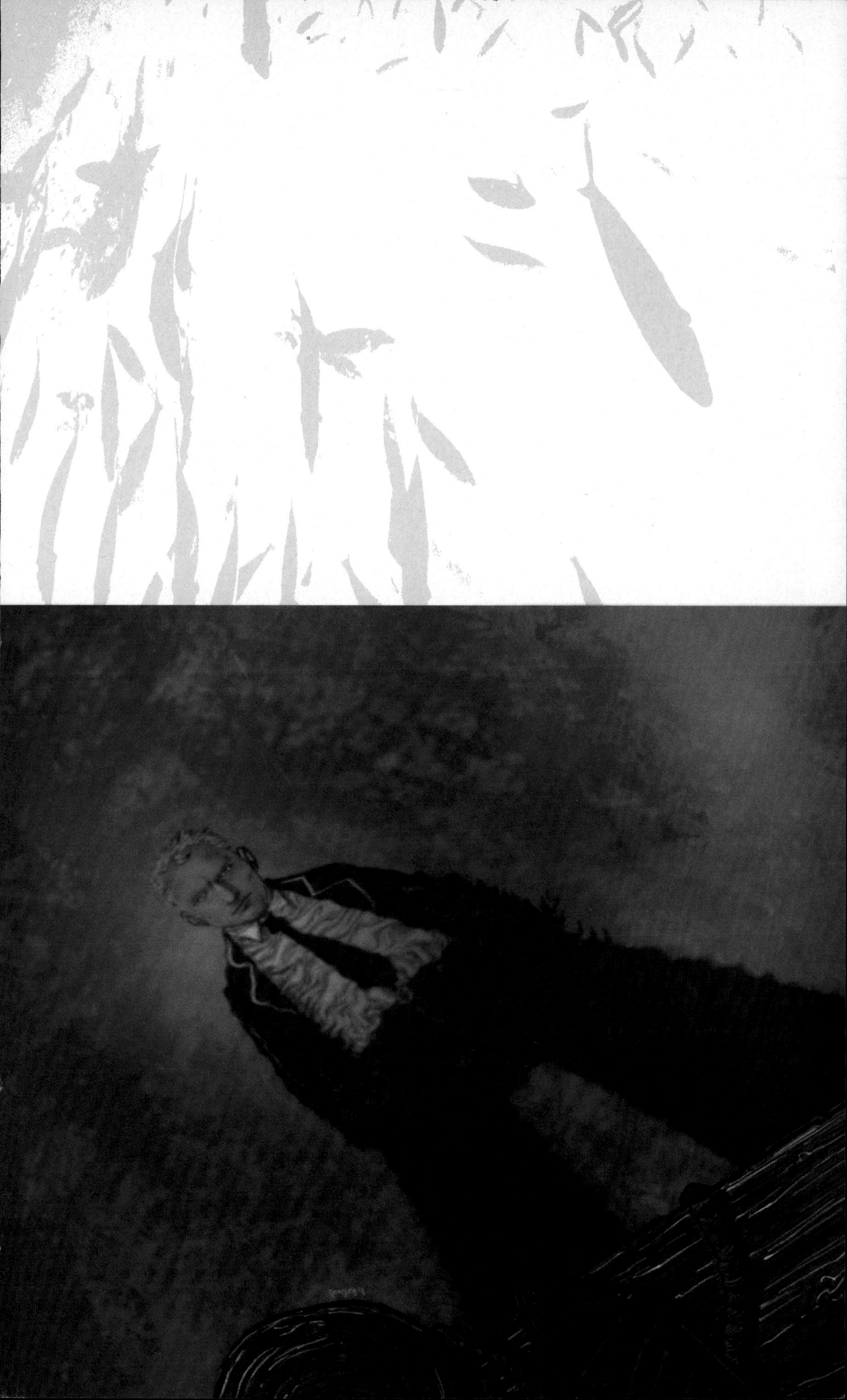

# FELL.™

## CHAPTER 4

They always say floaters are the worst.
GOD, THEY ALWAYS SMELL SO BAD...

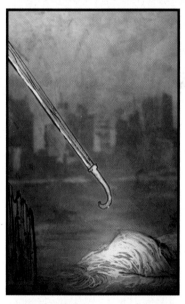

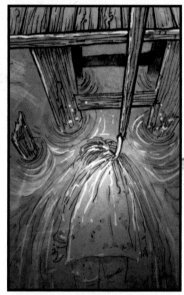

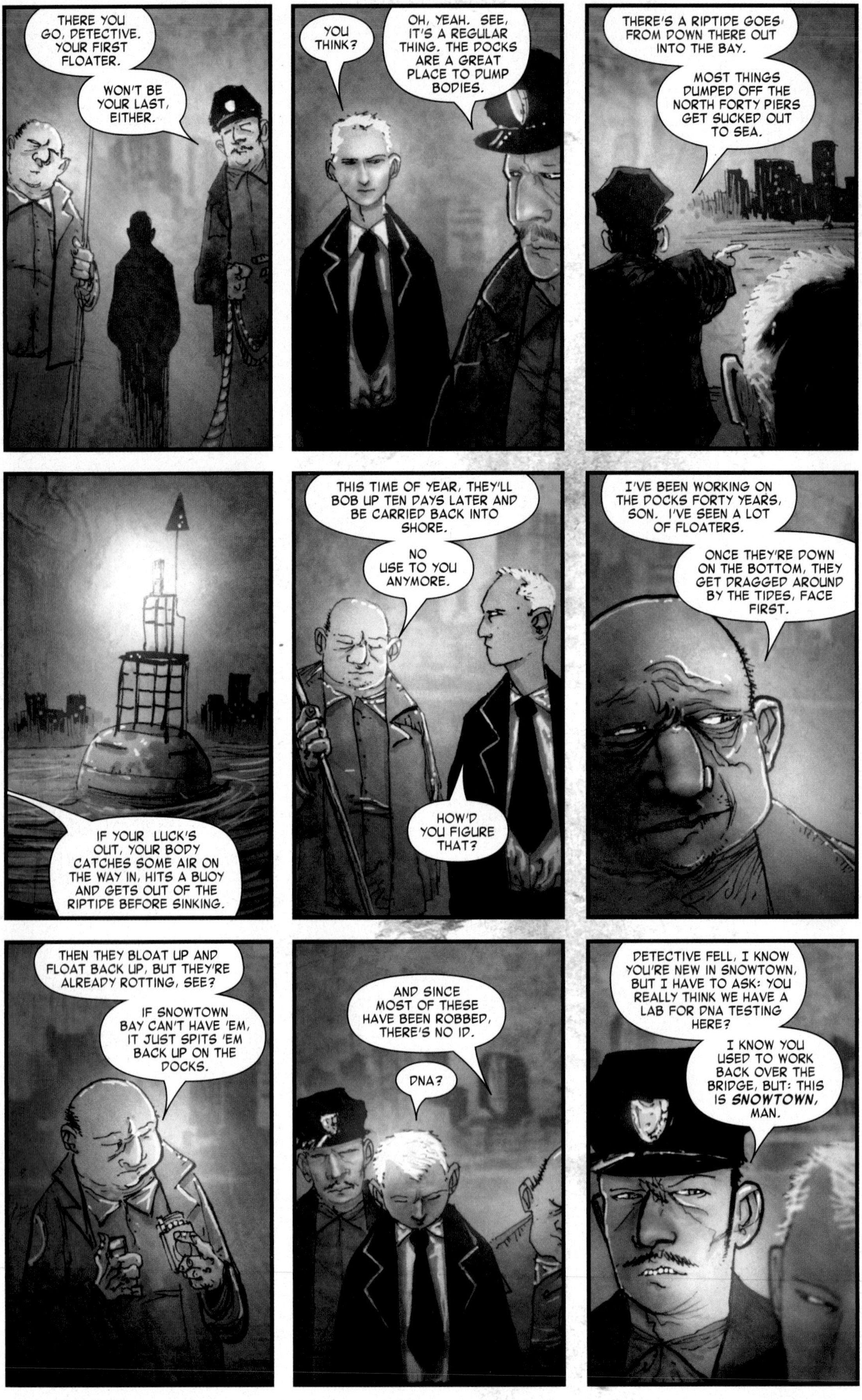
THERE YOU GO, DETECTIVE. YOUR FIRST FLOATER.
WON'T BE YOUR LAST, EITHER.
YOU THINK?
OH, YEAH. SEE, IT'S A REGULAR THING. THE DOCKS ARE A GREAT PLACE TO DUMP BODIES.
THERE'S A RIPTIDE GOES FROM DOWN THERE OUT INTO THE BAY.
MOST THINGS DUMPED OFF THE NORTH FORTY PIERS GET SUCKED OUT TO SEA.
IF YOUR LUCK'S OUT, YOUR BODY CATCHES SOME AIR ON THE WAY IN, HITS A BUOY AND GETS OUT OF THE RIPTIDE BEFORE SINKING.
THIS TIME OF YEAR, THEY'LL BOB UP TEN DAYS LATER AND BE CARRIED BACK INTO SHORE.
NO USE TO YOU ANYMORE.
HOW'D YOU FIGURE THAT?
I'VE BEEN WORKING ON THE DOCKS FORTY YEARS, SON. I'VE SEEN A LOT OF FLOATERS.
ONCE THEY'RE DOWN ON THE BOTTOM, THEY GET DRAGGED AROUND BY THE TIDES, FACE FIRST.
THEN THEY BLOAT UP AND FLOAT BACK UP, BUT THEY'RE ALREADY ROTTING, SEE?
IF SNOWTOWN BAY CAN'T HAVE 'EM, IT JUST SPITS 'EM BACK UP ON THE DOCKS.
AND SINCE MOST OF THESE HAVE BEEN ROBBED, THERE'S NO ID.
DNA?
DETECTIVE FELL, I KNOW YOU'RE NEW IN SNOWTOWN, BUT I HAVE TO ASK: YOU REALLY THINK WE HAVE A LAB FOR DNA TESTING HERE?
I KNOW YOU USED TO WORK BACK OVER THE BRIDGE, BUT: THIS IS SNOWTOWN, MAN.

SO WHAT DO YOU DO?

CALL THE MEAT WAGON, HAVE 'EM BAGGED AND STACKED IN THE HOSPITAL BASEMENT, BURN 'EM A YEAR LATER.

I'M GONNA ADVISE YOU DON'T TURN HIM OVER, DETECTIVE...

A YEAR?

WELL, THAT'S WHAT REGS SAY. MORE LIKE A MONTH, DEPENDING ON HOW FULL THE BASEMENT IS.

SERIOUSLY, DETECTIVE, YOU DON'T WANNA DO THAT.

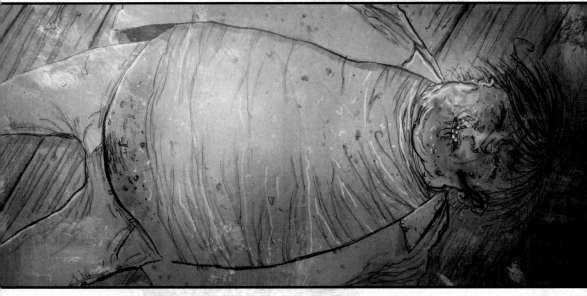

JESUS.

AIN'T NO JESUS IN SNOWTOWN, DETECTIVE.

CALL THE MEAT WAGON. HAVE THE BODY TAKEN TO THE CORONER.

DETECTIVE, THERE'S GONNA BE ANOTHER ONE JUST LIKE THIS NEXT WEEK. LEAVE IT.

NOT THIS ONE.

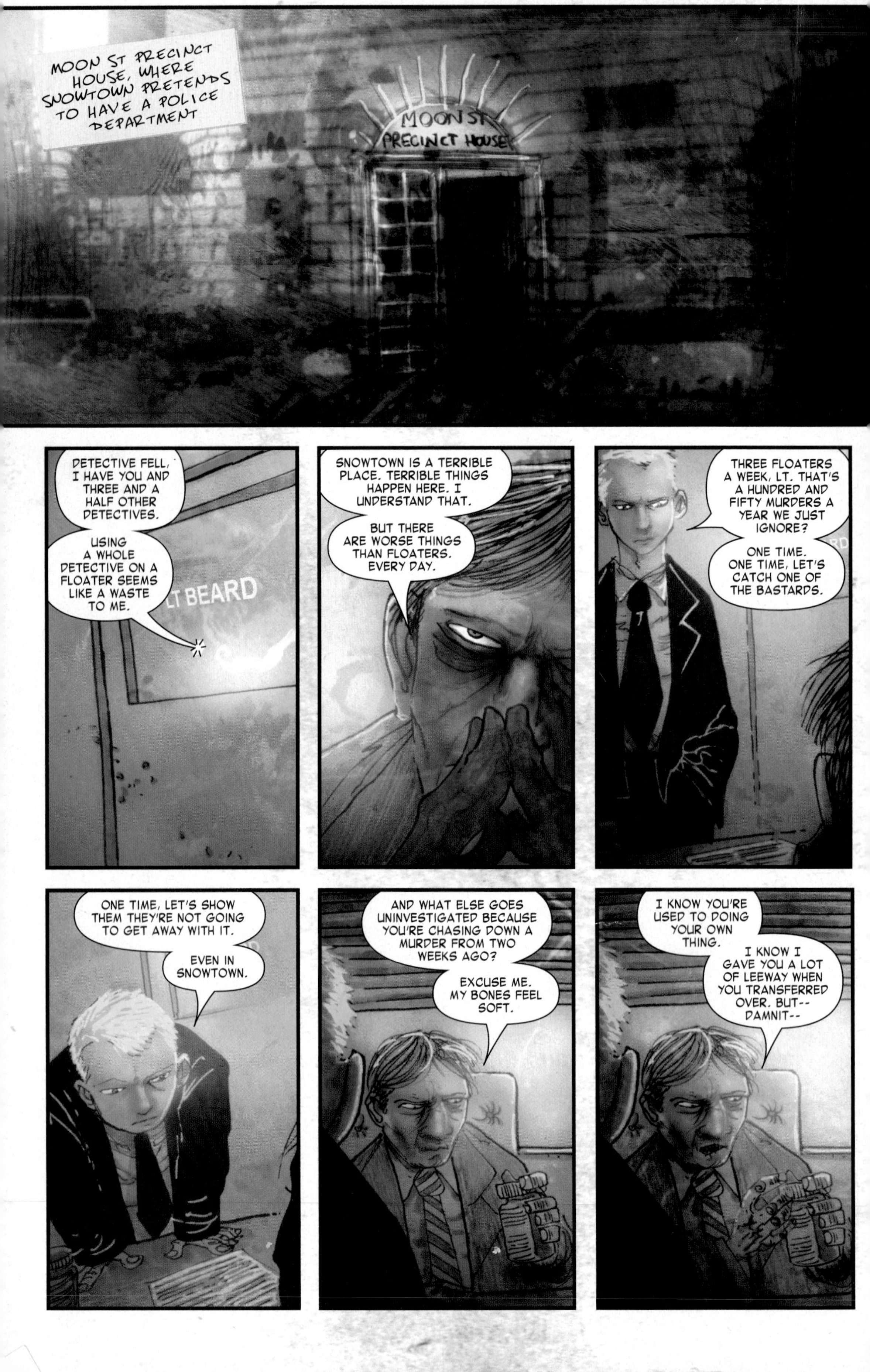
MOON ST PRECINCT HOUSE, WHERE SNOWTOWN PRETENDS TO HAVE A POLICE DEPARTMENT
MOON ST PRECINCT HOUSE
DETECTIVE FELL, I HAVE YOU AND THREE AND A HALF OTHER DETECTIVES.
USING A WHOLE DETECTIVE ON A FLOATER SEEMS LIKE A WASTE TO ME.
LT BEARD
SNOWTOWN IS A TERRIBLE PLACE. TERRIBLE THINGS HAPPEN HERE. I UNDERSTAND THAT.
BUT THERE ARE WORSE THINGS THAN FLOATERS. EVERY DAY.
THREE FLOATERS A WEEK, LT. THAT'S A HUNDRED AND FIFTY MURDERS A YEAR WE JUST IGNORE?
ONE TIME. ONE TIME, LET'S CATCH ONE OF THE BASTARDS.
ONE TIME, LET'S SHOW THEM THEY'RE NOT GOING TO GET AWAY WITH IT.
EVEN IN SNOWTOWN.
AND WHAT ELSE GOES UNINVESTIGATED BECAUSE YOU'RE CHASING DOWN A MURDER FROM TWO WEEKS AGO?
EXCUSE ME. MY BONES FEEL SOFT.
I KNOW YOU'RE USED TO DOING YOUR OWN THING.
I KNOW I GAVE YOU A LOT OF LEEWAY WHEN YOU TRANSFERRED OVER. BUT-- DAMNIT--

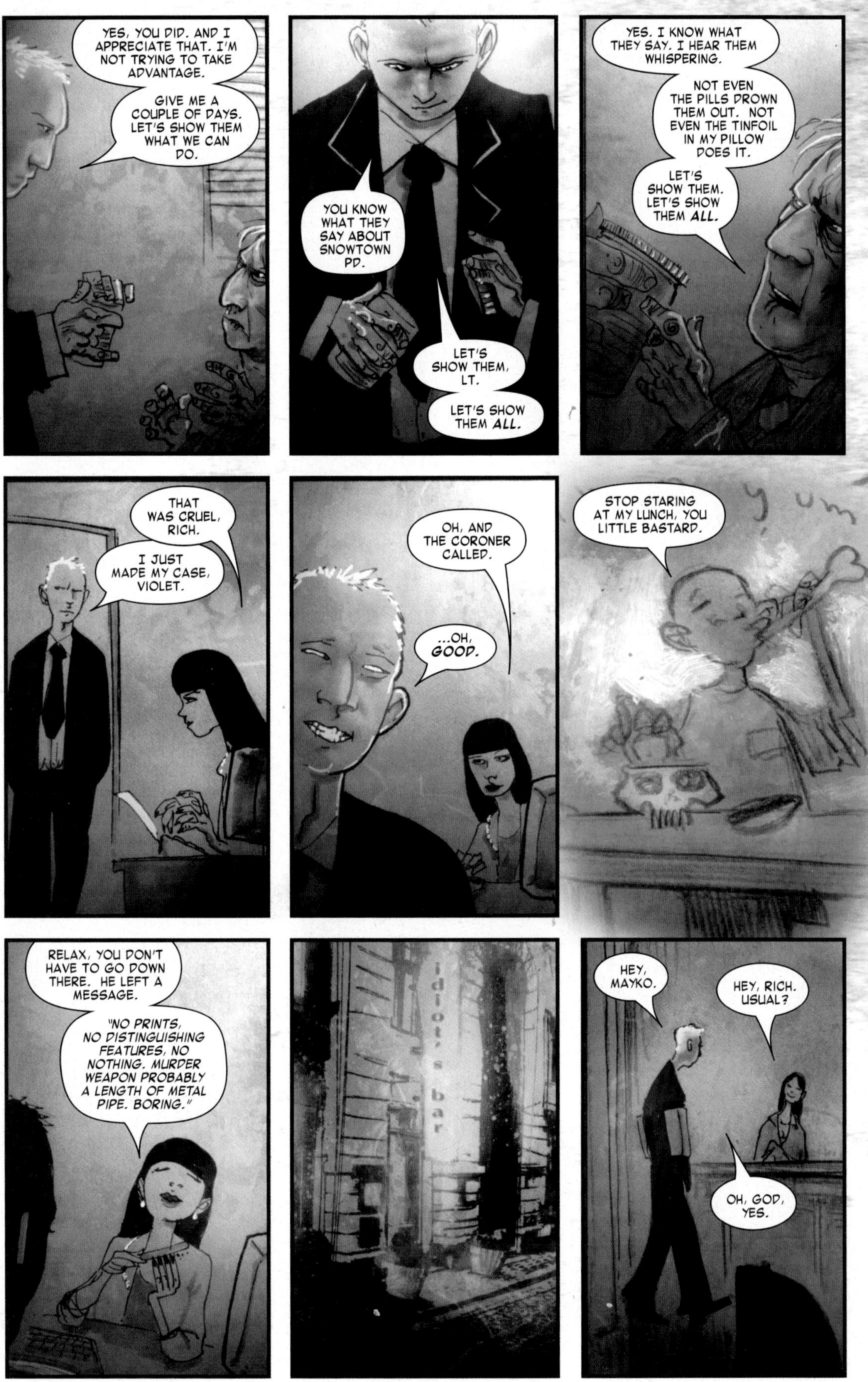
YES, YOU DID. AND I APPRECIATE THAT. I'M NOT TRYING TO TAKE ADVANTAGE.
GIVE ME A COUPLE OF DAYS. LET'S SHOW THEM WHAT WE CAN DO.
YOU KNOW WHAT THEY SAY ABOUT SNOWTOWN PD.
LET'S SHOW THEM, LT.
LET'S SHOW THEM ALL.
YES. I KNOW WHAT THEY SAY. I HEAR THEM WHISPERING.
NOT EVEN THE PILLS DROWN THEM OUT. NOT EVEN THE TINFOIL IN MY PILLOW DOES IT.
LET'S SHOW THEM. LET'S SHOW THEM ALL.
THAT WAS CRUEL, RICH.
I JUST MADE MY CASE, VIOLET.
OH, AND THE CORONER CALLED.
...OH, GOOD.
STOP STARING AT MY LUNCH, YOU LITTLE BASTARD.
RELAX, YOU DON'T HAVE TO GO DOWN THERE. HE LEFT A MESSAGE.
"NO PRINTS, NO DISTINGUISHING FEATURES, NO NOTHING. MURDER WEAPON PROBABLY A LENGTH OF METAL PIPE. BORING."
idiot's bar
HEY, MAYKO.
HEY, RICH. USUAL?
OH, GOD, YES.

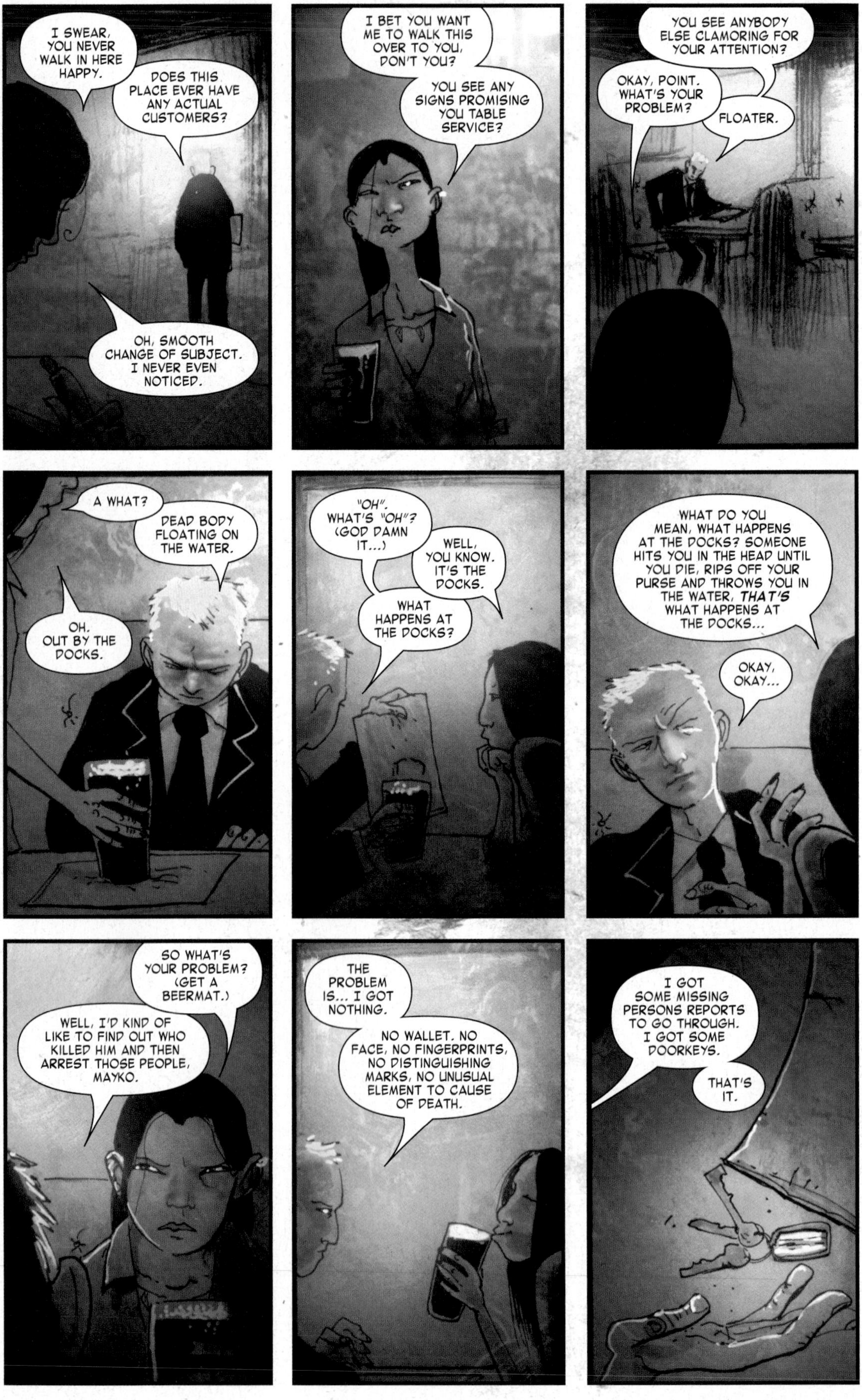
I SWEAR, YOU NEVER WALK IN HERE HAPPY.
DOES THIS PLACE EVER HAVE ANY ACTUAL CUSTOMERS?
OH, SMOOTH CHANGE OF SUBJECT. I NEVER EVEN NOTICED.
I BET YOU WANT ME TO WALK THIS OVER TO YOU, DON'T YOU?
YOU SEE ANY SIGNS PROMISING YOU TABLE SERVICE?
YOU SEE ANYBODY ELSE CLAMORING FOR YOUR ATTENTION?
OKAY, POINT. WHAT'S YOUR PROBLEM?
FLOATER.
A WHAT?
DEAD BODY FLOATING ON THE WATER.
OH. OUT BY THE DOCKS.
"OH". WHAT'S "OH"? (GOD DAMN IT...)
WELL, YOU KNOW. IT'S THE DOCKS.
WHAT HAPPENS AT THE DOCKS?
WHAT DO YOU MEAN, WHAT HAPPENS AT THE DOCKS? SOMEONE HITS YOU IN THE HEAD UNTIL YOU DIE, RIPS OFF YOUR PURSE AND THROWS YOU IN THE WATER, *THAT'S* WHAT HAPPENS AT THE DOCKS...
OKAY, OKAY...
SO WHAT'S YOUR PROBLEM? (GET A BEERMAT.)
WELL, I'D KIND OF LIKE TO FIND OUT WHO KILLED HIM AND THEN ARREST THOSE PEOPLE, MAYKO.
THE PROBLEM IS... I GOT NOTHING.
NO WALLET. NO FACE, NO FINGERPRINTS, NO DISTINGUISHING MARKS, NO UNUSUAL ELEMENT TO CAUSE OF DEATH.
I GOT SOME MISSING PERSONS REPORTS TO GO THROUGH. I GOT SOME DOORKEYS.
THAT'S IT.

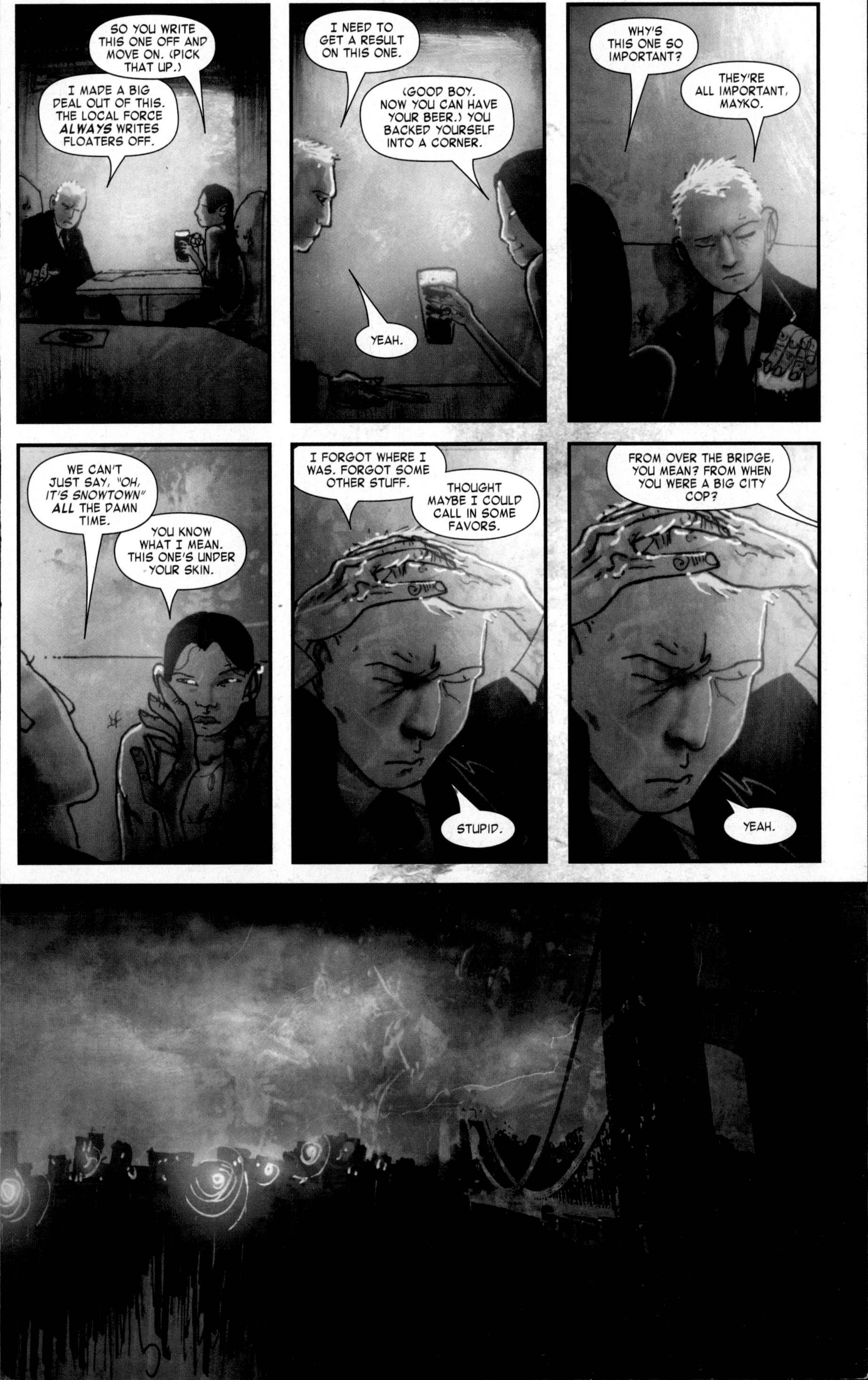

SO YOU WRITE THIS ONE OFF AND MOVE ON. (PICK THAT UP.)
I MADE A BIG DEAL OUT OF THIS. THE LOCAL FORCE ALWAYS WRITES FLOATERS OFF.
I NEED TO GET A RESULT ON THIS ONE.
(GOOD BOY. NOW YOU CAN HAVE YOUR BEER.) YOU BACKED YOURSELF INTO A CORNER.
YEAH.
WHY'S THIS ONE SO IMPORTANT?
THEY'RE ALL IMPORTANT, MAYKO.
WE CAN'T JUST SAY, "OH, IT'S SNOWTOWN" ALL THE DAMN TIME.
YOU KNOW WHAT I MEAN. THIS ONE'S UNDER YOUR SKIN.
I FORGOT WHERE I WAS. FORGOT SOME OTHER STUFF.
THOUGHT MAYBE I COULD CALL IN SOME FAVORS.
STUPID.
FROM OVER THE BRIDGE, YOU MEAN? FROM WHEN YOU WERE A BIG CITY COP?
YEAH.

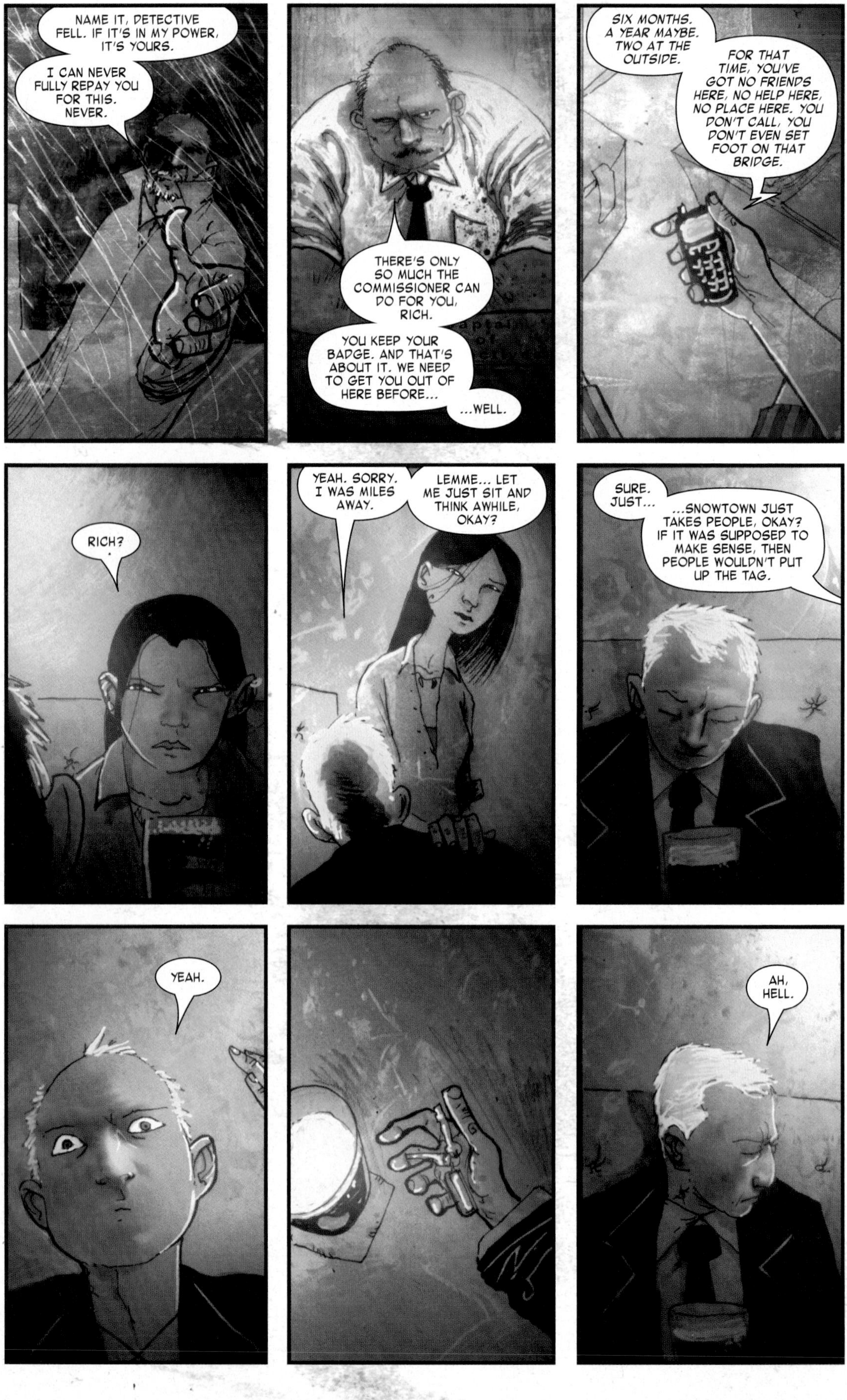
NAME IT, DETECTIVE FELL. IF IT'S IN MY POWER, IT'S YOURS.
I CAN NEVER FULLY REPAY YOU FOR THIS. NEVER.
THERE'S ONLY SO MUCH THE COMMISSIONER CAN DO FOR YOU, RICH.
YOU KEEP YOUR BADGE. AND THAT'S ABOUT IT. WE NEED TO GET YOU OUT OF HERE BEFORE...
...WELL.
SIX MONTHS. A YEAR MAYBE. TWO AT THE OUTSIDE.
FOR THAT TIME, YOU'VE GOT NO FRIENDS HERE, NO HELP HERE, NO PLACE HERE. YOU DON'T CALL, YOU DON'T EVEN SET FOOT ON THAT BRIDGE.
RICH?
YEAH. SORRY. I WAS MILES AWAY.
LEMME... LET ME JUST SIT AND THINK AWHILE, OKAY?
SURE. JUST...
...SNOWTOWN JUST TAKES PEOPLE, OKAY? IF IT WAS SUPPOSED TO MAKE SENSE, THEN PEOPLE WOULDN'T PUT UP THE TAG.
YEAH.
AH, HELL.

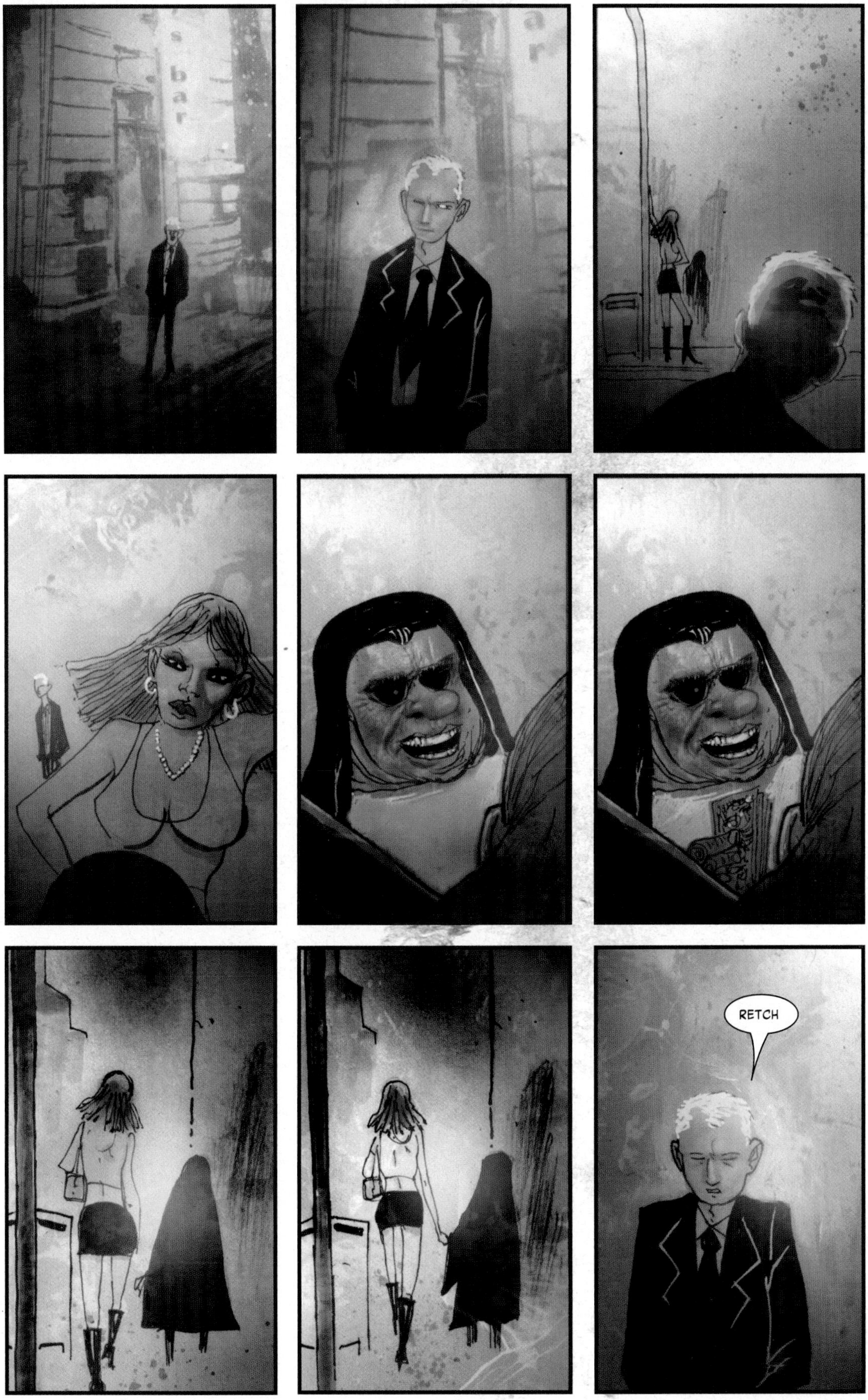
RETCH

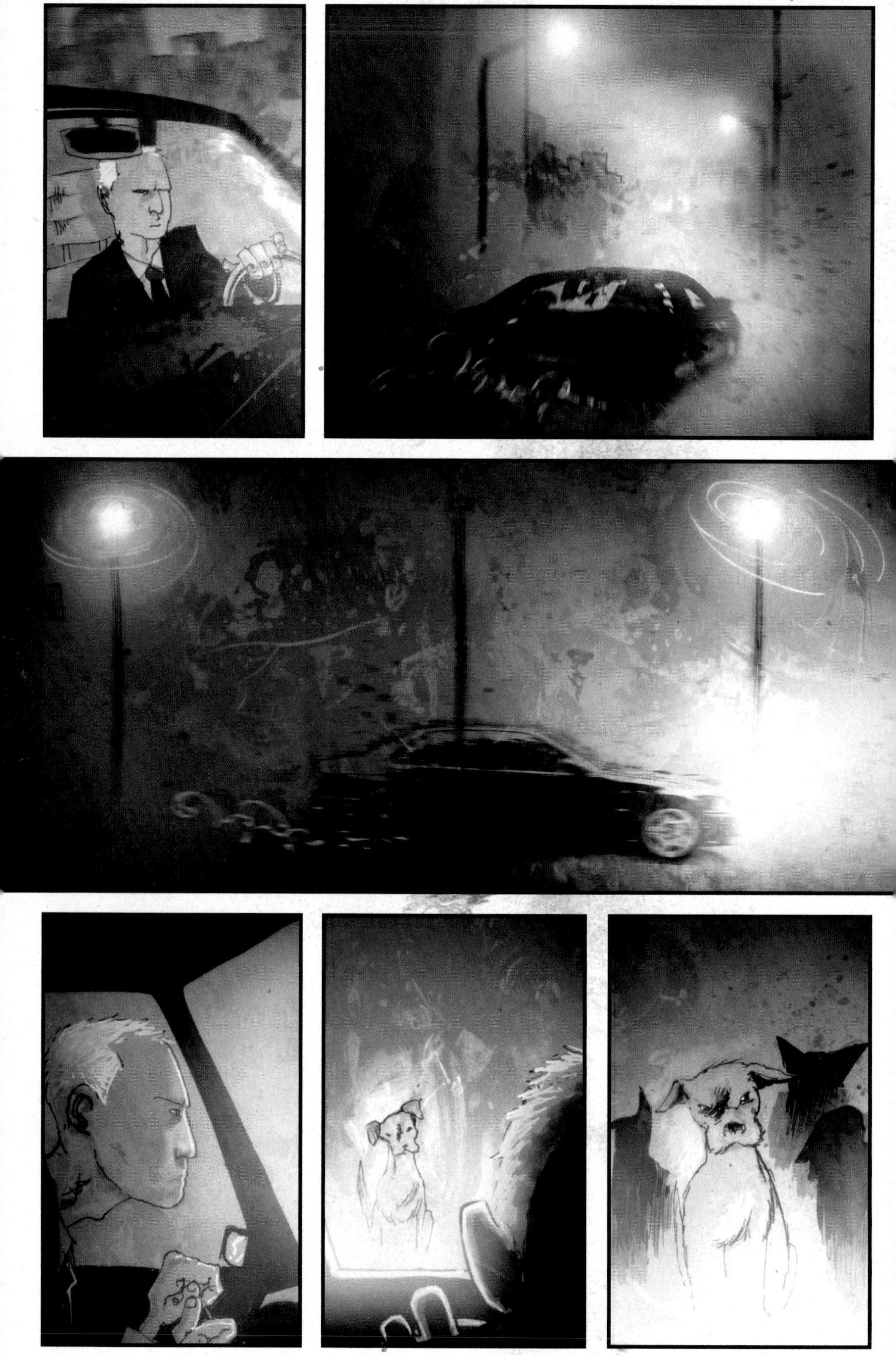

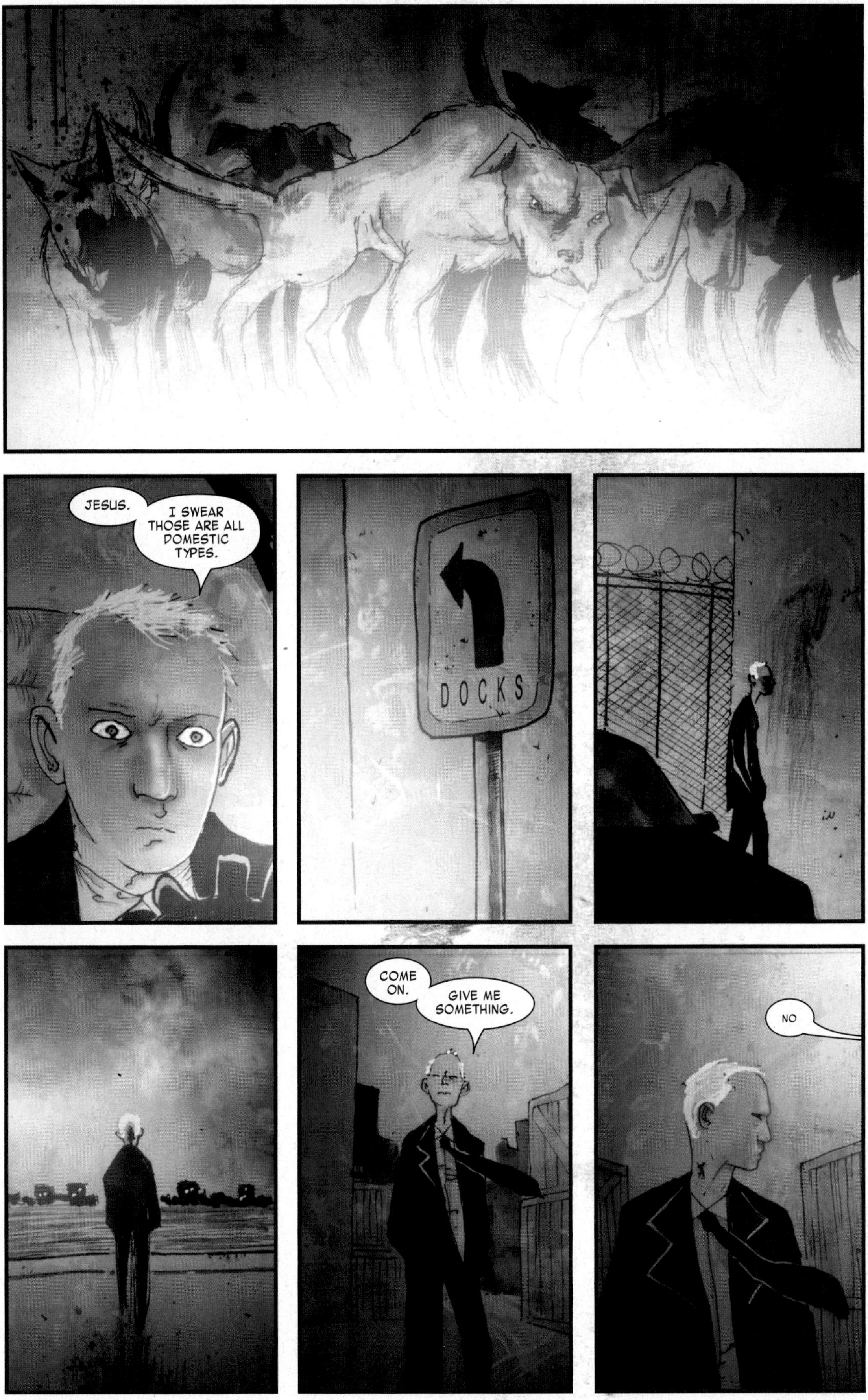
JESUS.
I SWEAR THOSE ARE ALL DOMESTIC TYPES.
DOCKS
COME ON.
GIVE ME SOMETHING.
NO

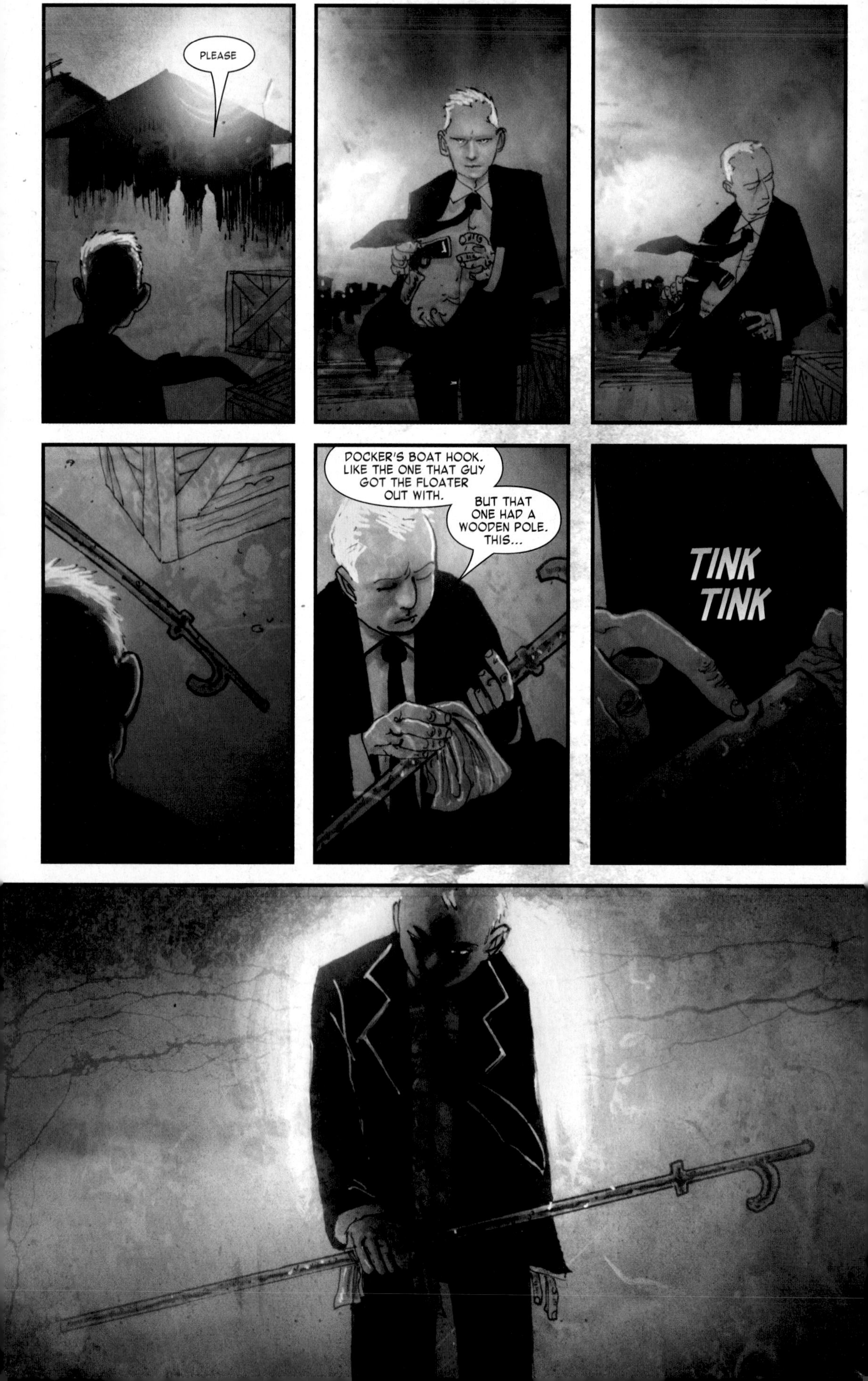
PLEASE
DOCKER'S BOAT HOOK. LIKE THE ONE THAT GUY GOT THE FLOATER OUT WITH.
BUT THAT ONE HAD A WOODEN POLE. THIS...
TINK TINK

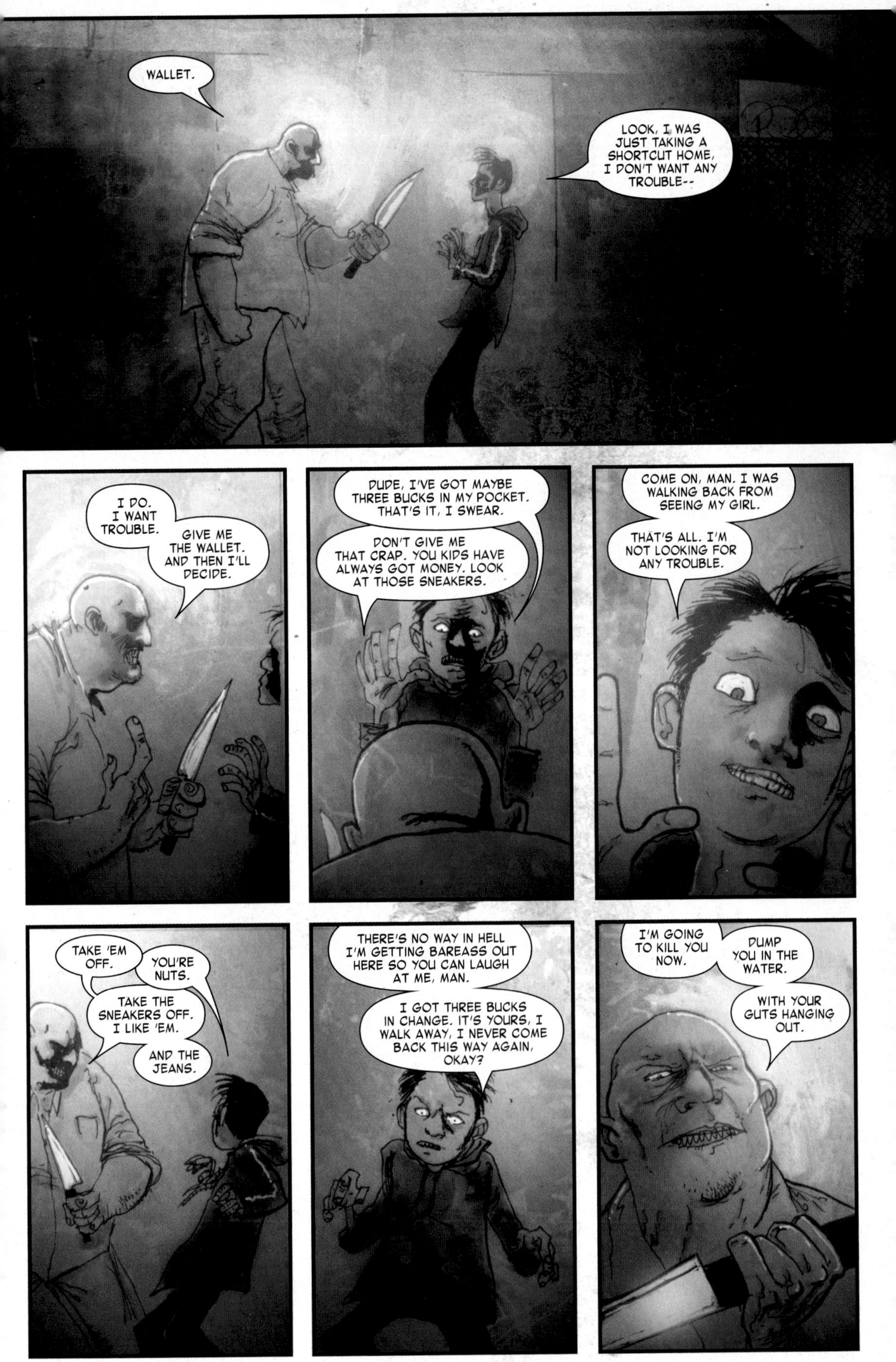
WALLET.
LOOK, I WAS JUST TAKING A SHORTCUT HOME, I DON'T WANT ANY TROUBLE--
I DO. I WANT TROUBLE.
GIVE ME THE WALLET. AND THEN I'LL DECIDE.
DUDE, I'VE GOT MAYBE THREE BUCKS IN MY POCKET. THAT'S IT, I SWEAR.
DON'T GIVE ME THAT CRAP. YOU KIDS HAVE ALWAYS GOT MONEY. LOOK AT THOSE SNEAKERS.
COME ON, MAN. I WAS WALKING BACK FROM SEEING MY GIRL.
THAT'S ALL. I'M NOT LOOKING FOR ANY TROUBLE.
TAKE 'EM OFF.
YOU'RE NUTS.
TAKE THE SNEAKERS OFF. I LIKE 'EM.
AND THE JEANS.
THERE'S NO WAY IN HELL I'M GETTING BAREASS OUT HERE SO YOU CAN LAUGH AT ME, MAN.
I GOT THREE BUCKS IN CHANGE. IT'S YOURS, I WALK AWAY, I NEVER COME BACK THIS WAY AGAIN, OKAY?
I'M GOING TO KILL YOU NOW.
DUMP YOU IN THE WATER.
WITH YOUR GUTS HANGING OUT.

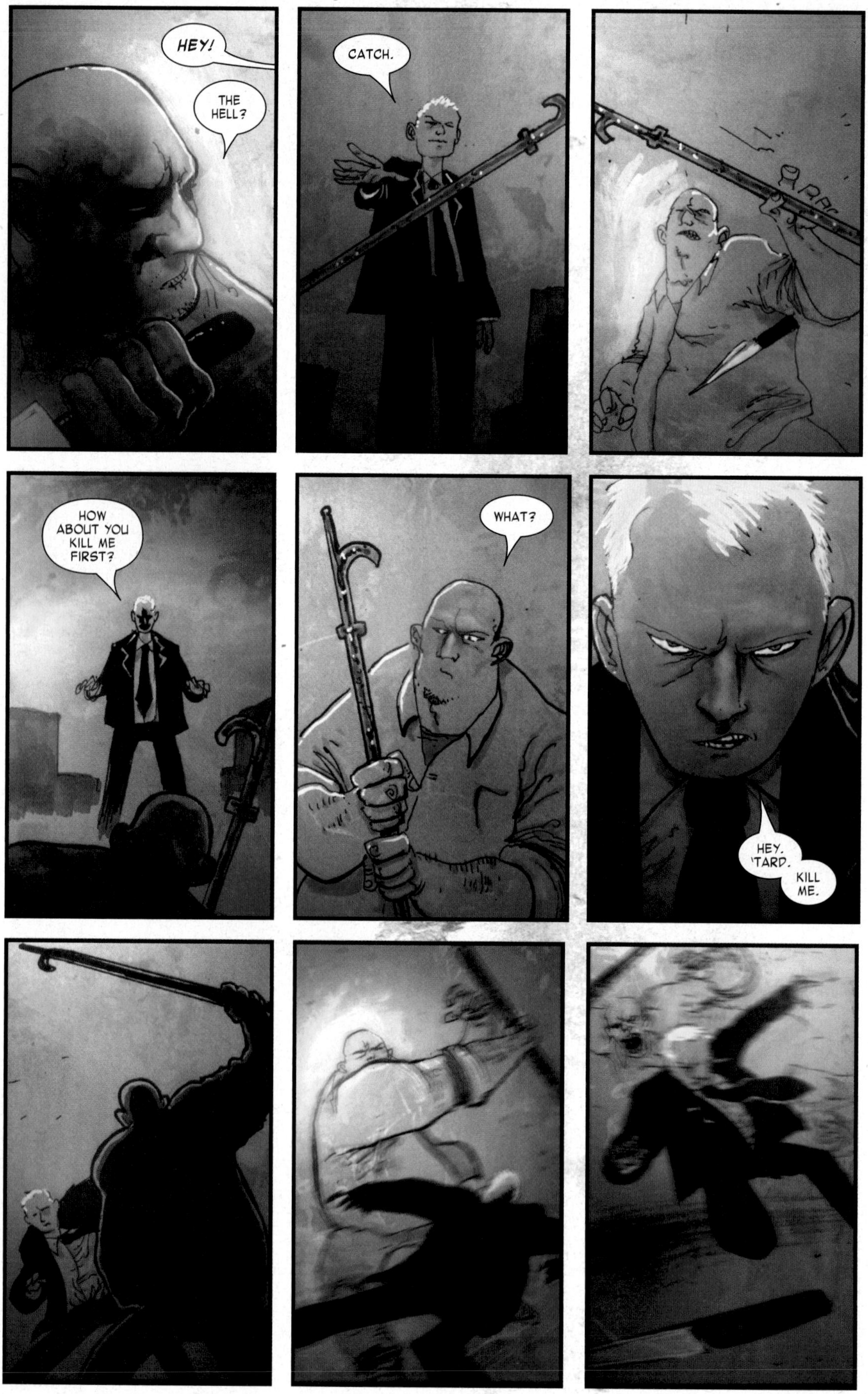
HEY!
THE HELL?
CATCH.
HOW ABOUT YOU KILL ME FIRST?
WHAT?
HEY. 'TARD.
KILL ME.

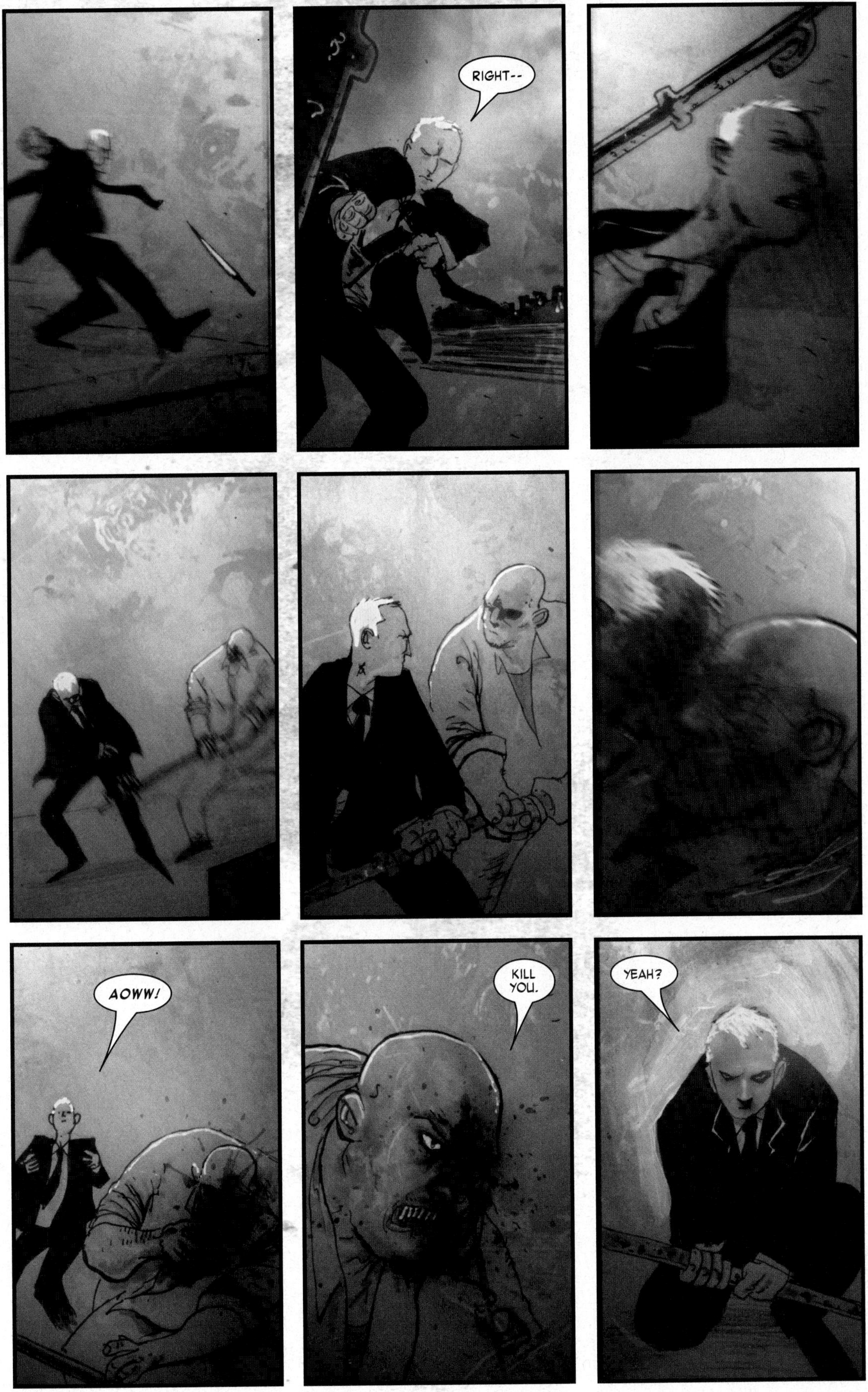
RIGHT--
AOWW!
KILL YOU.
YEAH?

KILL ME! COME ON!

SHOW ME HOW YOU'RE GONNA KILL ME!

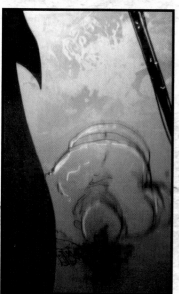

YOU'RE UNDER ARREST FOR ATTEMPTED ARMED ROBBERY, ASSAULTING A POLICE OFFICER--

--AND ON SUSPICION OF MURDER IN THE CASE OF JOHN DOE 478/05 DEATH CAUSED BY METAL PIPE-LIKE OBJECT.

LIKE THIS ONE.

DETECTIVE FELL, SNOWTOWN PD. PLEASE STAY PUT WHILE I CALL THIS IN.

WE'LL GET YOU A RIDE HOME AFTERWARDS. BUT ONE THING --

WHENEVER YOU'RE ASKED ABOUT HOW THIS MAN THREATENED YOU... DON'T MENTION THE KNIFE.

HE HAD A BOAT HOOK. HE WAS GOING TO GUT YOU WITH THAT BOAT HOOK. AND THEN I DISARMED HIM. CLEAR?

...SURE. WHATEVER YOU SAY.

THANK YOU, SIR. IT'S IMPORTANT.

YOU HEAR THAT? EVERY TIME YOU TAKE ONE...

...I'M GOING TO TAKE ONE BACK.

END

# FELL.™

## CHAPTER 5

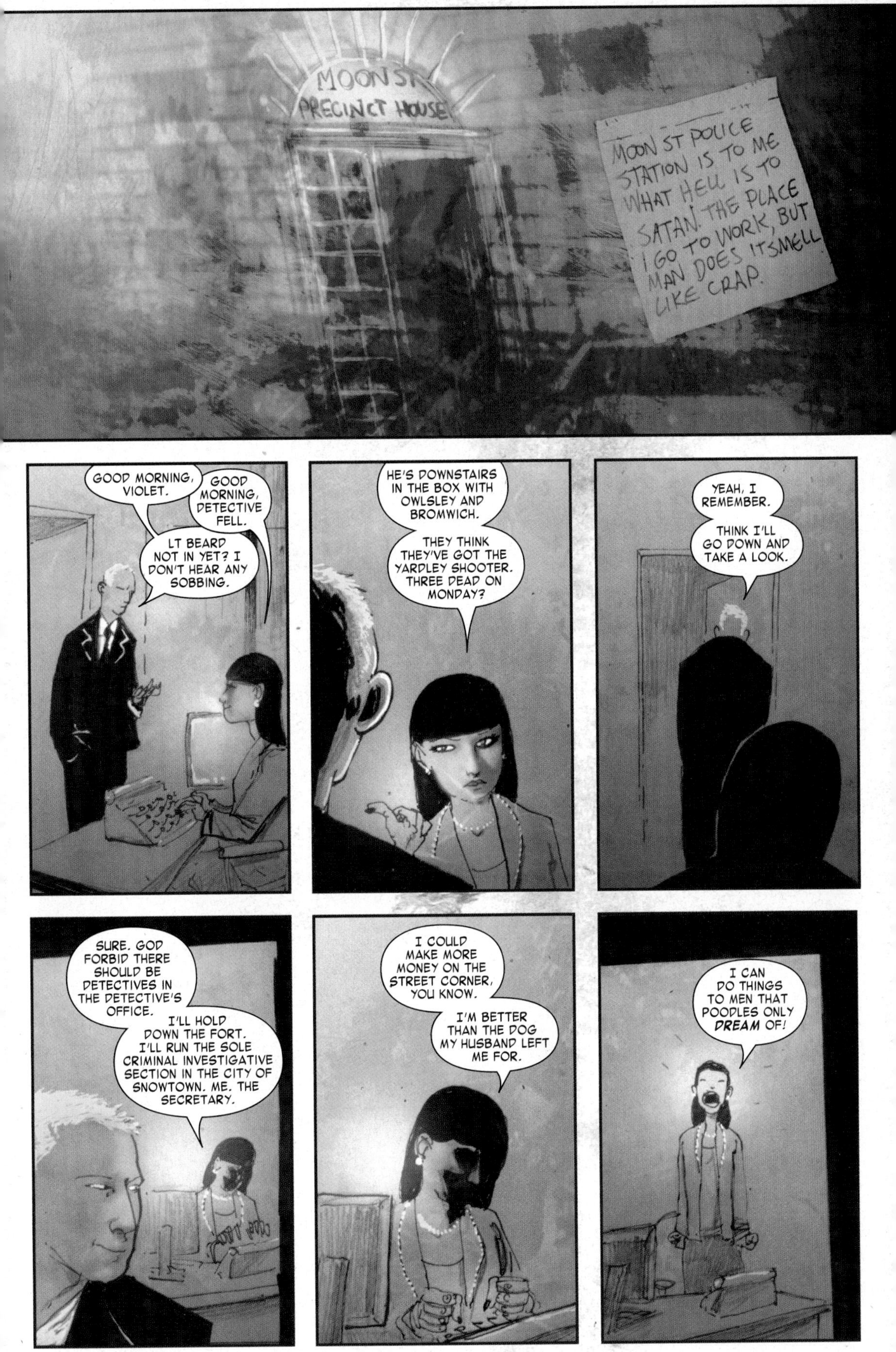
MOON ST PRECINCT HOUSE
MOON ST POLICE STATION IS TO ME WHAT HELL IS TO SATAN. THE PLACE I GO TO WORK, BUT MAN DOES IT SMELL LIKE CRAP.
GOOD MORNING, VIOLET.
GOOD MORNING, DETECTIVE FELL.
LT BEARD NOT IN YET? I DON'T HEAR ANY SOBBING.
HE'S DOWNSTAIRS IN THE BOX WITH OWLSLEY AND BROMWICH.
THEY THINK THEY'VE GOT THE YARDLEY SHOOTER. THREE DEAD ON MONDAY?
YEAH, I REMEMBER.
THINK I'LL GO DOWN AND TAKE A LOOK.
SURE. GOD FORBID THERE SHOULD BE DETECTIVES IN THE DETECTIVE'S OFFICE.
I'LL HOLD DOWN THE FORT. I'LL RUN THE SOLE CRIMINAL INVESTIGATIVE SECTION IN THE CITY OF SNOWTOWN. ME. THE SECRETARY.
I COULD MAKE MORE MONEY ON THE STREET CORNER, YOU KNOW.
I'M BETTER THAN THE DOG MY HUSBAND LEFT ME FOR.
I CAN DO THINGS TO MEN THAT POODLES ONLY *DREAM* OF!

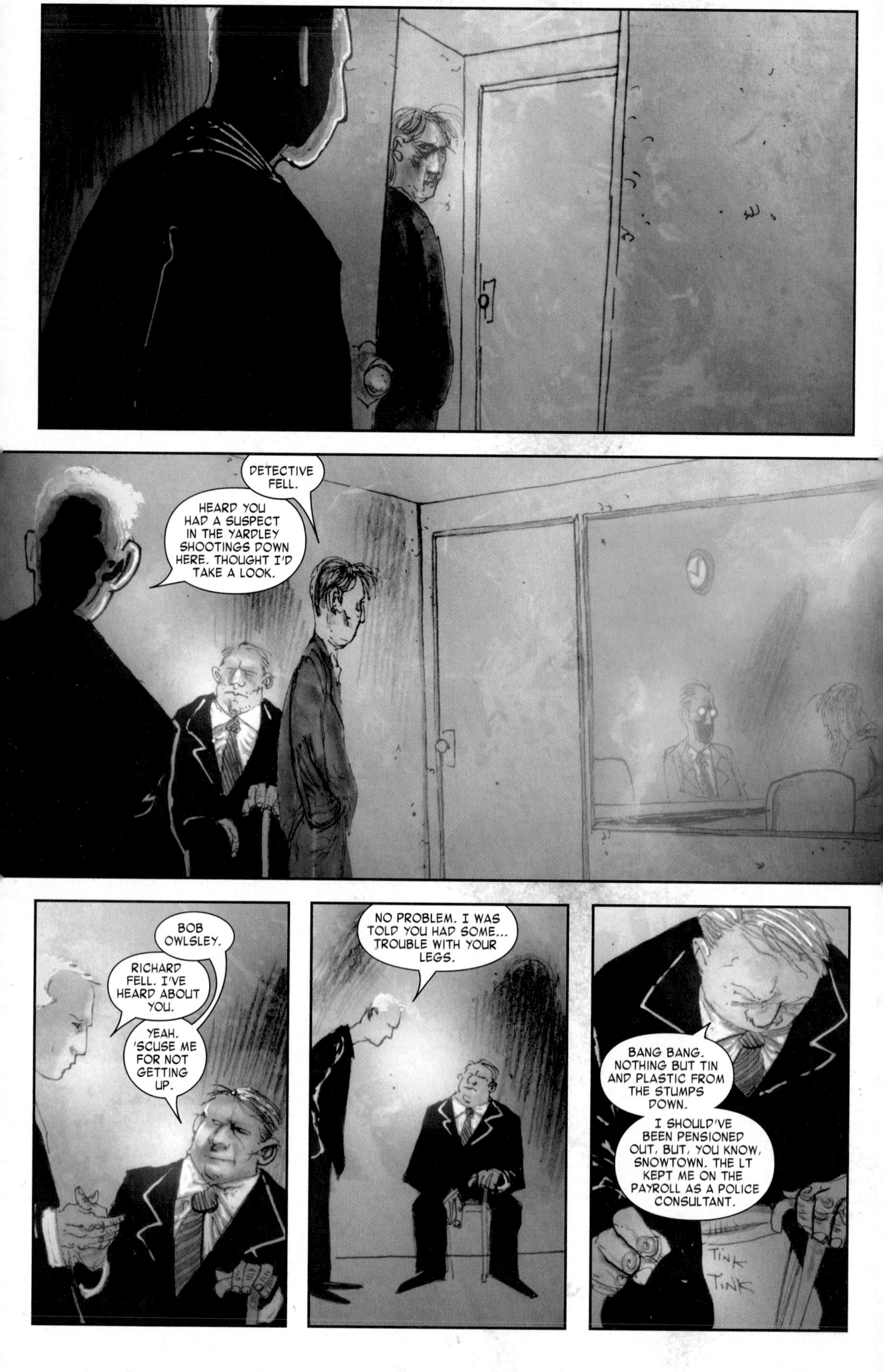
DETECTIVE FELL.
HEARD YOU HAD A SUSPECT IN THE YARDLEY SHOOTINGS DOWN HERE. THOUGHT I'D TAKE A LOOK.
BOB OWLSLEY.
RICHARD FELL. I'VE HEARD ABOUT YOU.
YEAH. 'SCUSE ME FOR NOT GETTING UP.
NO PROBLEM. I WAS TOLD YOU HAD SOME... TROUBLE WITH YOUR LEGS.
BANG BANG. NOTHING BUT TIN AND PLASTIC FROM THE STUMPS DOWN.
I SHOULD'VE BEEN PENSIONED OUT, BUT, YOU KNOW, SNOWTOWN. THE LT KEPT ME ON THE PAYROLL AS A POLICE CONSULTANT.
TINK
TINK

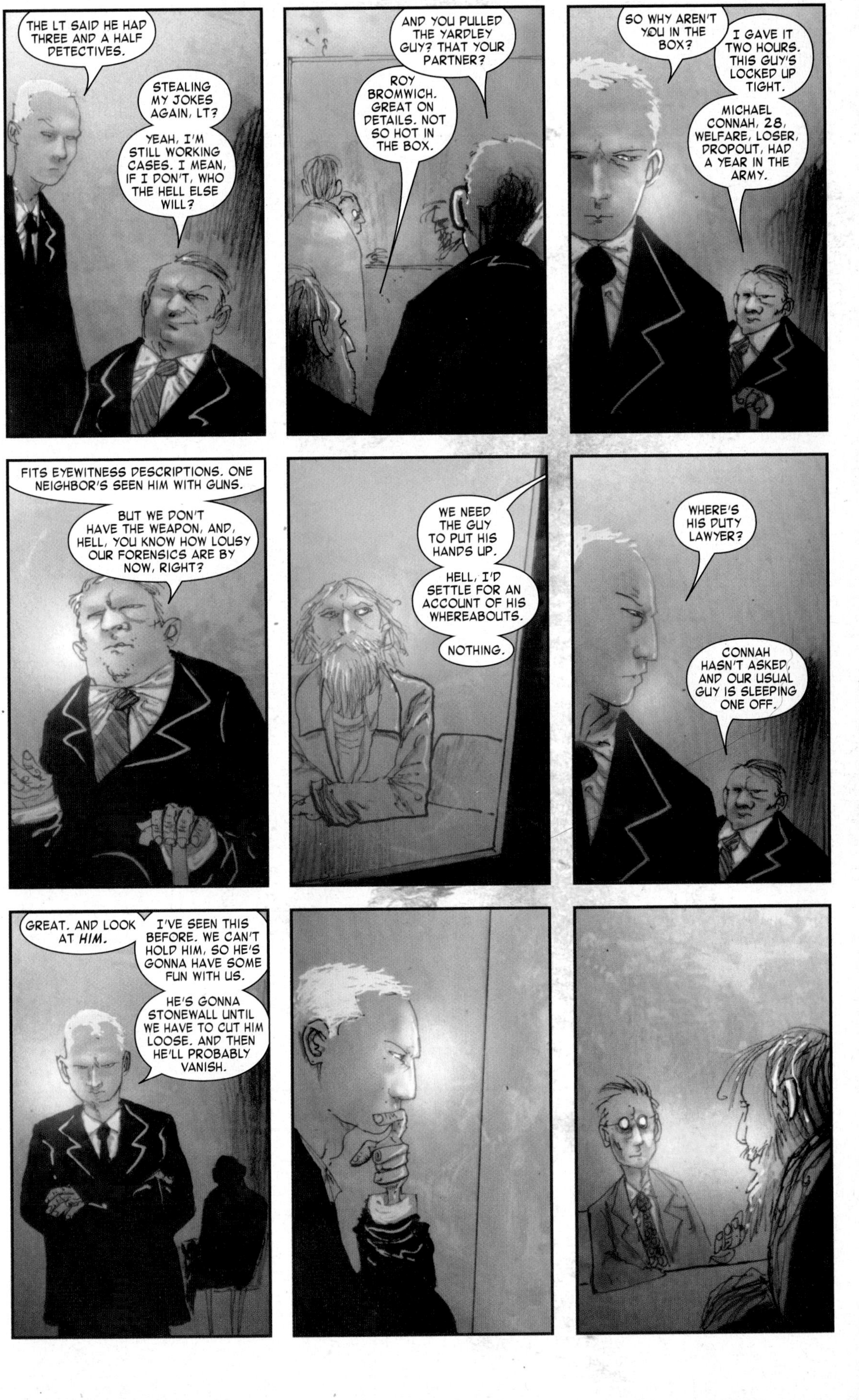
THE LT SAID HE HAD THREE AND A HALF DETECTIVES.
STEALING MY JOKES AGAIN, LT?
YEAH, I'M STILL WORKING CASES. I MEAN, IF I DON'T, WHO THE HELL ELSE WILL?
AND YOU PULLED THE YARDLEY GUY? THAT YOUR PARTNER?
ROY BROMWICH. GREAT ON DETAILS. NOT SO HOT IN THE BOX.
SO WHY AREN'T YOU IN THE BOX?
I GAVE IT TWO HOURS. THIS GUY'S LOCKED UP TIGHT.
MICHAEL CONNAH, 28, WELFARE, LOSER, DROPOUT, HAD A YEAR IN THE ARMY.
FITS EYEWITNESS DESCRIPTIONS. ONE NEIGHBOR'S SEEN HIM WITH GUNS.
BUT WE DON'T HAVE THE WEAPON, AND, HELL, YOU KNOW HOW LOUSY OUR FORENSICS ARE BY NOW, RIGHT?
WE NEED THE GUY TO PUT HIS HANDS UP.
HELL, I'D SETTLE FOR AN ACCOUNT OF HIS WHEREABOUTS.
NOTHING.
WHERE'S HIS DUTY LAWYER?
CONNAH HASN'T ASKED, AND OUR USUAL GUY IS SLEEPING ONE OFF.
GREAT. AND LOOK AT *HIM*.
I'VE SEEN THIS BEFORE. WE CAN'T HOLD HIM, SO HE'S GONNA HAVE SOME FUN WITH US.
HE'S GONNA STONEWALL UNTIL WE HAVE TO CUT HIM LOOSE. AND THEN HE'LL PROBABLY VANISH.

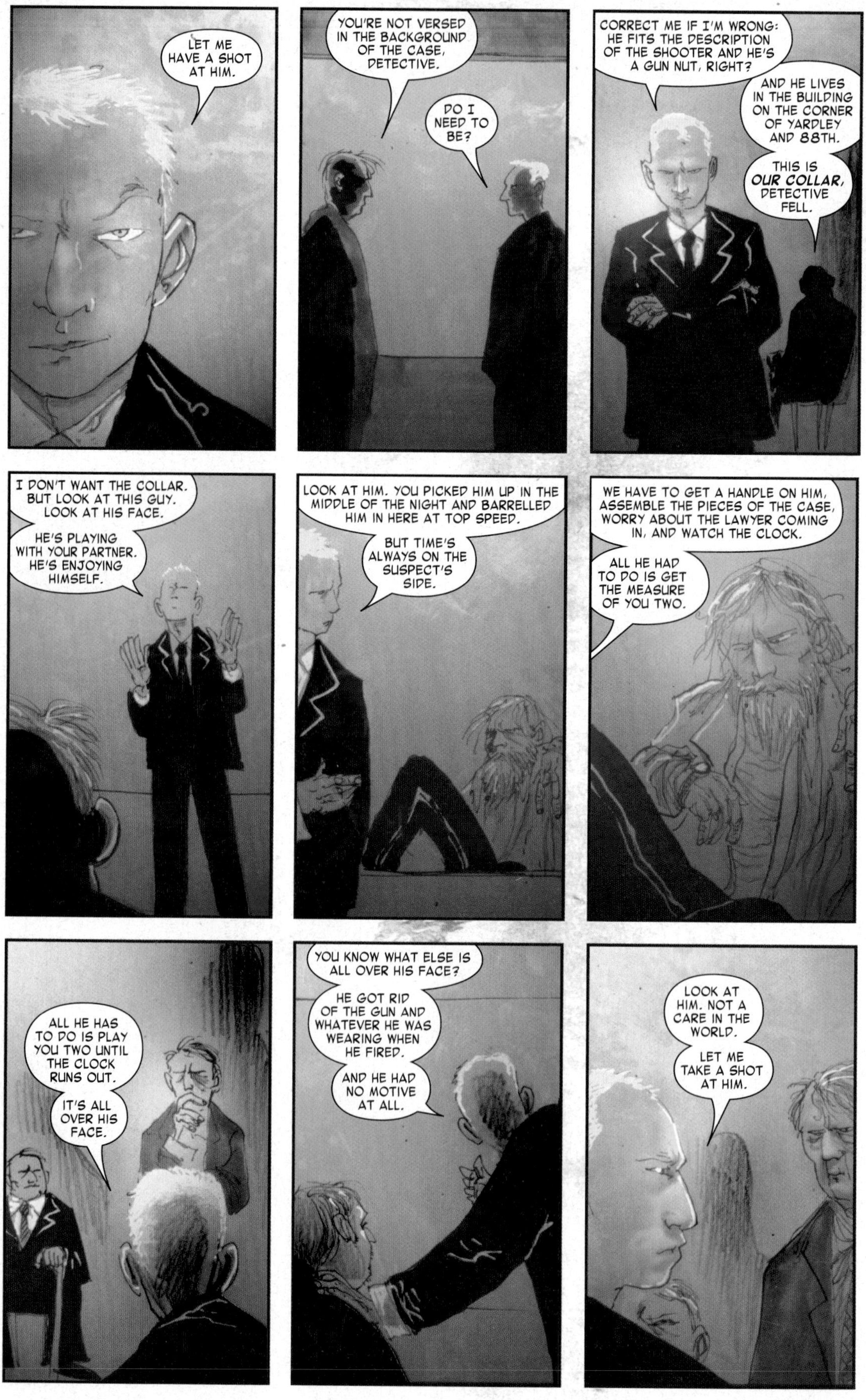
LET ME HAVE A SHOT AT HIM.
YOU'RE NOT VERSED IN THE BACKGROUND OF THE CASE, DETECTIVE.
DO I NEED TO BE?
CORRECT ME IF I'M WRONG: HE FITS THE DESCRIPTION OF THE SHOOTER AND HE'S A GUN NUT, RIGHT?
AND HE LIVES IN THE BUILDING ON THE CORNER OF YARDLEY AND 88TH.
THIS IS **OUR COLLAR,** DETECTIVE FELL.
I DON'T WANT THE COLLAR. BUT LOOK AT THIS GUY. LOOK AT HIS FACE.
HE'S PLAYING WITH YOUR PARTNER. HE'S ENJOYING HIMSELF.
LOOK AT HIM. YOU PICKED HIM UP IN THE MIDDLE OF THE NIGHT AND BARRELLED HIM IN HERE AT TOP SPEED.
BUT TIME'S ALWAYS ON THE SUSPECT'S SIDE.
WE HAVE TO GET A HANDLE ON HIM, ASSEMBLE THE PIECES OF THE CASE, WORRY ABOUT THE LAWYER COMING IN, AND WATCH THE CLOCK.
ALL HE HAD TO DO IS GET THE MEASURE OF YOU TWO.
ALL HE HAS TO DO IS PLAY YOU TWO UNTIL THE CLOCK RUNS OUT.
IT'S ALL OVER HIS FACE.
YOU KNOW WHAT ELSE IS ALL OVER HIS FACE?
HE GOT RID OF THE GUN AND WHATEVER HE WAS WEARING WHEN HE FIRED.
AND HE HAD NO MOTIVE AT ALL.
LOOK AT HIM. NOT A CARE IN THE WORLD.
LET ME TAKE A SHOT AT HIM.

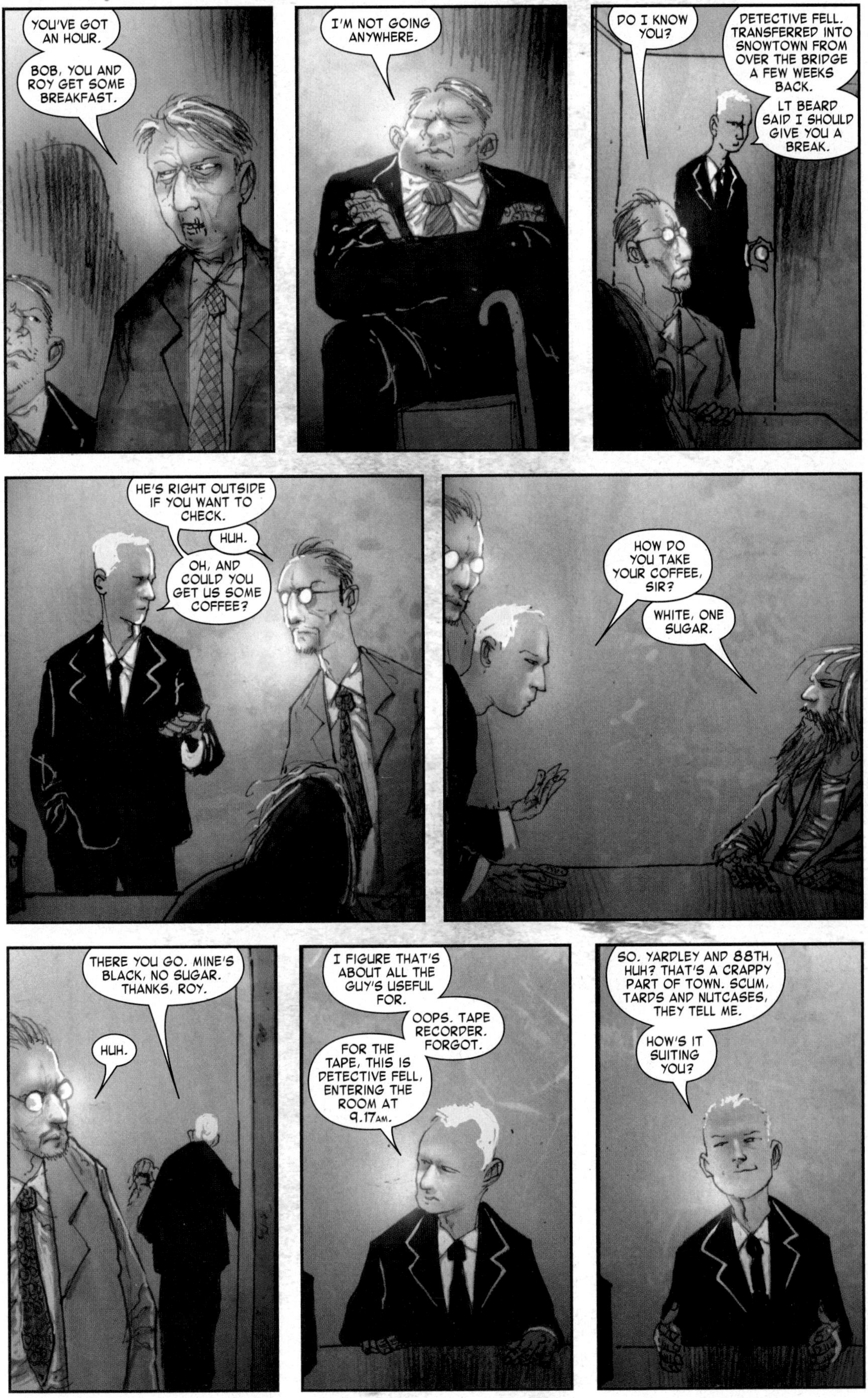
YOU'VE GOT AN HOUR.
BOB, YOU AND ROY GET SOME BREAKFAST.
I'M NOT GOING ANYWHERE.
DO I KNOW YOU?
DETECTIVE FELL. TRANSFERRED INTO SNOWTOWN FROM OVER THE BRIDGE A FEW WEEKS BACK.
LT BEARD SAID I SHOULD GIVE YOU A BREAK.
HE'S RIGHT OUTSIDE IF YOU WANT TO CHECK.
HUH.
OH, AND COULD YOU GET US SOME COFFEE?
HOW DO YOU TAKE YOUR COFFEE, SIR?
WHITE, ONE SUGAR.
THERE YOU GO. MINE'S BLACK, NO SUGAR. THANKS, ROY.
HUH.
I FIGURE THAT'S ABOUT ALL THE GUY'S USEFUL FOR.
OOPS. TAPE RECORDER. FORGOT.
FOR THE TAPE, THIS IS DETECTIVE FELL, ENTERING THE ROOM AT 9.17AM.
SO. YARDLEY AND 88TH, HUH? THAT'S A CRAPPY PART OF TOWN. SCUM, TARDS AND NUTCASES, THEY TELL ME.
HOW'S IT SUITING YOU?

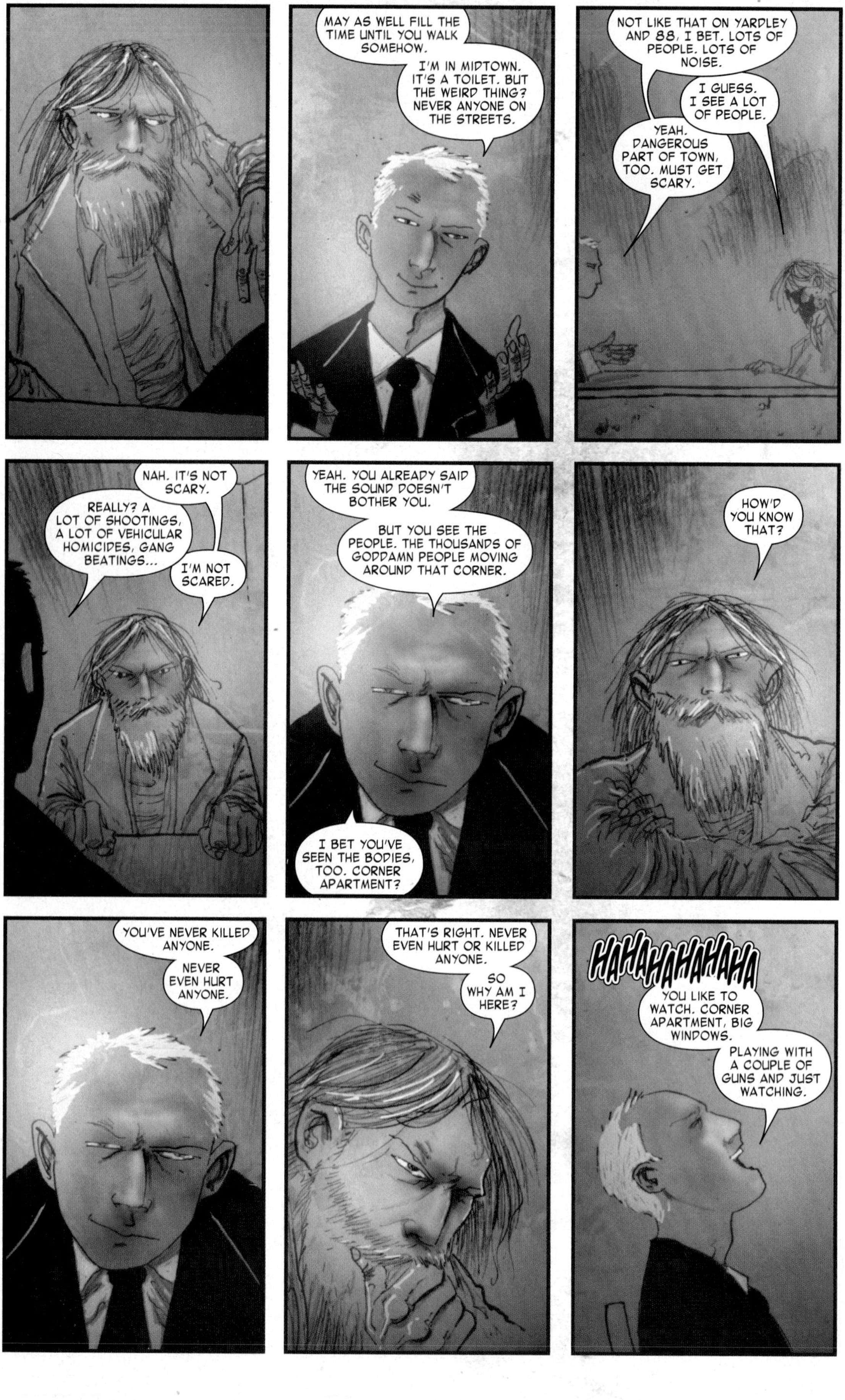

MAY AS WELL FILL THE TIME UNTIL YOU WALK SOMEHOW.
I'M IN MIDTOWN. IT'S A TOILET. BUT THE WEIRD THING? NEVER ANYONE ON THE STREETS.
NOT LIKE THAT ON YARDLEY AND 88, I BET. LOTS OF PEOPLE. LOTS OF NOISE.
I GUESS. I SEE A LOT OF PEOPLE.
YEAH. DANGEROUS PART OF TOWN, TOO. MUST GET SCARY.
NAH. IT'S NOT SCARY.
REALLY? A LOT OF SHOOTINGS, A LOT OF VEHICULAR HOMICIDES, GANG BEATINGS...
I'M NOT SCARED.
YEAH. YOU ALREADY SAID THE SOUND DOESN'T BOTHER YOU.
BUT YOU SEE THE PEOPLE. THE THOUSANDS OF GODDAMN PEOPLE MOVING AROUND THAT CORNER.
I BET YOU'VE SEEN THE BODIES, TOO. CORNER APARTMENT?
HOW'D YOU KNOW THAT?
YOU'VE NEVER KILLED ANYONE.
NEVER EVEN HURT ANYONE.
THAT'S RIGHT. NEVER EVEN HURT OR KILLED ANYONE.
SO WHY AM I HERE?
HAHAHAHAHAHAHA
YOU LIKE TO WATCH. CORNER APARTMENT, BIG WINDOWS.
PLAYING WITH A COUPLE OF GUNS AND JUST WATCHING.

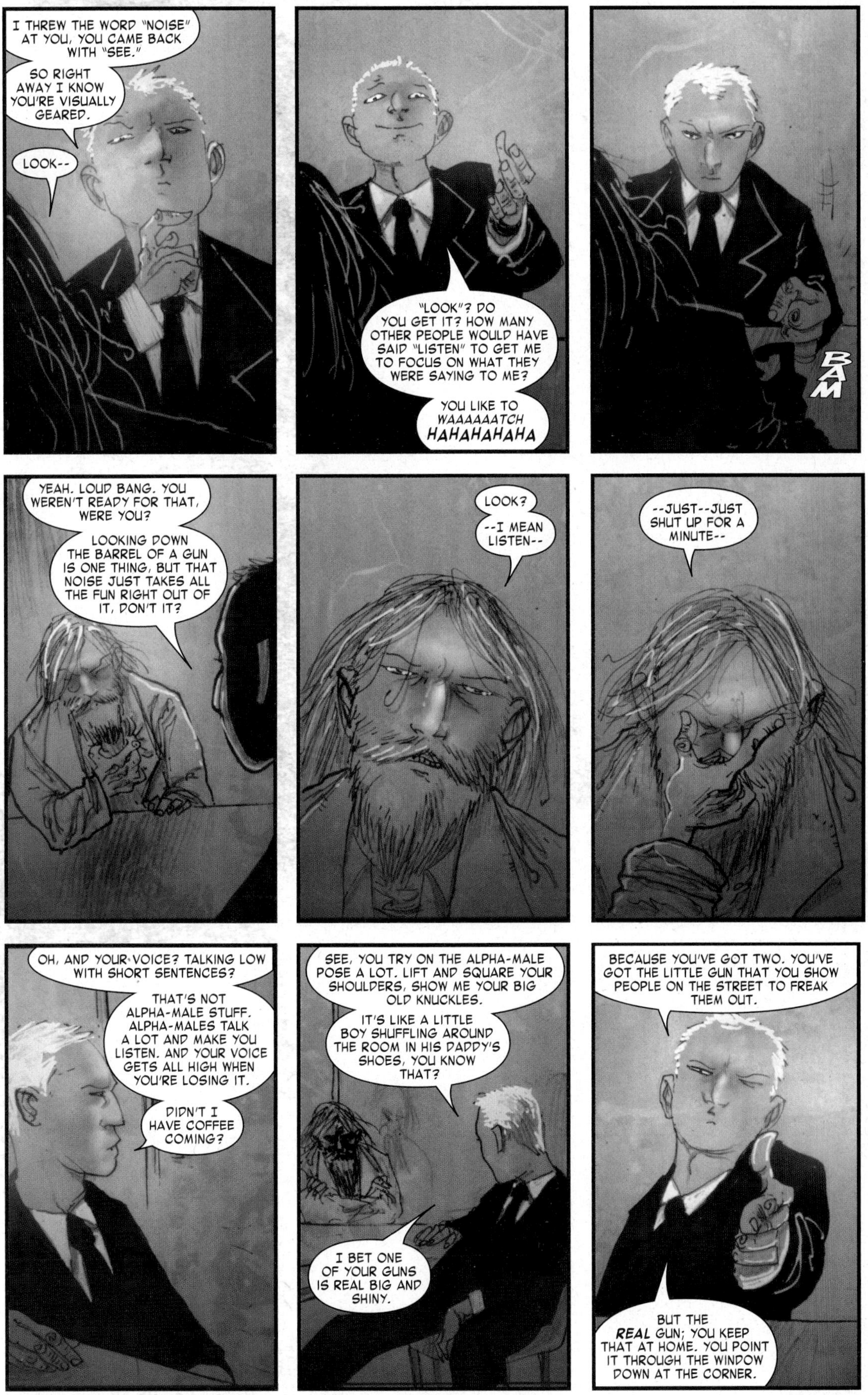
I THREW THE WORD "NOISE" AT YOU, YOU CAME BACK WITH "SEE."
SO RIGHT AWAY I KNOW YOU'RE VISUALLY GEARED.
LOOK--
"LOOK"? DO YOU GET IT? HOW MANY OTHER PEOPLE WOULD HAVE SAID "LISTEN" TO GET ME TO FOCUS ON WHAT THEY WERE SAYING TO ME?
YOU LIKE TO WAAAAAATCH HAHAHAHAHA
BAM
YEAH. LOUD BANG. YOU WEREN'T READY FOR THAT, WERE YOU?
LOOKING DOWN THE BARREL OF A GUN IS ONE THING, BUT THAT NOISE JUST TAKES ALL THE FUN RIGHT OUT OF IT, DON'T IT?
LOOK?
--I MEAN LISTEN--
--JUST--JUST SHUT UP FOR A MINUTE--
OH, AND YOUR VOICE? TALKING LOW WITH SHORT SENTENCES?
THAT'S NOT ALPHA-MALE STUFF. ALPHA-MALES TALK A LOT AND MAKE YOU LISTEN. AND YOUR VOICE GETS ALL HIGH WHEN YOU'RE LOSING IT.
DIDN'T I HAVE COFFEE COMING?
SEE, YOU TRY ON THE ALPHA-MALE POSE A LOT. LIFT AND SQUARE YOUR SHOULDERS, SHOW ME YOUR BIG OLD KNUCKLES.
IT'S LIKE A LITTLE BOY SHUFFLING AROUND THE ROOM IN HIS DADDY'S SHOES, YOU KNOW THAT?
I BET ONE OF YOUR GUNS IS REAL BIG AND SHINY.
BECAUSE YOU'VE GOT TWO. YOU'VE GOT THE LITTLE GUN THAT YOU SHOW PEOPLE ON THE STREET TO FREAK THEM OUT.
BUT THE REAL GUN; YOU KEEP THAT AT HOME. YOU POINT IT THROUGH THE WINDOW DOWN AT THE CORNER.

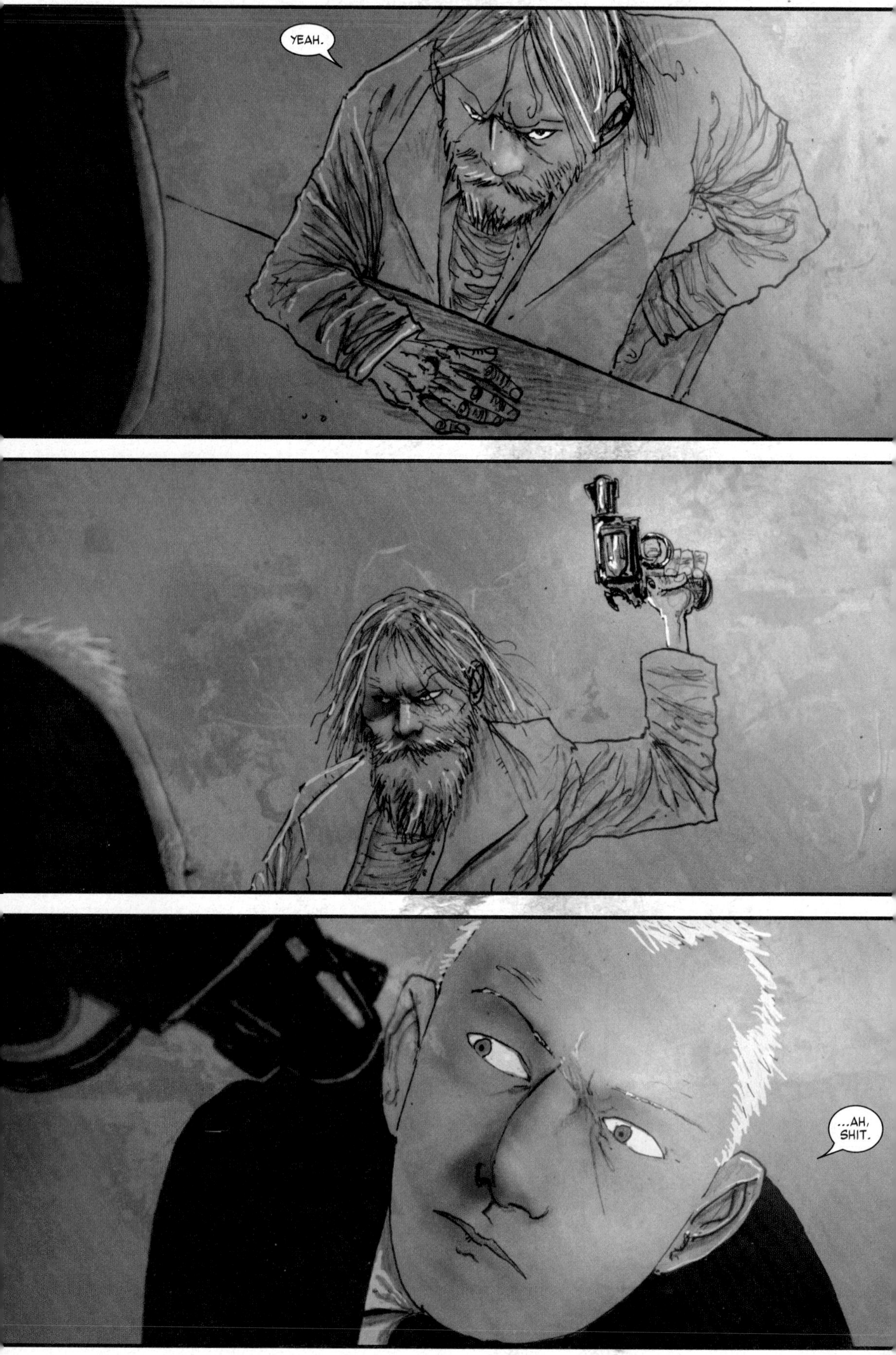
YEAH.
...AH, SHIT.

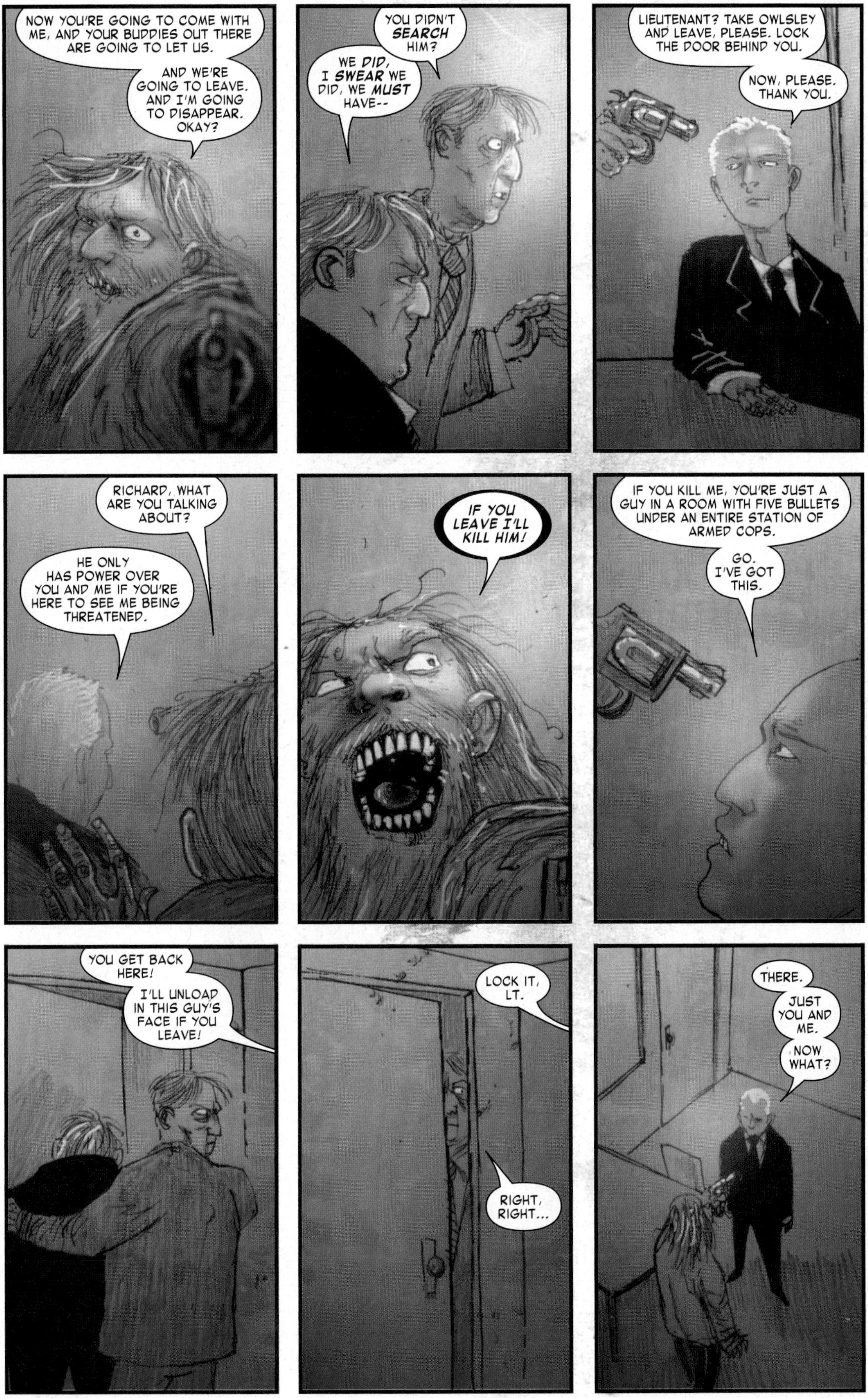
NOW YOU'RE GOING TO COME WITH ME, AND YOUR BUDDIES OUT THERE ARE GOING TO LET US.
AND WE'RE GOING TO LEAVE. AND I'M GOING TO DISAPPEAR. OKAY?
YOU DIDN'T SEARCH HIM?
WE DID, I SWEAR WE DID, WE MUST HAVE--
LIEUTENANT? TAKE OWLSLEY AND LEAVE, PLEASE. LOCK THE DOOR BEHIND YOU.
NOW, PLEASE. THANK YOU.
RICHARD, WHAT ARE YOU TALKING ABOUT?
HE ONLY HAS POWER OVER YOU AND ME IF YOU'RE HERE TO SEE ME BEING THREATENED.
IF YOU LEAVE I'LL KILL HIM!
IF YOU KILL ME, YOU'RE JUST A GUY IN A ROOM WITH FIVE BULLETS UNDER AN ENTIRE STATION OF ARMED COPS.
GO. I'VE GOT THIS.
YOU GET BACK HERE!
I'LL UNLOAD IN THIS GUY'S FACE IF YOU LEAVE!
LOCK IT, LT.
RIGHT, RIGHT...
THERE.
JUST YOU AND ME.
NOW WHAT?

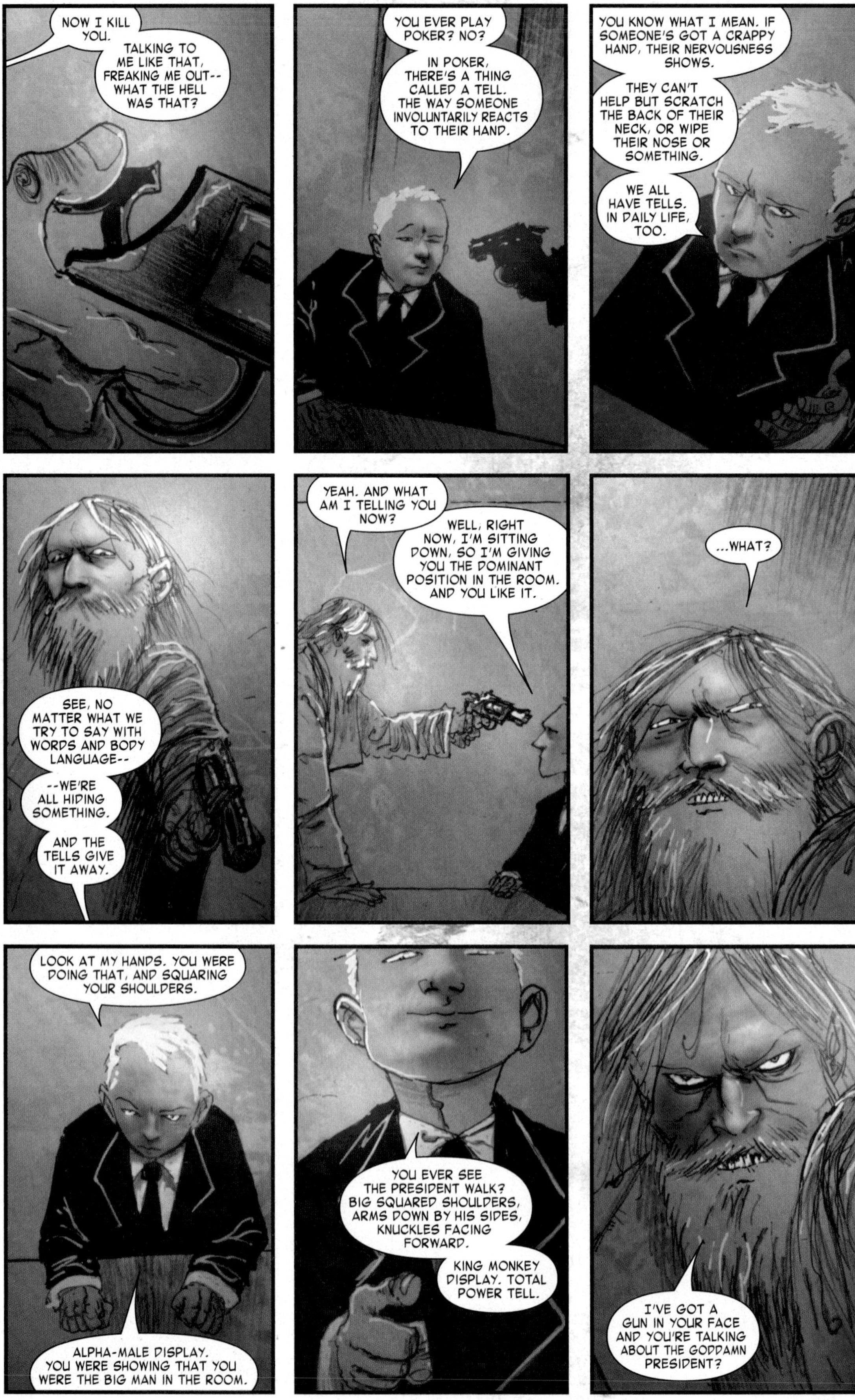
NOW I KILL YOU.
TALKING TO ME LIKE THAT, FREAKING ME OUT--WHAT THE HELL WAS THAT?
YOU EVER PLAY POKER? NO?
IN POKER, THERE'S A THING CALLED A TELL. THE WAY SOMEONE INVOLUNTARILY REACTS TO THEIR HAND.
YOU KNOW WHAT I MEAN. IF SOMEONE'S GOT A CRAPPY HAND, THEIR NERVOUSNESS SHOWS.
THEY CAN'T HELP BUT SCRATCH THE BACK OF THEIR NECK, OR WIPE THEIR NOSE OR SOMETHING.
WE ALL HAVE TELLS. IN DAILY LIFE, TOO.
SEE, NO MATTER WHAT WE TRY TO SAY WITH WORDS AND BODY LANGUAGE--
--WE'RE ALL HIDING SOMETHING.
AND THE TELLS GIVE IT AWAY.
YEAH. AND WHAT AM I TELLING YOU NOW?
WELL, RIGHT NOW, I'M SITTING DOWN, SO I'M GIVING YOU THE DOMINANT POSITION IN THE ROOM. AND YOU LIKE IT.
...WHAT?
LOOK AT MY HANDS. YOU WERE DOING THAT, AND SQUARING YOUR SHOULDERS.
ALPHA-MALE DISPLAY. YOU WERE SHOWING THAT YOU WERE THE BIG MAN IN THE ROOM.
YOU EVER SEE THE PRESIDENT WALK? BIG SQUARED SHOULDERS, ARMS DOWN BY HIS SIDES, KNUCKLES FACING FORWARD.
KING MONKEY DISPLAY. TOTAL POWER TELL.
I'VE GOT A GUN IN YOUR FACE AND YOU'RE TALKING ABOUT THE GODDAMN PRESIDENT?

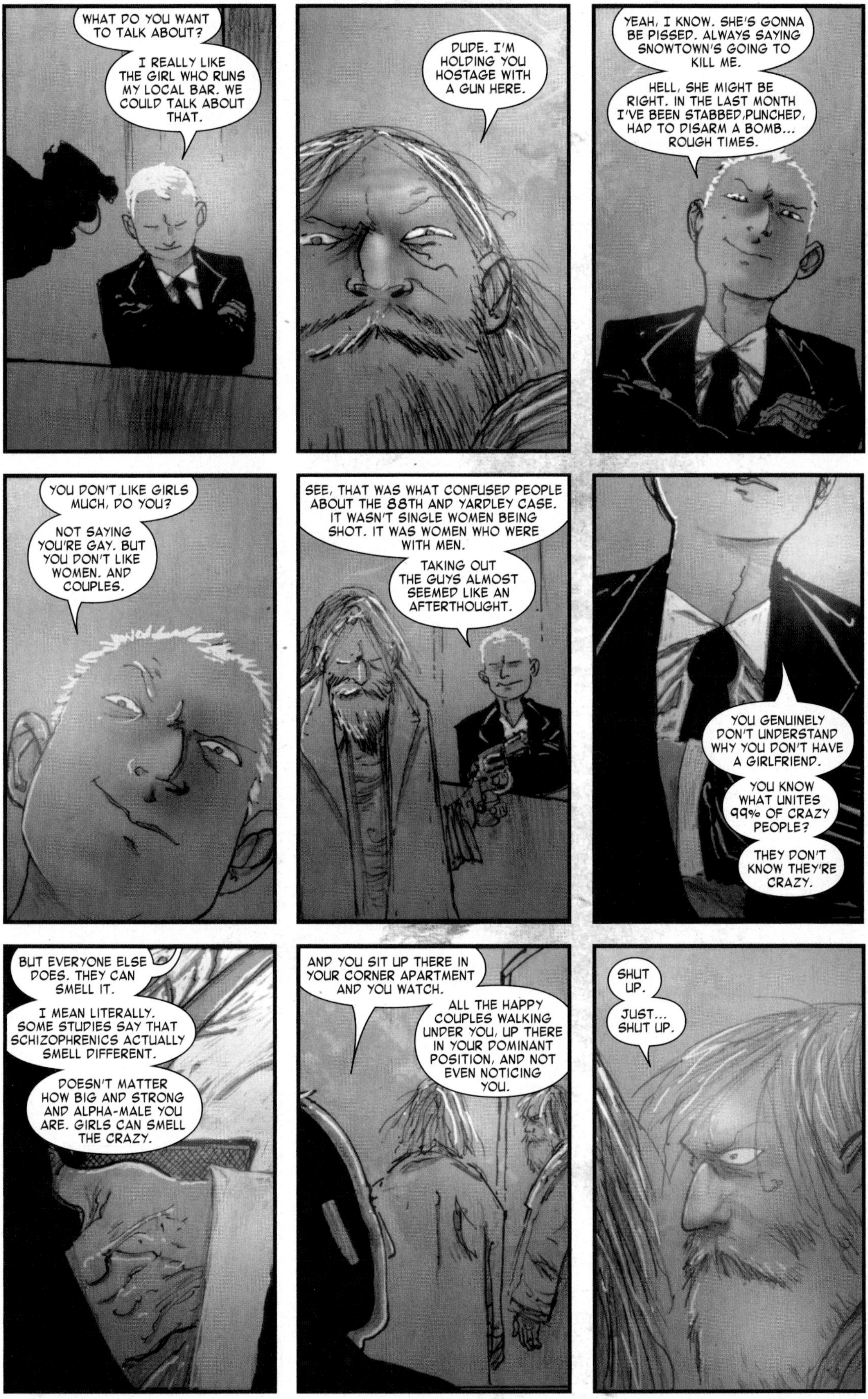
WHAT DO YOU WANT TO TALK ABOUT?
I REALLY LIKE THE GIRL WHO RUNS MY LOCAL BAR. WE COULD TALK ABOUT THAT.
DUDE. I'M HOLDING YOU HOSTAGE WITH A GUN HERE.
YEAH, I KNOW. SHE'S GONNA BE PISSED. ALWAYS SAYING SNOWTOWN'S GOING TO KILL ME.
HELL, SHE MIGHT BE RIGHT. IN THE LAST MONTH I'VE BEEN STABBED, PUNCHED, HAD TO DISARM A BOMB... ROUGH TIMES.
YOU DON'T LIKE GIRLS MUCH, DO YOU?
NOT SAYING YOU'RE GAY. BUT YOU DON'T LIKE WOMEN. AND COUPLES.
SEE, THAT WAS WHAT CONFUSED PEOPLE ABOUT THE 88TH AND YARDLEY CASE. IT WASN'T SINGLE WOMEN BEING SHOT. IT WAS WOMEN WHO WERE WITH MEN.
TAKING OUT THE GUYS ALMOST SEEMED LIKE AN AFTERTHOUGHT.
YOU GENUINELY DON'T UNDERSTAND WHY YOU DON'T HAVE A GIRLFRIEND.
YOU KNOW WHAT UNITES 99% OF CRAZY PEOPLE?
THEY DON'T KNOW THEY'RE CRAZY.
BUT EVERYONE ELSE DOES. THEY CAN SMELL IT.
I MEAN LITERALLY. SOME STUDIES SAY THAT SCHIZOPHRENICS ACTUALLY SMELL DIFFERENT.
DOESN'T MATTER HOW BIG AND STRONG AND ALPHA-MALE YOU ARE. GIRLS CAN SMELL THE CRAZY.
AND YOU SIT UP THERE IN YOUR CORNER APARTMENT AND YOU WATCH.
ALL THE HAPPY COUPLES WALKING UNDER YOU, UP THERE IN YOUR DOMINANT POSITION, AND NOT EVEN NOTICING YOU.
SHUT UP.
JUST... SHUT UP.

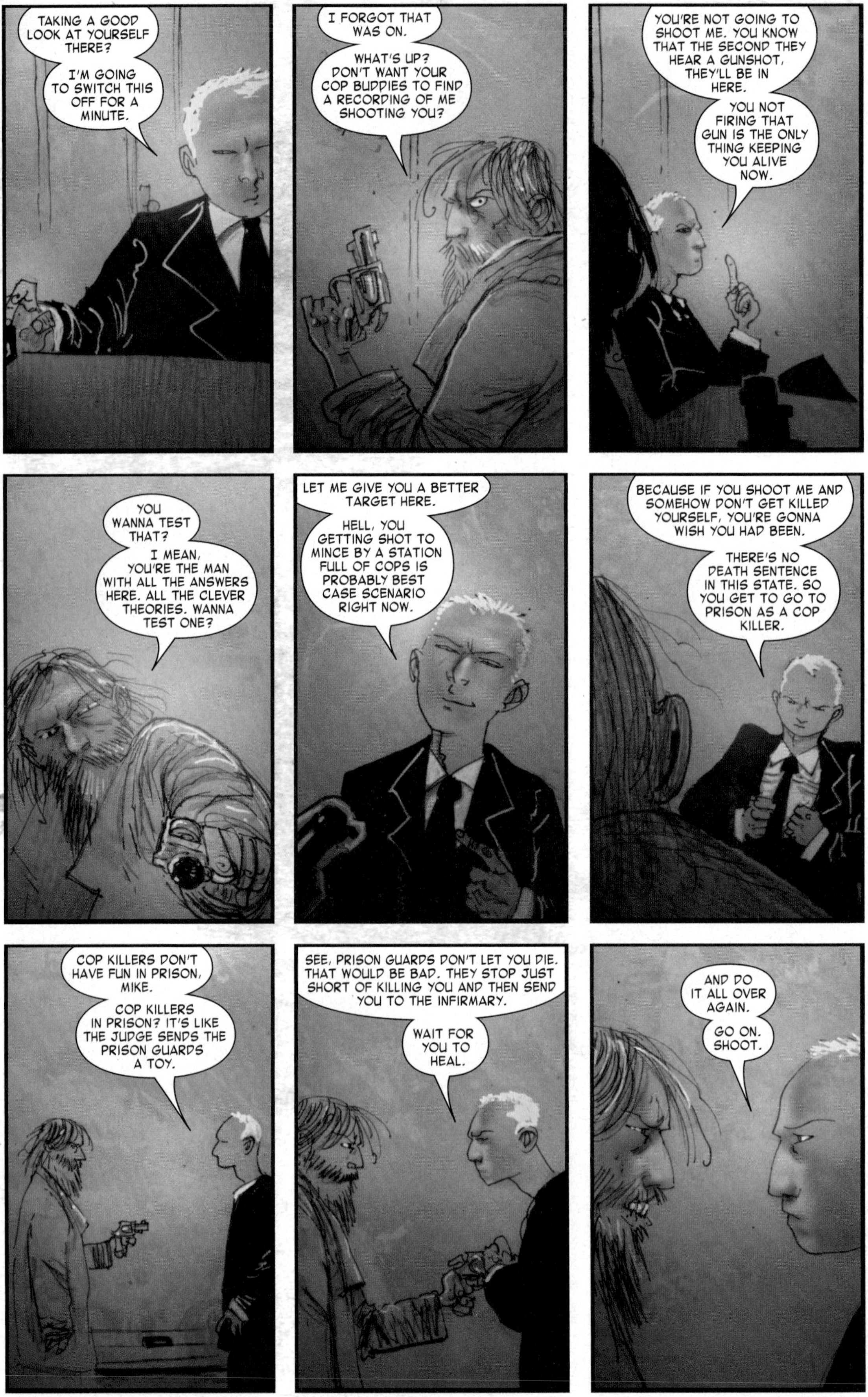
TAKING A GOOD LOOK AT YOURSELF THERE?
I'M GOING TO SWITCH THIS OFF FOR A MINUTE.
I FORGOT THAT WAS ON.
WHAT'S UP? DON'T WANT YOUR COP BUDDIES TO FIND A RECORDING OF ME SHOOTING YOU?
YOU'RE NOT GOING TO SHOOT ME. YOU KNOW THAT THE SECOND THEY HEAR A GUNSHOT, THEY'LL BE IN HERE.
YOU NOT FIRING THAT GUN IS THE ONLY THING KEEPING YOU ALIVE NOW.
YOU WANNA TEST THAT?
I MEAN, YOU'RE THE MAN WITH ALL THE ANSWERS HERE. ALL THE CLEVER THEORIES. WANNA TEST ONE?
LET ME GIVE YOU A BETTER TARGET HERE.
HELL, YOU GETTING SHOT TO MINCE BY A STATION FULL OF COPS IS PROBABLY BEST CASE SCENARIO RIGHT NOW.
BECAUSE IF YOU SHOOT ME AND SOMEHOW DON'T GET KILLED YOURSELF, YOU'RE GONNA WISH YOU HAD BEEN.
THERE'S NO DEATH SENTENCE IN THIS STATE. SO YOU GET TO GO TO PRISON AS A COP KILLER.
COP KILLERS DON'T HAVE FUN IN PRISON, MIKE.
COP KILLERS IN PRISON? IT'S LIKE THE JUDGE SENDS THE PRISON GUARDS A TOY.
SEE, PRISON GUARDS DON'T LET YOU DIE. THAT WOULD BE BAD. THEY STOP JUST SHORT OF KILLING YOU AND THEN SEND YOU TO THE INFIRMARY.
WAIT FOR YOU TO HEAL.
AND DO IT ALL OVER AGAIN.
GO ON. SHOOT.

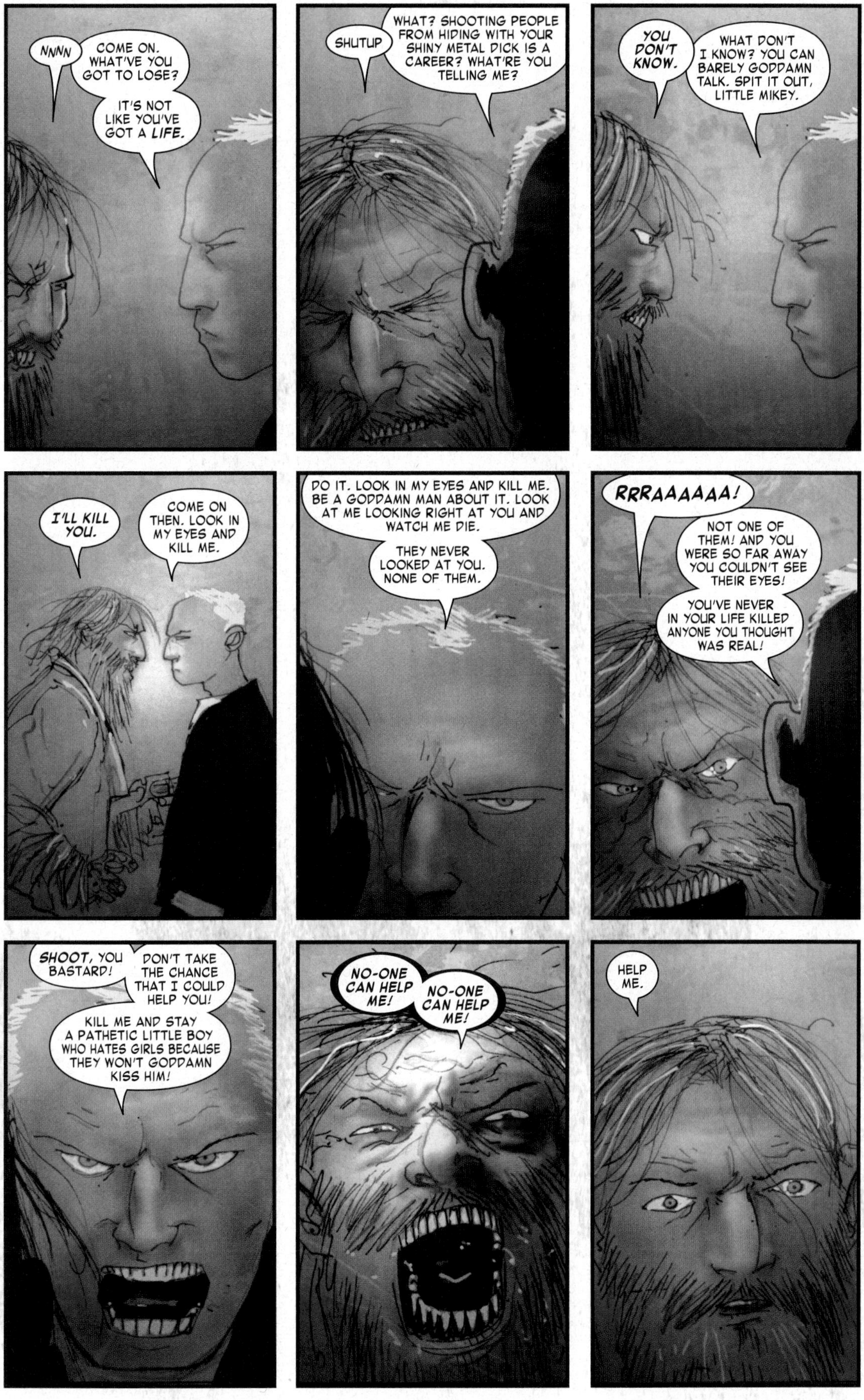
NNNN
COME ON. WHAT'VE YOU GOT TO LOSE?
IT'S NOT LIKE YOU'VE GOT A LIFE.
SHUTUP
WHAT? SHOOTING PEOPLE FROM HIDING WITH YOUR SHINY METAL DICK IS A CAREER? WHAT'RE YOU TELLING ME?
YOU DON'T KNOW.
WHAT DON'T I KNOW? YOU CAN BARELY GODDAMN TALK. SPIT IT OUT, LITTLE MIKEY.
I'LL KILL YOU.
COME ON THEN. LOOK IN MY EYES AND KILL ME.
DO IT. LOOK IN MY EYES AND KILL ME. BE A GODDAMN MAN ABOUT IT. LOOK AT ME LOOKING RIGHT AT YOU AND WATCH ME DIE.
THEY NEVER LOOKED AT YOU. NONE OF THEM.
RRRAAAAAA!
NOT ONE OF THEM! AND YOU WERE SO FAR AWAY YOU COULDN'T SEE THEIR EYES!
YOU'VE NEVER IN YOUR LIFE KILLED ANYONE YOU THOUGHT WAS REAL!
SHOOT, YOU BASTARD!
DON'T TAKE THE CHANCE THAT I COULD HELP YOU!
KILL ME AND STAY A PATHETIC LITTLE BOY WHO HATES GIRLS BECAUSE THEY WON'T GODDAMN KISS HIM!
NO-ONE CAN HELP ME!
NO-ONE CAN HELP ME!
HELP ME.

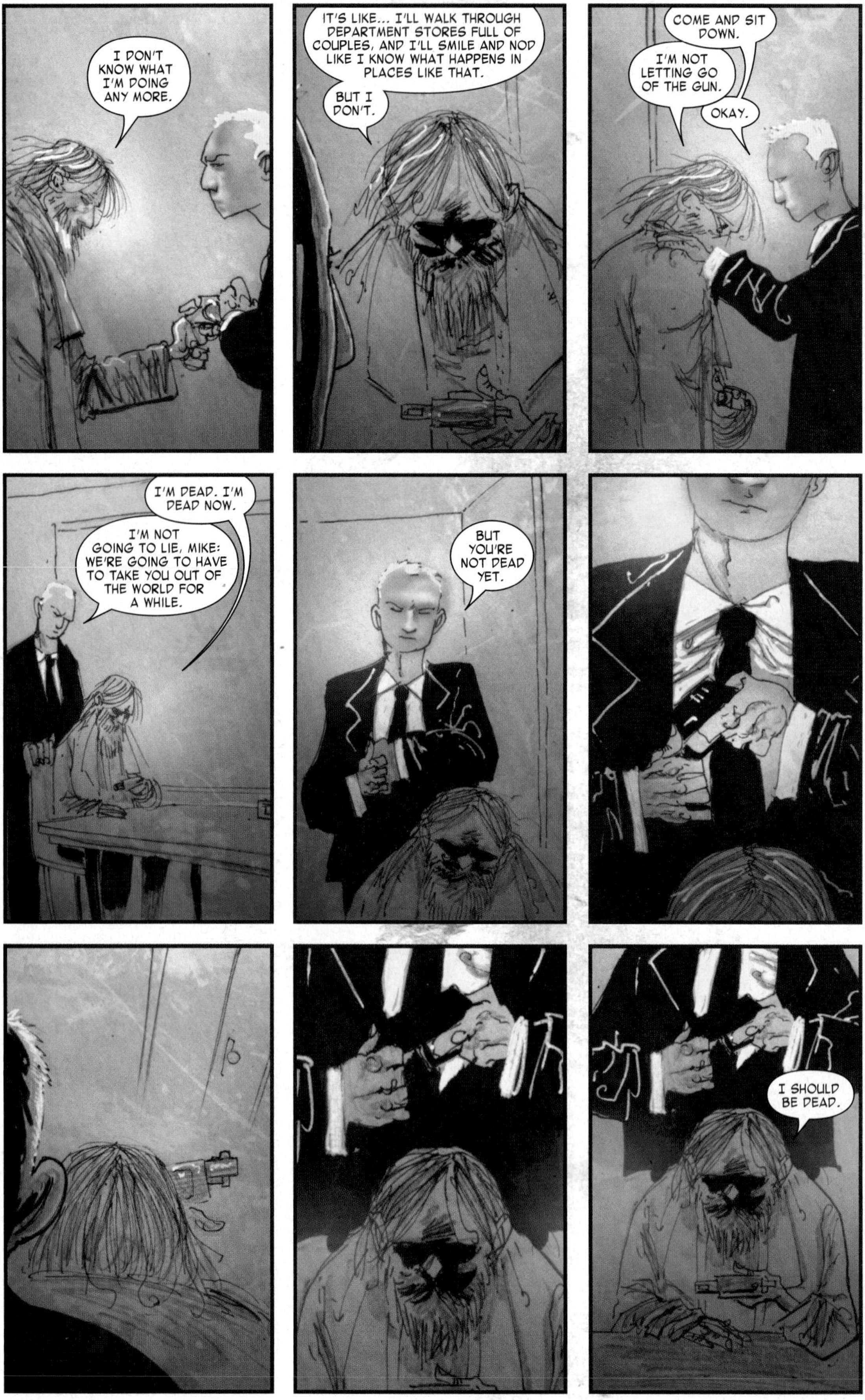
I DON'T KNOW WHAT I'M DOING ANY MORE.
IT'S LIKE... I'LL WALK THROUGH DEPARTMENT STORES FULL OF COUPLES, AND I'LL SMILE AND NOD LIKE I KNOW WHAT HAPPENS IN PLACES LIKE THAT.
BUT I DON'T.
COME AND SIT DOWN.
I'M NOT LETTING GO OF THE GUN.
OKAY.
I'M DEAD. I'M DEAD NOW.
I'M NOT GOING TO LIE, MIKE: WE'RE GOING TO HAVE TO TAKE YOU OUT OF THE WORLD FOR A WHILE.
BUT YOU'RE NOT DEAD YET.
I SHOULD BE DEAD.

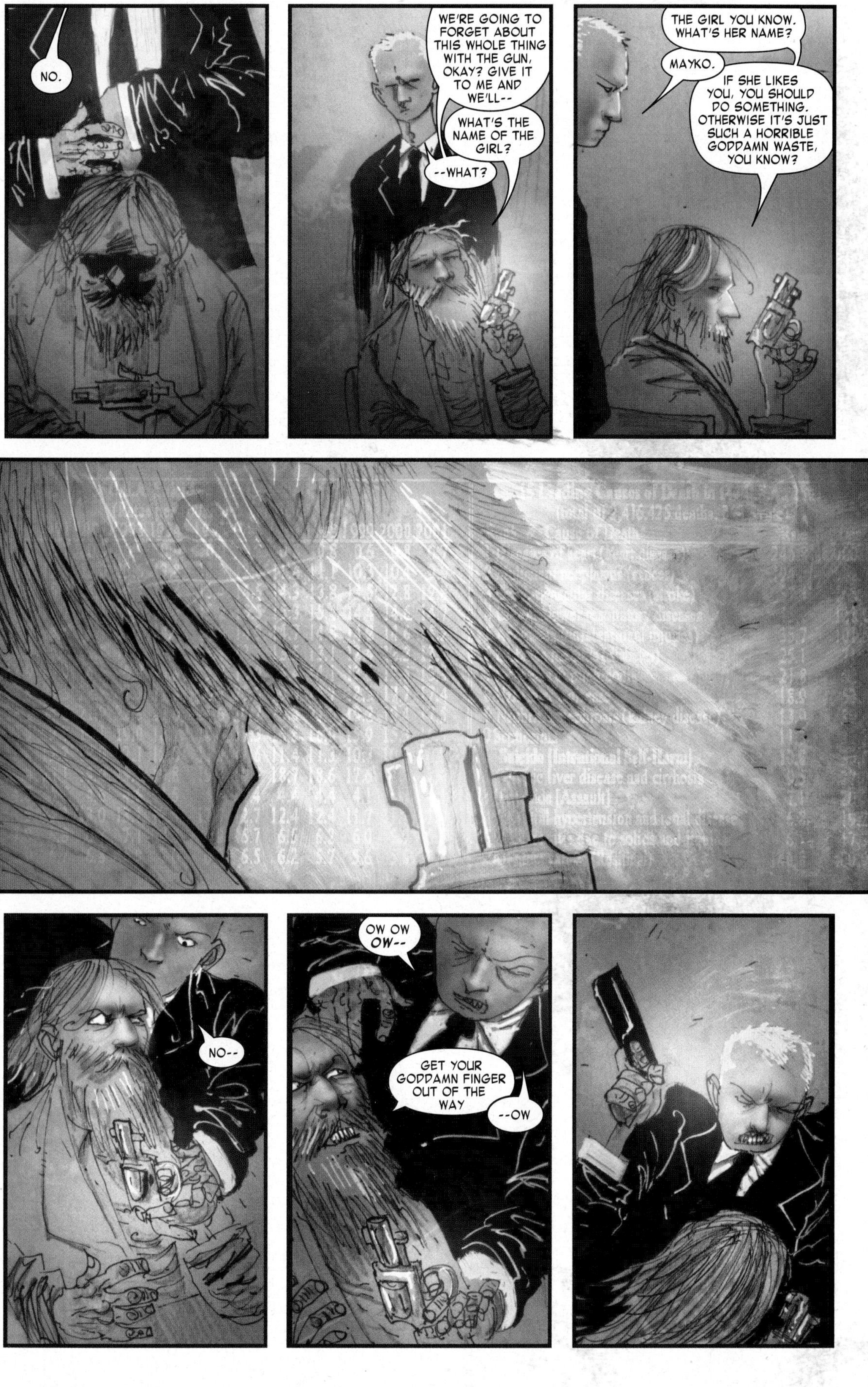
NO.
WE'RE GOING TO FORGET ABOUT THIS WHOLE THING WITH THE GUN, OKAY? GIVE IT TO ME AND WE'LL--
WHAT'S THE NAME OF THE GIRL?
--WHAT?
THE GIRL YOU KNOW. WHAT'S HER NAME?
MAYKO.
IF SHE LIKES YOU, YOU SHOULD DO SOMETHING. OTHERWISE IT'S JUST SUCH A HORRIBLE GODDAMN WASTE, YOU KNOW?
NO--
OW OW OW--
GET YOUR GODDAMN FINGER OUT OF THE WAY
--OW

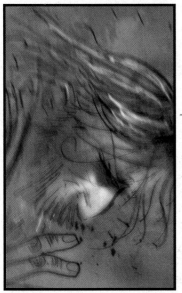

OW OW OW OW OW OW.

INTERVIEW CONCLUDED, 9:29AM.

SUSPECT TOOK A SHORT NAP.

MAYKO.

GOOD EVENING, RICH. I WAS JUST LEAVING, BUT--

NO, IT'S OKAY, I'VE HAD A REALLY LONG DAY, AND, UM... WOULD YOU LIKE TO GET SOMETHING TO EAT?

I REALLY WOULD.

END

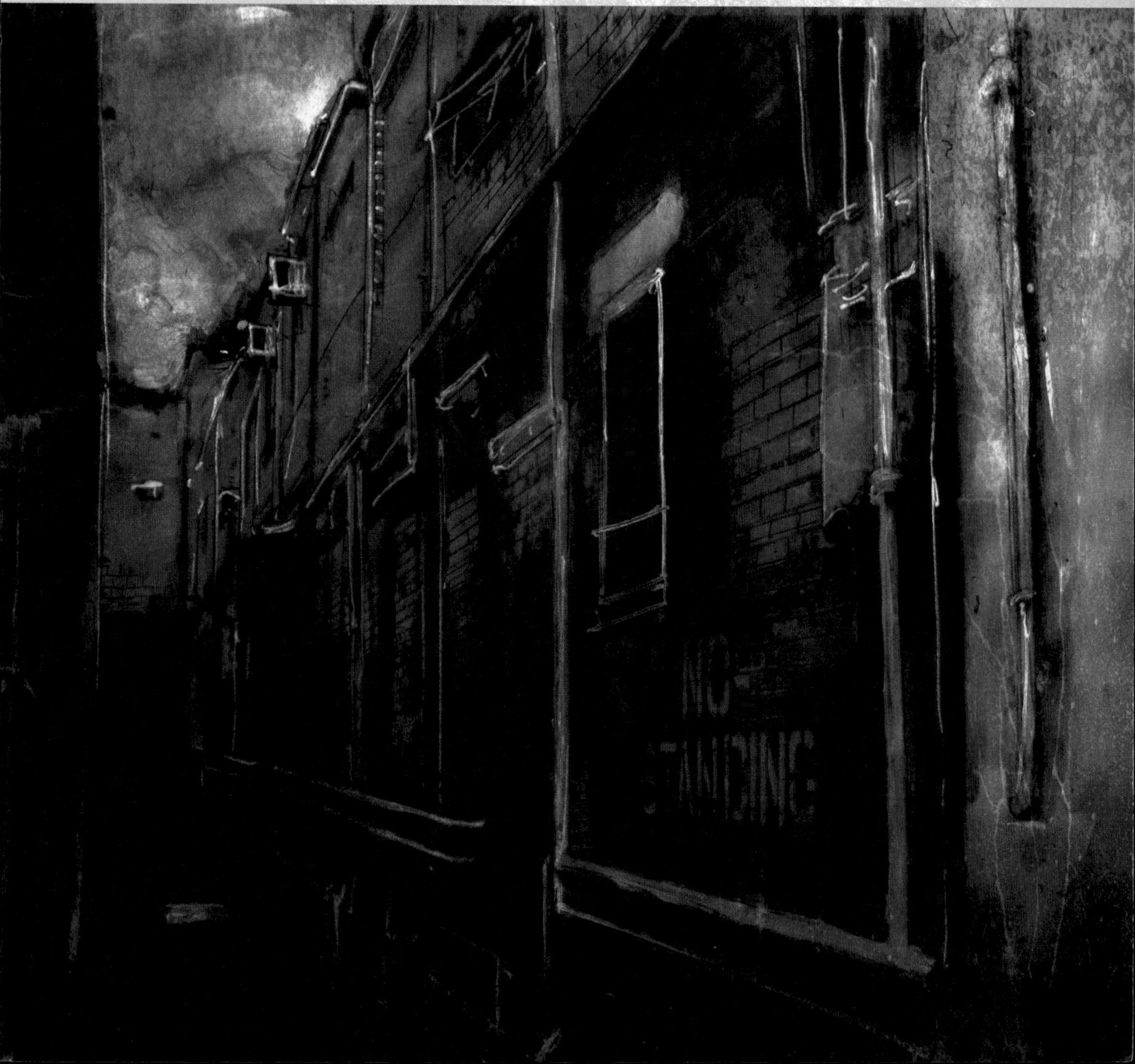
NO
STANDING

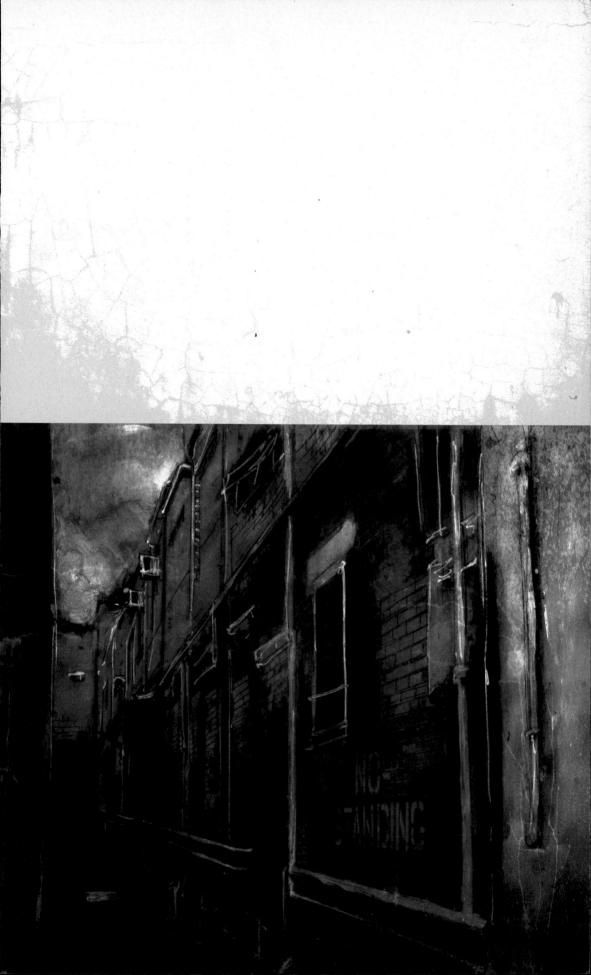

# FELL.

## CHAPTER 6

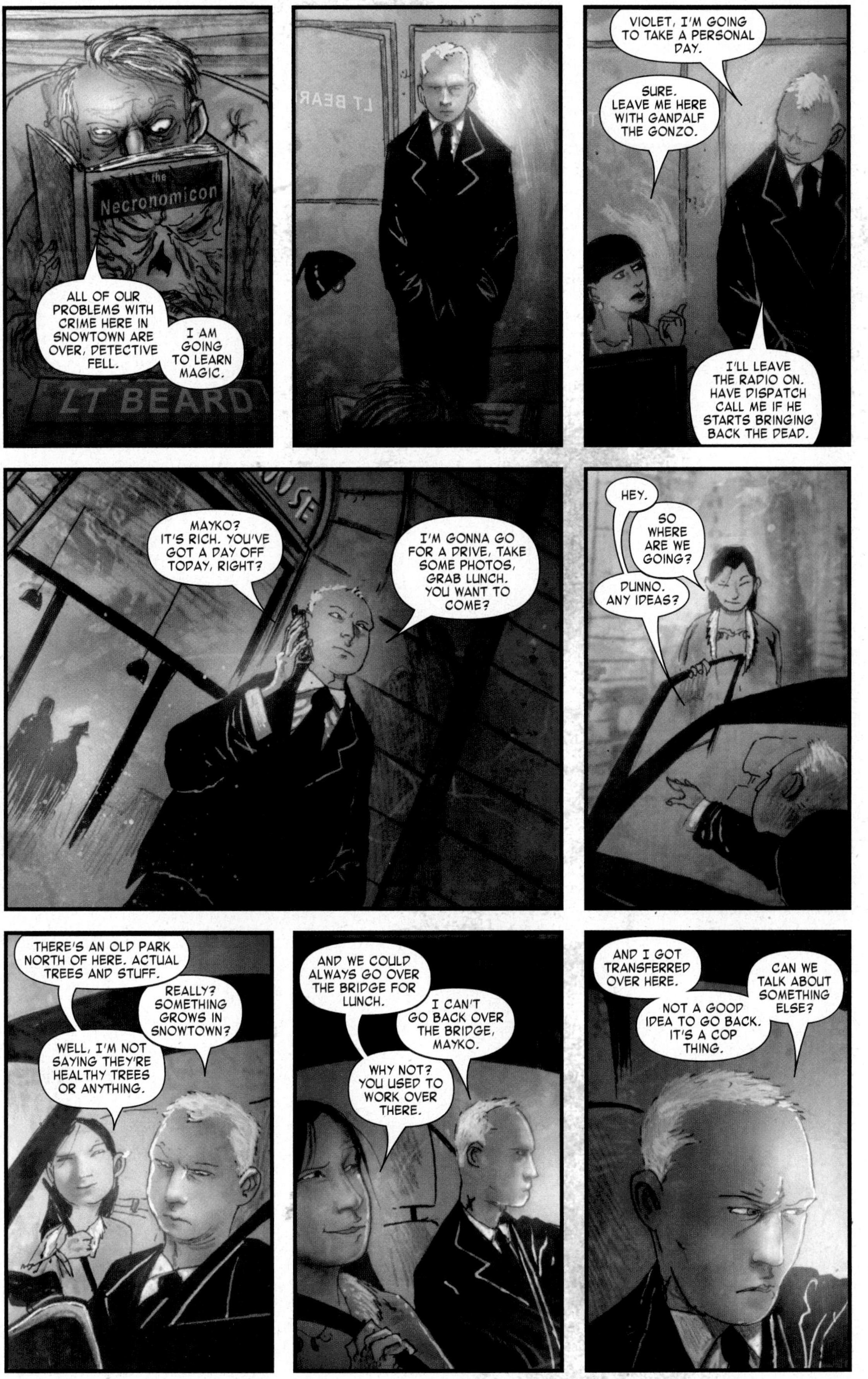
the Necronomicon
ALL OF OUR PROBLEMS WITH CRIME HERE IN SNOWTOWN ARE OVER, DETECTIVE FELL.
I AM GOING TO LEARN MAGIC.
LT BEARD
VIOLET, I'M GOING TO TAKE A PERSONAL DAY.
SURE. LEAVE ME HERE WITH GANDALF THE GONZO.
I'LL LEAVE THE RADIO ON. HAVE DISPATCH CALL ME IF HE STARTS BRINGING BACK THE DEAD.
MAYKO? IT'S RICH. YOU'VE GOT A DAY OFF TODAY, RIGHT?
I'M GONNA GO FOR A DRIVE, TAKE SOME PHOTOS, GRAB LUNCH. YOU WANT TO COME?
HEY.
SO WHERE ARE WE GOING?
DUNNO. ANY IDEAS?
THERE'S AN OLD PARK NORTH OF HERE. ACTUAL TREES AND STUFF.
REALLY? SOMETHING GROWS IN SNOWTOWN?
WELL, I'M NOT SAYING THEY'RE HEALTHY TREES OR ANYTHING.
AND WE COULD ALWAYS GO OVER THE BRIDGE FOR LUNCH.
I CAN'T GO BACK OVER THE BRIDGE, MAYKO.
WHY NOT? YOU USED TO WORK OVER THERE.
AND I GOT TRANSFERRED OVER HERE.
NOT A GOOD IDEA TO GO BACK. IT'S A COP THING.
CAN WE TALK ABOUT SOMETHING ELSE?

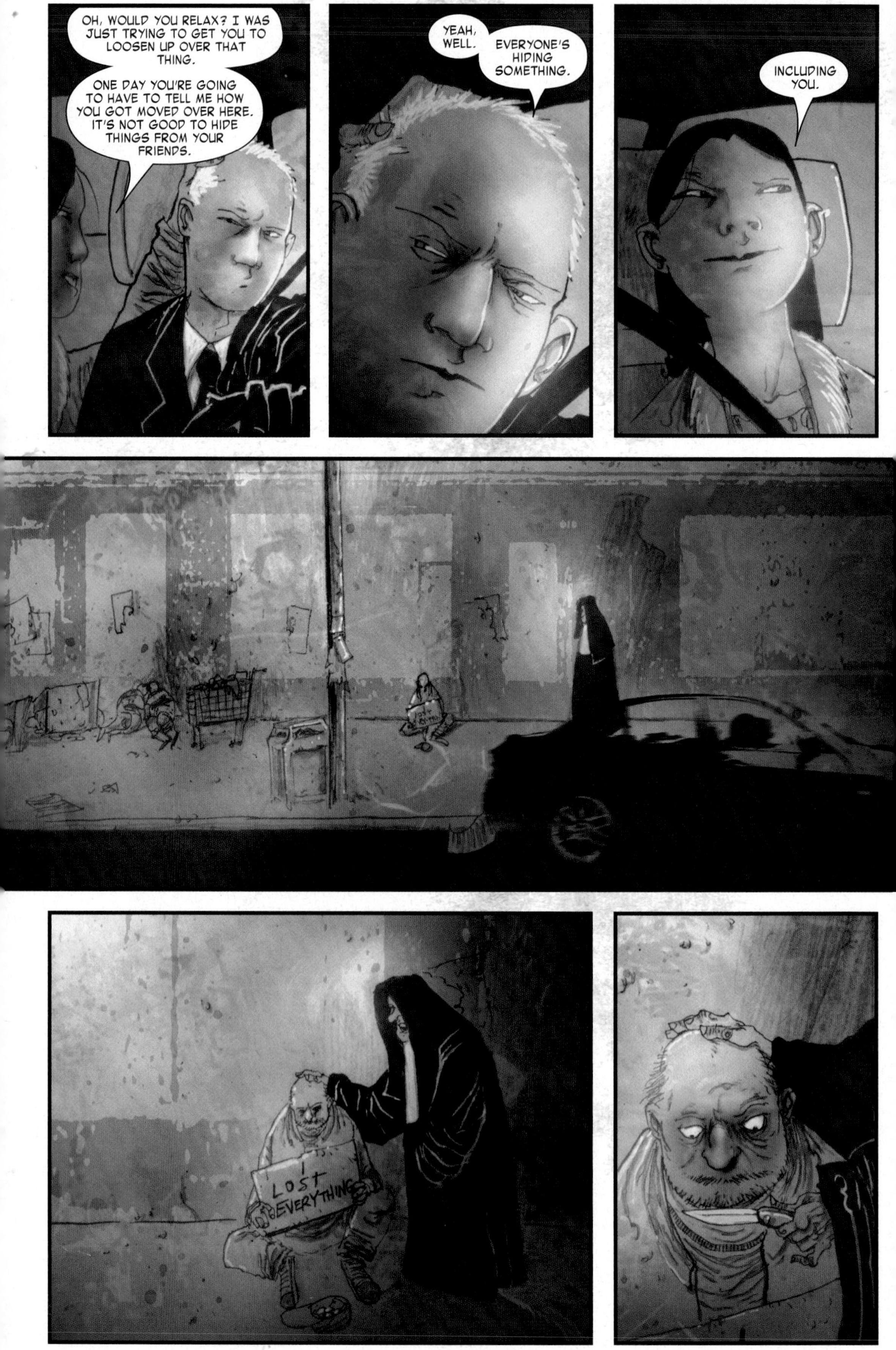
OH, WOULD YOU RELAX? I WAS JUST TRYING TO GET YOU TO LOOSEN UP OVER THAT THING.
ONE DAY YOU'RE GOING TO HAVE TO TELL ME HOW YOU GOT MOVED OVER HERE. IT'S NOT GOOD TO HIDE THINGS FROM YOUR FRIENDS.
YEAH, WELL.
EVERYONE'S HIDING SOMETHING.
INCLUDING YOU.
I LOST EVERYTHING

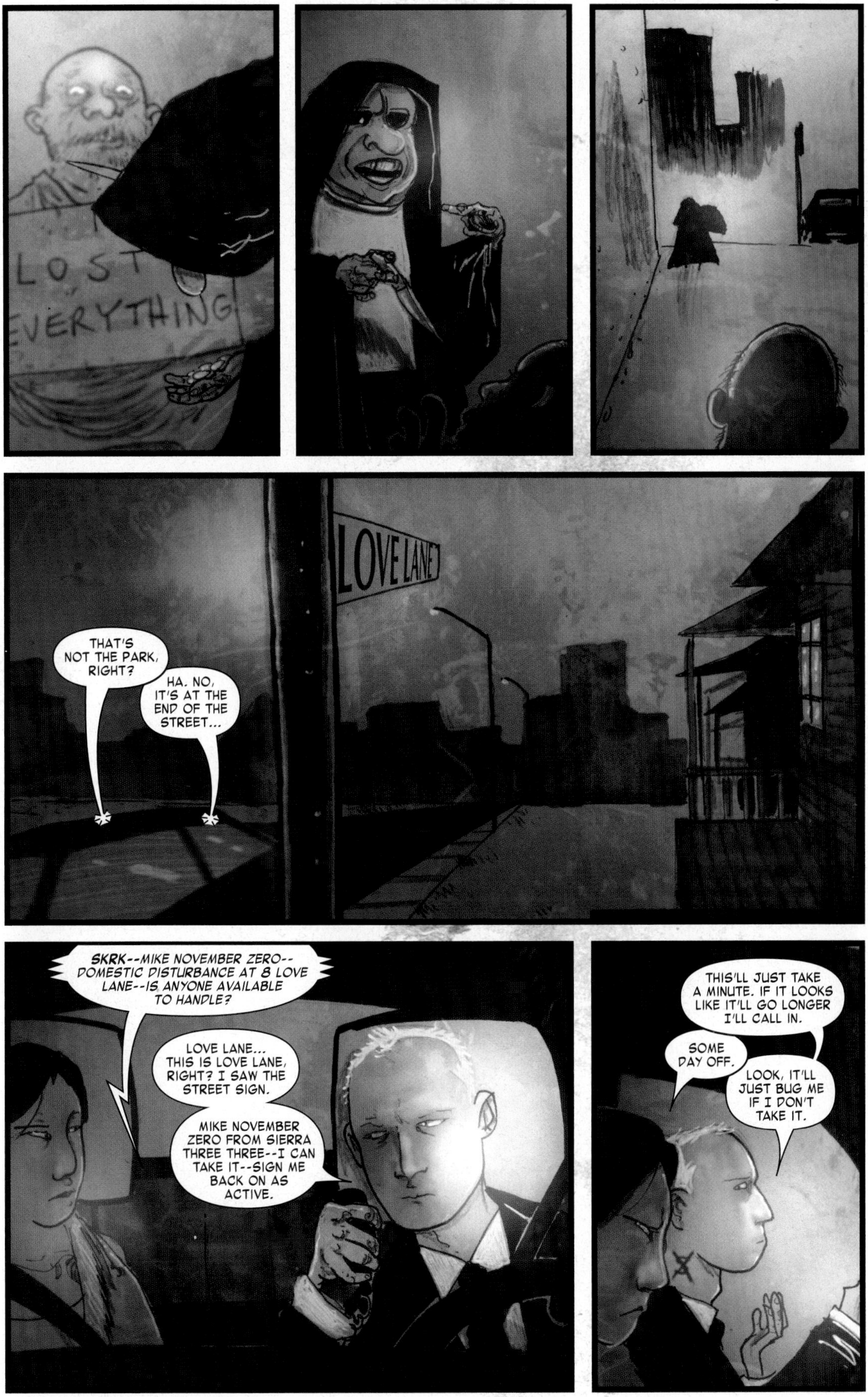
LOST EVERYTHING
LOVE LANE
THAT'S NOT THE PARK, RIGHT?
HA. NO, IT'S AT THE END OF THE STREET...
SKRK--MIKE NOVEMBER ZERO--DOMESTIC DISTURBANCE AT 8 LOVE LANE--IS ANYONE AVAILABLE TO HANDLE?
LOVE LANE... THIS IS LOVE LANE, RIGHT? I SAW THE STREET SIGN.
MIKE NOVEMBER ZERO FROM SIERRA THREE THREE--I CAN TAKE IT--SIGN ME BACK ON AS ACTIVE.
THIS'LL JUST TAKE A MINUTE. IF IT LOOKS LIKE IT'LL GO LONGER I'LL CALL IN.
SOME DAY OFF.
LOOK, IT'LL JUST BUG ME IF I DON'T TAKE IT.

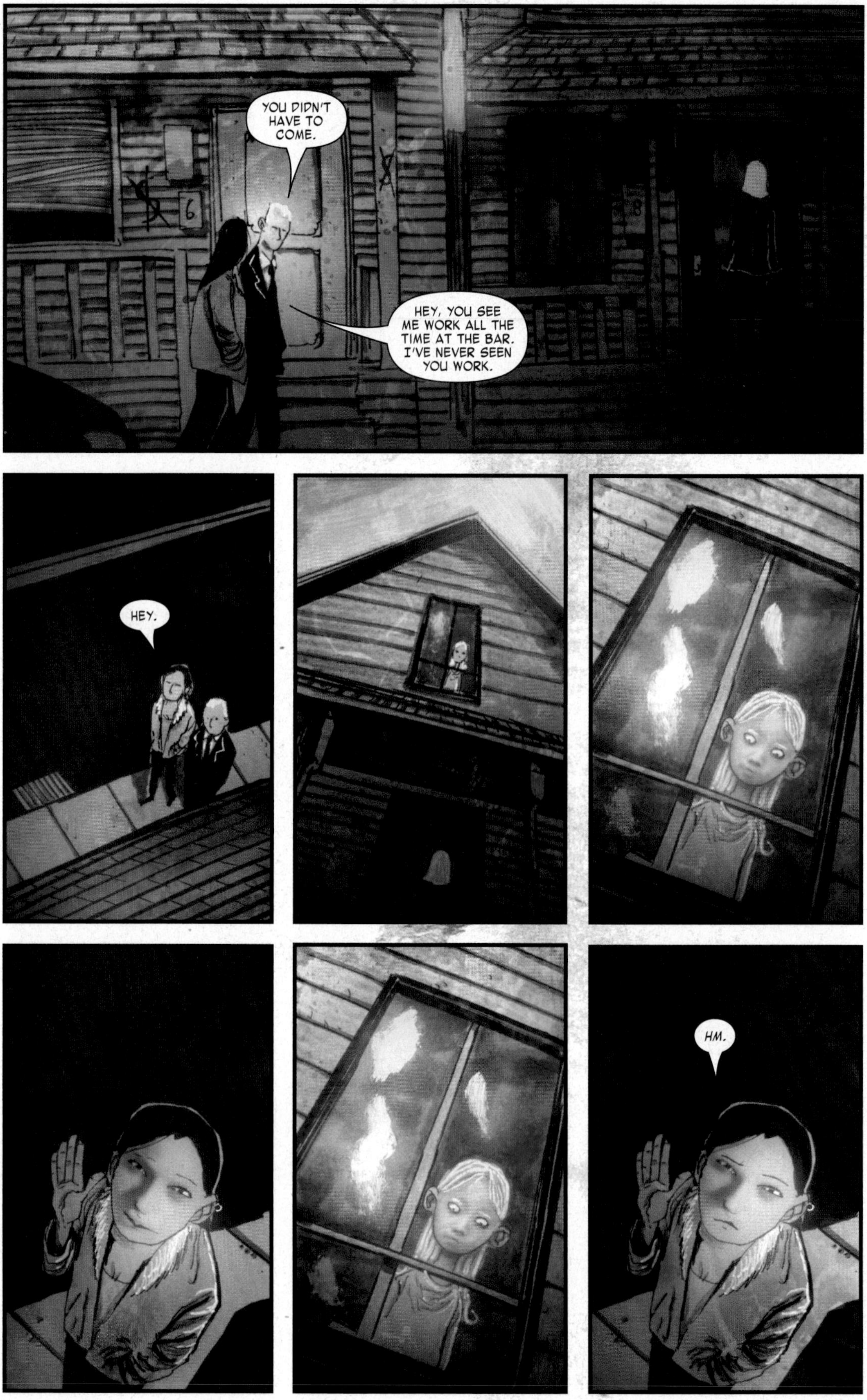
YOU DIDN'T HAVE TO COME.
HEY, YOU SEE ME WORK ALL THE TIME AT THE BAR. I'VE NEVER SEEN YOU WORK.
HEY.
HM.

CHET, YOU OPEN UP THIS GODDAMN DOOR! YOU OPEN IT UP OR I'M CALLING MY BROTHERS, AND YOU KNOW WHAT THAT MEANS!

YOU LET ME SEE HER AND YOU LET ME SEE HER NOW!

DETECTIVE FELL, SNOWTOWN PD. WHAT SEEMS TO BE THE PROBLEM, MA'AM?

HE WON'T LET ME SEE MY DAUGHTER!

CALM IS BEST, MA'AM. JUST EXPLAIN THE SITUATION TO ME AND I'LL SEE WHAT I CAN DO.

CHET, THAT'S MY EX-HUSBAND, HE GOT TEMPORARY CUSTODY OF OUR DAUGHTER WHILE I, Y'KNOW, GOT MYSELF TOGETHER.

I GOT VISITATION RIGHTS. BUT HE WON'T LET ME SEE HER. EVER. IT'S BEEN MONTHS.

WELL, LET'S SEE WHAT CHET'S GOT TO SAY.

POLICE. PLEASE OPEN THE DOOR.

THAT'S NOW, SIR. I CAN HEAR YOU BREATHING BEHIND THE DOOR.

HERE. DOCTOR'S REPORT. SHE'S TOO ILL TO LEAVE THE HOUSE. DIABETES.

RESTRAINING ORDER TOO. BANNING HER FROM APPROACHING THE HOUSE AFTER THE TIME SHE CAME WITH HER BROTHERS TO COMMIT ASSAULT.

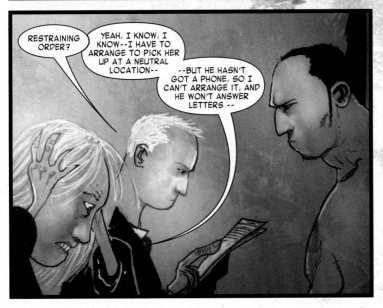

RESTRAINING ORDER?

YEAH, I KNOW, I KNOW--I HAVE TO ARRANGE TO PICK HER UP AT A NEUTRAL LOCATION--

--BUT HE HASN'T GOT A PHONE, SO I CAN'T ARRANGE IT, AND HE WON'T ANSWER LETTERS --

BECAUSE SHE'S TOO ILL TO LEAVE THE HOUSE.

I LOOK AFTER HER.

BECAUSE YOU'RE A CRACKHEAD.

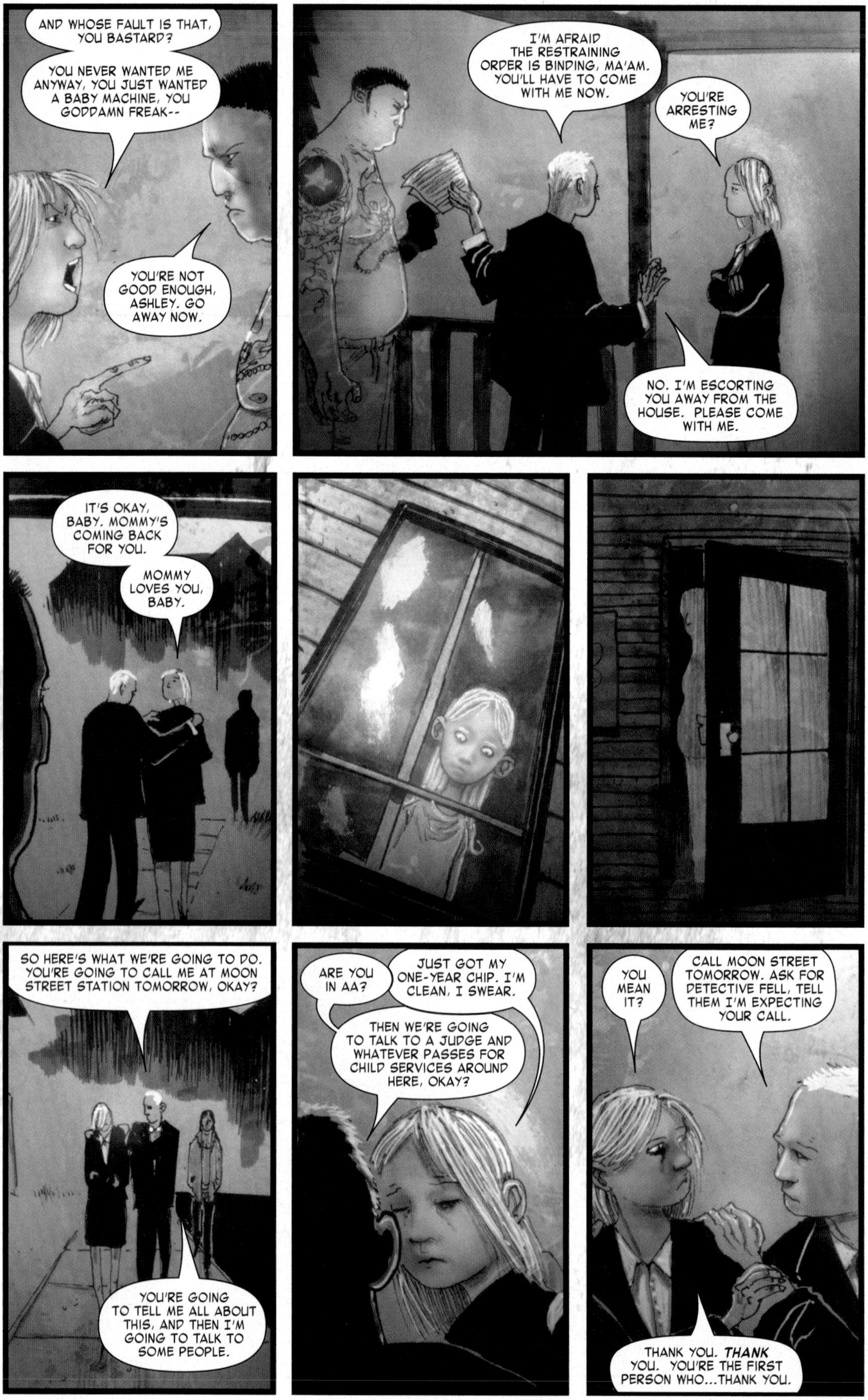
AND WHOSE FAULT IS THAT, YOU BASTARD?
YOU NEVER WANTED ME ANYWAY, YOU JUST WANTED A BABY MACHINE, YOU GODDAMN FREAK--
YOU'RE NOT GOOD ENOUGH, ASHLEY. GO AWAY NOW.
I'M AFRAID THE RESTRAINING ORDER IS BINDING, MA'AM. YOU'LL HAVE TO COME WITH ME NOW.
YOU'RE ARRESTING ME?
NO. I'M ESCORTING YOU AWAY FROM THE HOUSE. PLEASE COME WITH ME.
IT'S OKAY, BABY. MOMMY'S COMING BACK FOR YOU.
MOMMY LOVES YOU, BABY.
SO HERE'S WHAT WE'RE GOING TO DO. YOU'RE GOING TO CALL ME AT MOON STREET STATION TOMORROW, OKAY?
YOU'RE GOING TO TELL ME ALL ABOUT THIS, AND THEN I'M GOING TO TALK TO SOME PEOPLE.
ARE YOU IN AA?
JUST GOT MY ONE-YEAR CHIP. I'M CLEAN, I SWEAR.
THEN WE'RE GOING TO TALK TO A JUDGE AND WHATEVER PASSES FOR CHILD SERVICES AROUND HERE, OKAY?
YOU MEAN IT?
CALL MOON STREET TOMORROW. ASK FOR DETECTIVE FELL, TELL THEM I'M EXPECTING YOUR CALL.
THANK YOU. *THANK* YOU. YOU'RE THE FIRST PERSON WHO...THANK YOU.

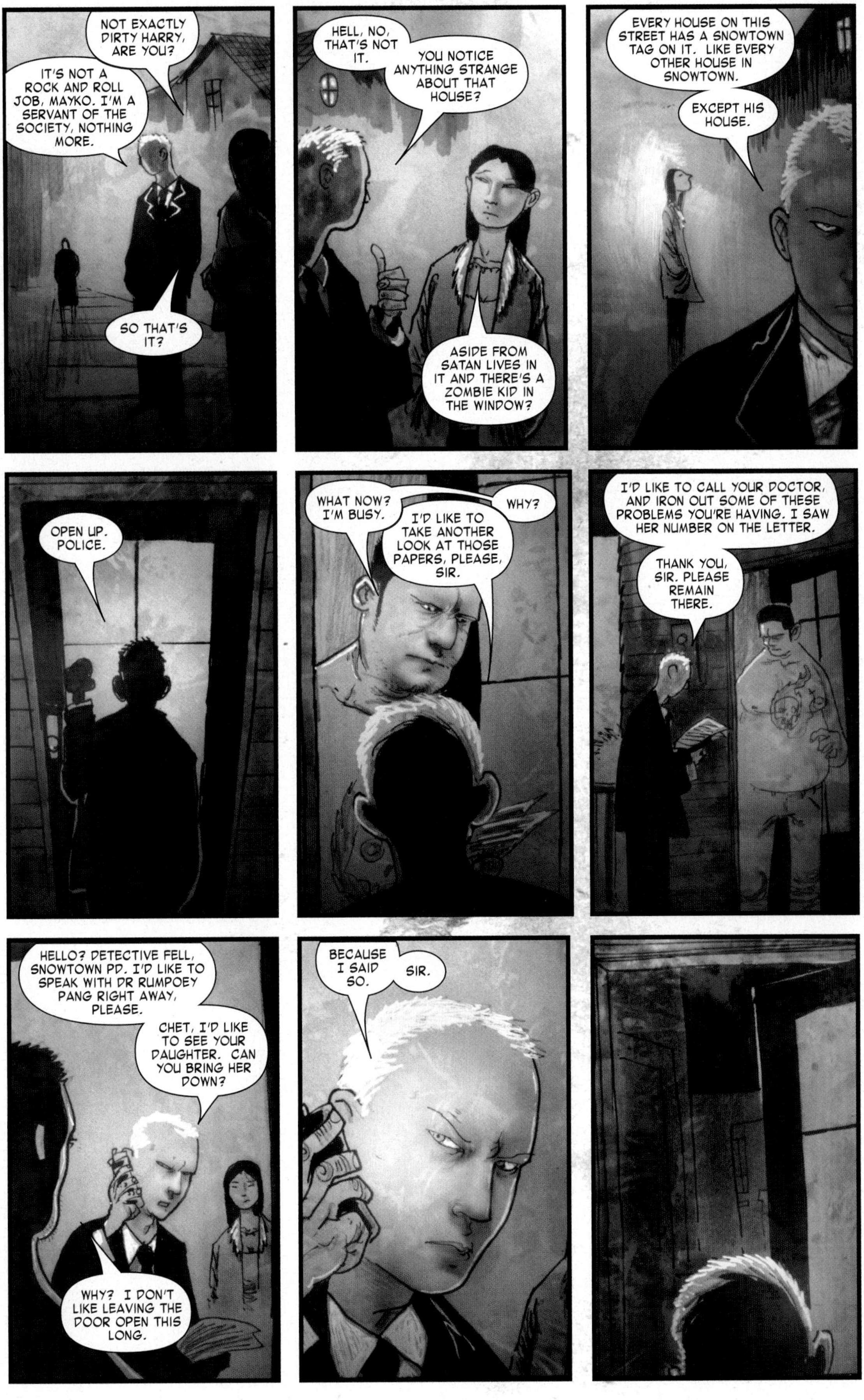
NOT EXACTLY DIRTY HARRY, ARE YOU?
IT'S NOT A ROCK AND ROLL JOB, MAYKO. I'M A SERVANT OF THE SOCIETY, NOTHING MORE.
SO THAT'S IT?
HELL, NO, THAT'S NOT IT.
YOU NOTICE ANYTHING STRANGE ABOUT THAT HOUSE?
ASIDE FROM SATAN LIVES IN IT AND THERE'S A ZOMBIE KID IN THE WINDOW?
EVERY HOUSE ON THIS STREET HAS A SNOWTOWN TAG ON IT. LIKE EVERY OTHER HOUSE IN SNOWTOWN.
EXCEPT HIS HOUSE.
OPEN UP. POLICE.
WHAT NOW? I'M BUSY.
I'D LIKE TO TAKE ANOTHER LOOK AT THOSE PAPERS, PLEASE, SIR.
WHY?
I'D LIKE TO CALL YOUR DOCTOR, AND IRON OUT SOME OF THESE PROBLEMS YOU'RE HAVING. I SAW HER NUMBER ON THE LETTER.
THANK YOU, SIR. PLEASE REMAIN THERE.
HELLO? DETECTIVE FELL, SNOWTOWN PD. I'D LIKE TO SPEAK WITH DR RUMPOEY PANG RIGHT AWAY, PLEASE.
CHET, I'D LIKE TO SEE YOUR DAUGHTER. CAN YOU BRING HER DOWN?
WHY? I DON'T LIKE LEAVING THE DOOR OPEN THIS LONG.
BECAUSE I SAID SO.
SIR.

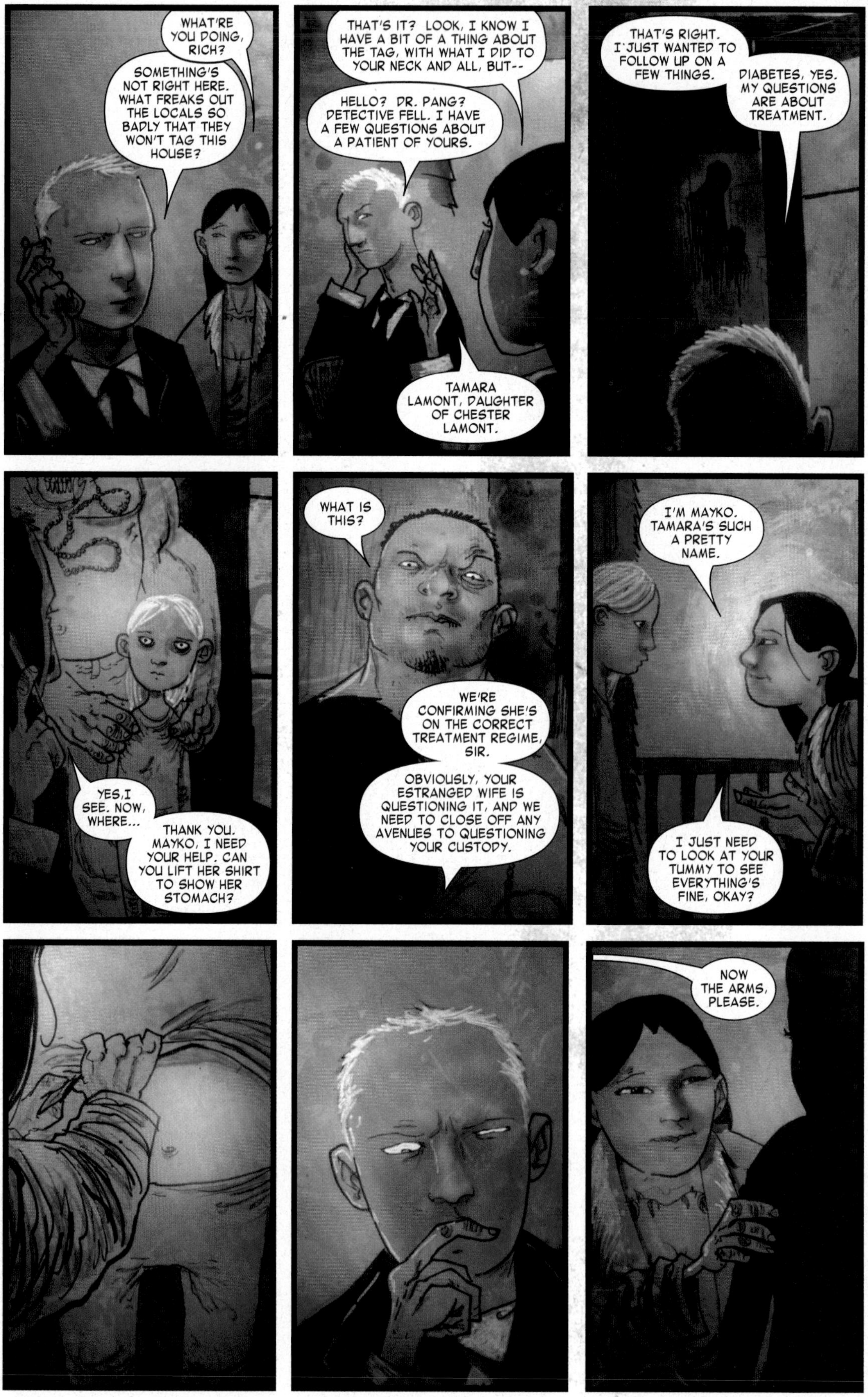
WHAT'RE YOU DOING, RICH?
SOMETHING'S NOT RIGHT HERE. WHAT FREAKS OUT THE LOCALS SO BADLY THAT THEY WON'T TAG THIS HOUSE?
THAT'S IT? LOOK, I KNOW I HAVE A BIT OF A THING ABOUT THE TAG, WITH WHAT I DID TO YOUR NECK AND ALL, BUT--
HELLO? DR. PANG? DETECTIVE FELL. I HAVE A FEW QUESTIONS ABOUT A PATIENT OF YOURS.
TAMARA LAMONT, DAUGHTER OF CHESTER LAMONT.
THAT'S RIGHT. I JUST WANTED TO FOLLOW UP ON A FEW THINGS.
DIABETES, YES. MY QUESTIONS ARE ABOUT TREATMENT.
YES, I SEE. NOW, WHERE...
THANK YOU. MAYKO, I NEED YOUR HELP. CAN YOU LIFT HER SHIRT TO SHOW HER STOMACH?
WHAT IS THIS?
WE'RE CONFIRMING SHE'S ON THE CORRECT TREATMENT REGIME, SIR.
OBVIOUSLY, YOUR ESTRANGED WIFE IS QUESTIONING IT, AND WE NEED TO CLOSE OFF ANY AVENUES TO QUESTIONING YOUR CUSTODY.
I'M MAYKO. TAMARA'S SUCH A PRETTY NAME.
I JUST NEED TO LOOK AT YOUR TUMMY TO SEE EVERYTHING'S FINE, OKAY?
NOW THE ARMS, PLEASE.

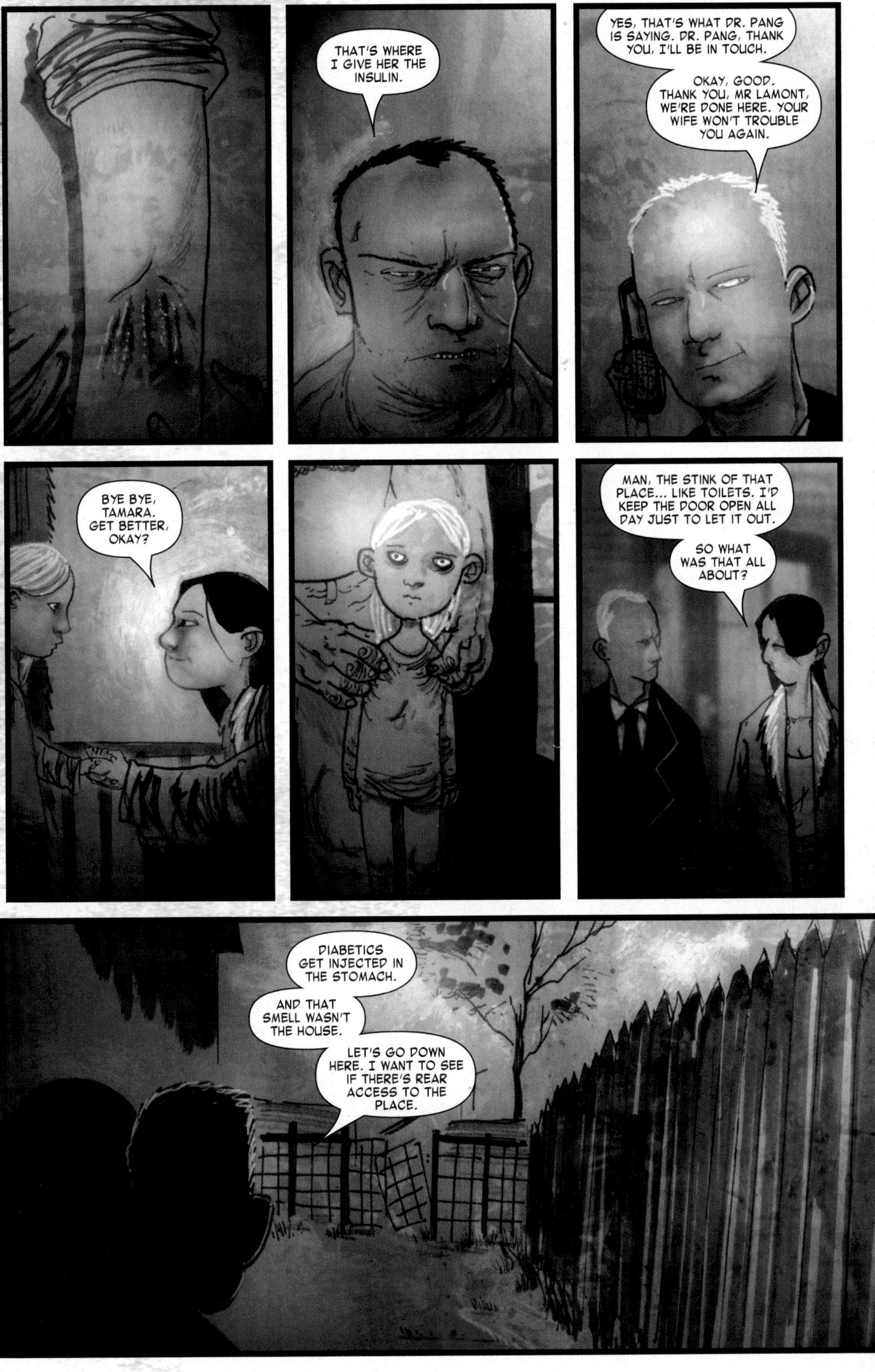
THAT'S WHERE I GIVE HER THE INSULIN.
YES, THAT'S WHAT DR. PANG IS SAYING. DR. PANG, THANK YOU, I'LL BE IN TOUCH.
OKAY, GOOD. THANK YOU, MR LAMONT, WE'RE DONE HERE. YOUR WIFE WON'T TROUBLE YOU AGAIN.
BYE BYE, TAMARA. GET BETTER, OKAY?
MAN, THE STINK OF THAT PLACE... LIKE TOILETS. I'D KEEP THE DOOR OPEN ALL DAY JUST TO LET IT OUT.
SO WHAT WAS THAT ALL ABOUT?
DIABETICS GET INJECTED IN THE STOMACH.
AND THAT SMELL WASN'T THE HOUSE.
LET'S GO DOWN HERE. I WANT TO SEE IF THERE'S REAR ACCESS TO THE PLACE.

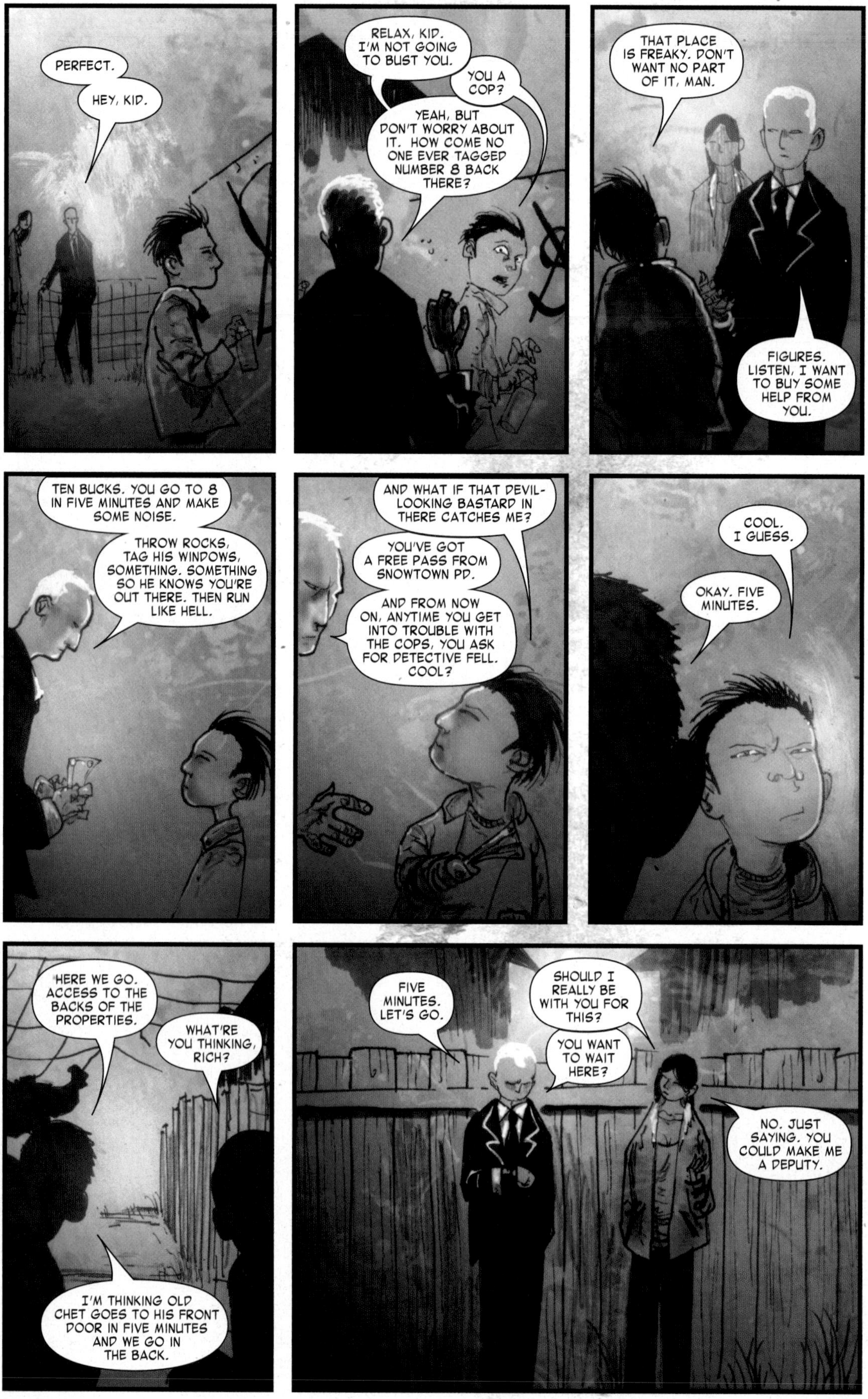
PERFECT.
HEY, KID.
RELAX, KID. I'M NOT GOING TO BUST YOU.
YOU A COP?
YEAH, BUT DON'T WORRY ABOUT IT. HOW COME NO ONE EVER TAGGED NUMBER 8 BACK THERE?
THAT PLACE IS FREAKY. DON'T WANT NO PART OF IT, MAN.
FIGURES. LISTEN, I WANT TO BUY SOME HELP FROM YOU.
TEN BUCKS. YOU GO TO 8 IN FIVE MINUTES AND MAKE SOME NOISE.
THROW ROCKS, TAG HIS WINDOWS, SOMETHING. SOMETHING SO HE KNOWS YOU'RE OUT THERE. THEN RUN LIKE HELL.
AND WHAT IF THAT DEVIL-LOOKING BASTARD IN THERE CATCHES ME?
YOU'VE GOT A FREE PASS FROM SNOWTOWN PD.
AND FROM NOW ON, ANYTIME YOU GET INTO TROUBLE WITH THE COPS, YOU ASK FOR DETECTIVE FELL. COOL?
COOL. I GUESS.
OKAY. FIVE MINUTES.
HERE WE GO. ACCESS TO THE BACKS OF THE PROPERTIES.
WHAT'RE YOU THINKING, RICH?
I'M THINKING OLD CHET GOES TO HIS FRONT DOOR IN FIVE MINUTES AND WE GO IN THE BACK.
FIVE MINUTES. LET'S GO.
SHOULD I REALLY BE WITH YOU FOR THIS?
YOU WANT TO WAIT HERE?
NO. JUST SAYING. YOU COULD MAKE ME A DEPUTY.

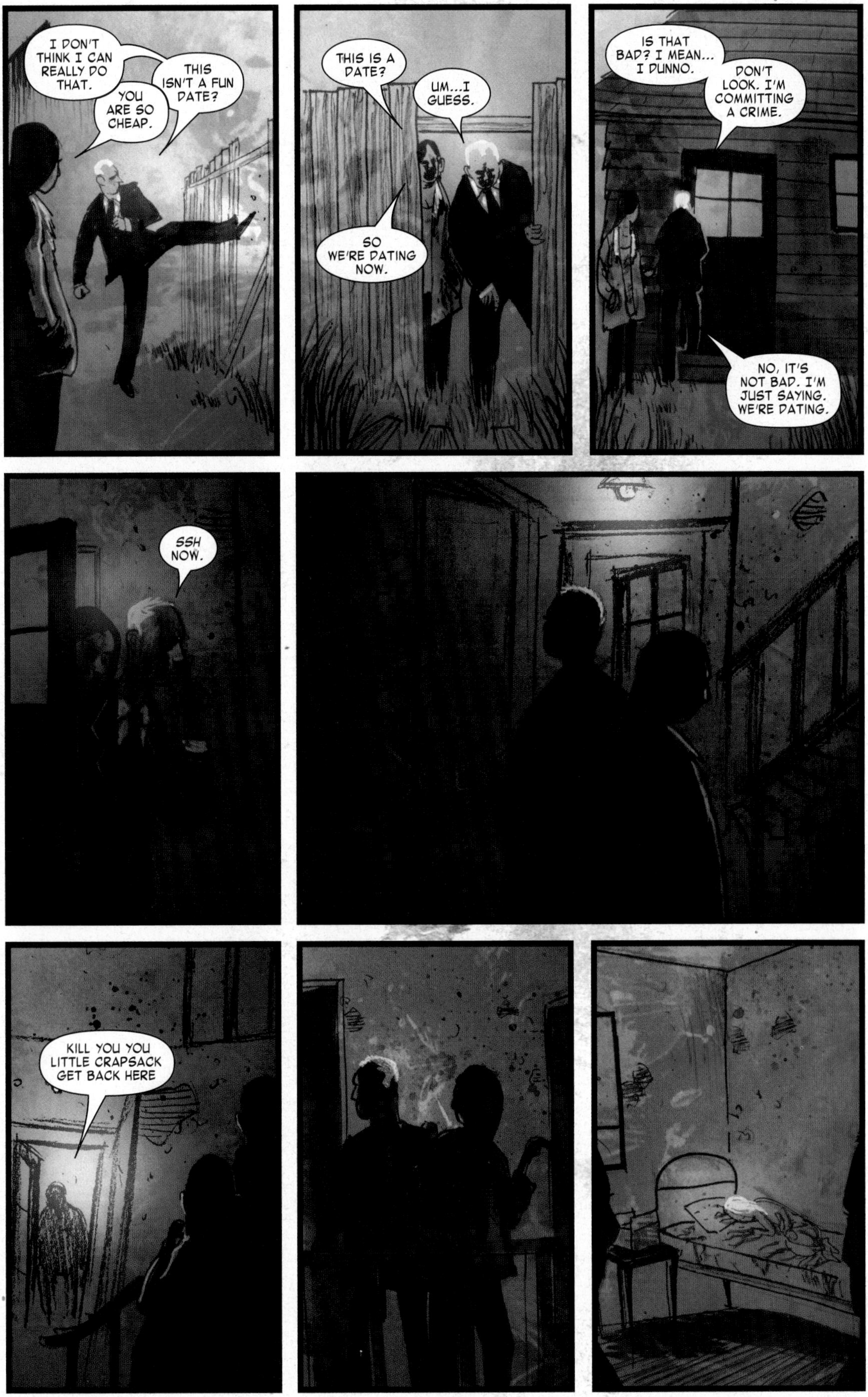
I DON'T THINK I CAN REALLY DO THAT.
THIS ISN'T A FUN DATE?
YOU ARE SO CHEAP.
THIS IS A DATE?
UM...I GUESS.
SO WE'RE DATING NOW.
IS THAT BAD? I MEAN... I DUNNO.
DON'T LOOK. I'M COMMITTING A CRIME.
NO, IT'S NOT BAD. I'M JUST SAYING. WE'RE DATING.
SSH NOW.
KILL YOU YOU LITTLE CRAPSACK GET BACK HERE

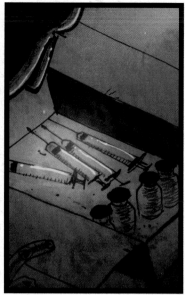

SNFF DISPATCH? THIS IS SIERRA THREE THREE. I'M GOING TO NEED A WAGON TO 8 LOVE LANE SOONEST. ALSO AN AMBULANCE. URGENT.

WE NINJA ALL THE WAY UP HERE AND THEN YOU USE YOUR CELL?

IS THAT SOMEONE UP THERE? WHO HE HELL'S UP THERE?

WHAT THE HELL IS THIS? I'LL KILL YOU AND YOUR BITCH WITH MY BARE HANDS--

COME ON, THEN. KILL ME. I WANT TO SEE IT.

ME NOT BEING EIGHT YEARS OLD AND ALL, YOU DISGUSTING FREAK OF NATURE.

I OUGHT TO EXECUTE YOU RIGHT HERE.

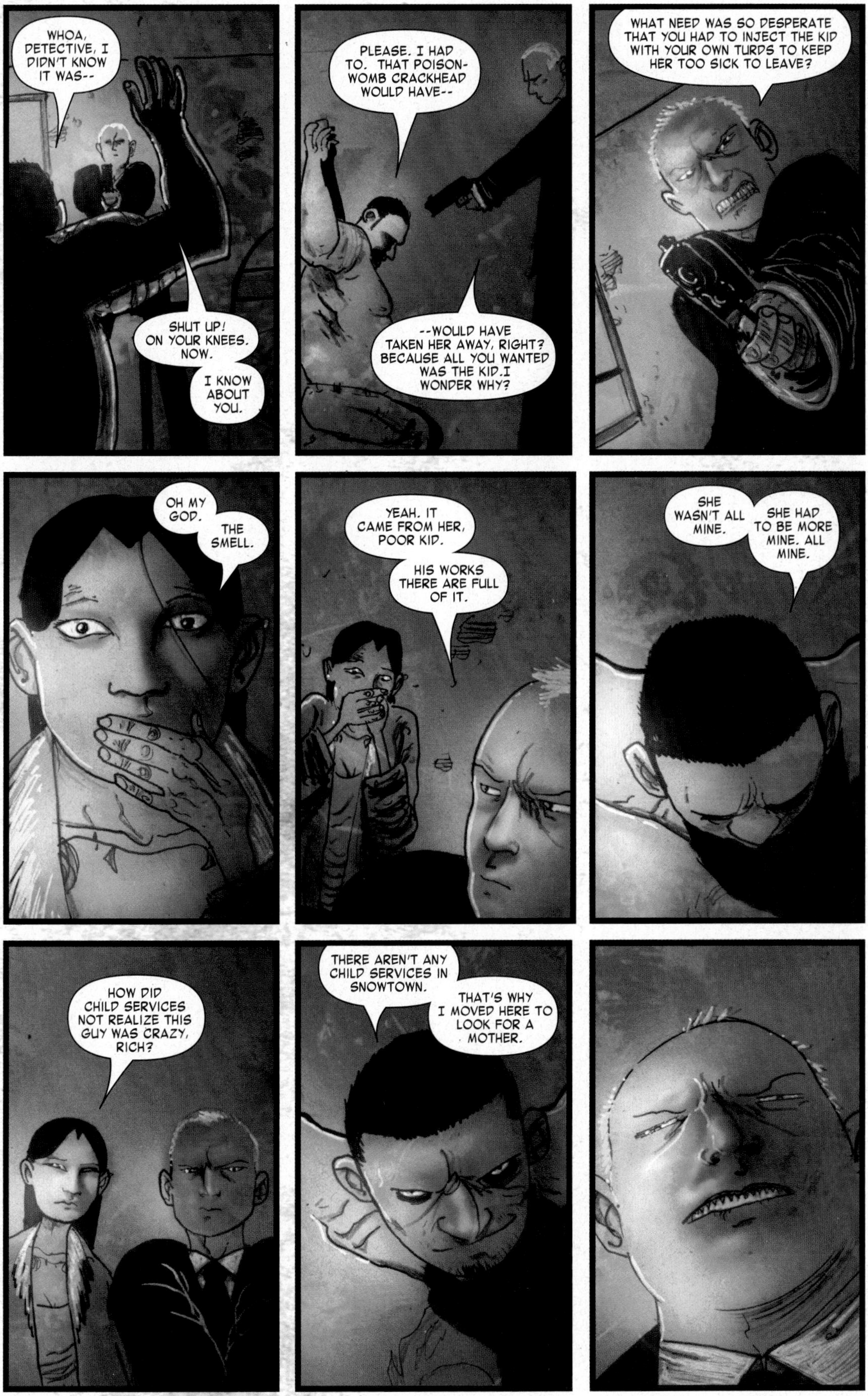
WHOA, DETECTIVE, I DIDN'T KNOW IT WAS--
SHUT UP! ON YOUR KNEES. NOW.
I KNOW ABOUT YOU.
PLEASE. I HAD TO. THAT POISON-WOMB CRACKHEAD WOULD HAVE--
--WOULD HAVE TAKEN HER AWAY, RIGHT? BECAUSE ALL YOU WANTED WAS THE KID. I WONDER WHY?
WHAT NEED WAS SO DESPERATE THAT YOU HAD TO INJECT THE KID WITH YOUR OWN TURDS TO KEEP HER TOO SICK TO LEAVE?
OH MY GOD.
THE SMELL.
YEAH. IT CAME FROM HER, POOR KID.
HIS WORKS THERE ARE FULL OF IT.
SHE WASN'T ALL MINE.
SHE HAD TO BE MORE MINE. ALL MINE.
HOW DID CHILD SERVICES NOT REALIZE THIS GUY WAS CRAZY, RICH?
THERE AREN'T ANY CHILD SERVICES IN SNOWTOWN.
THAT'S WHY I MOVED HERE TO LOOK FOR A MOTHER.

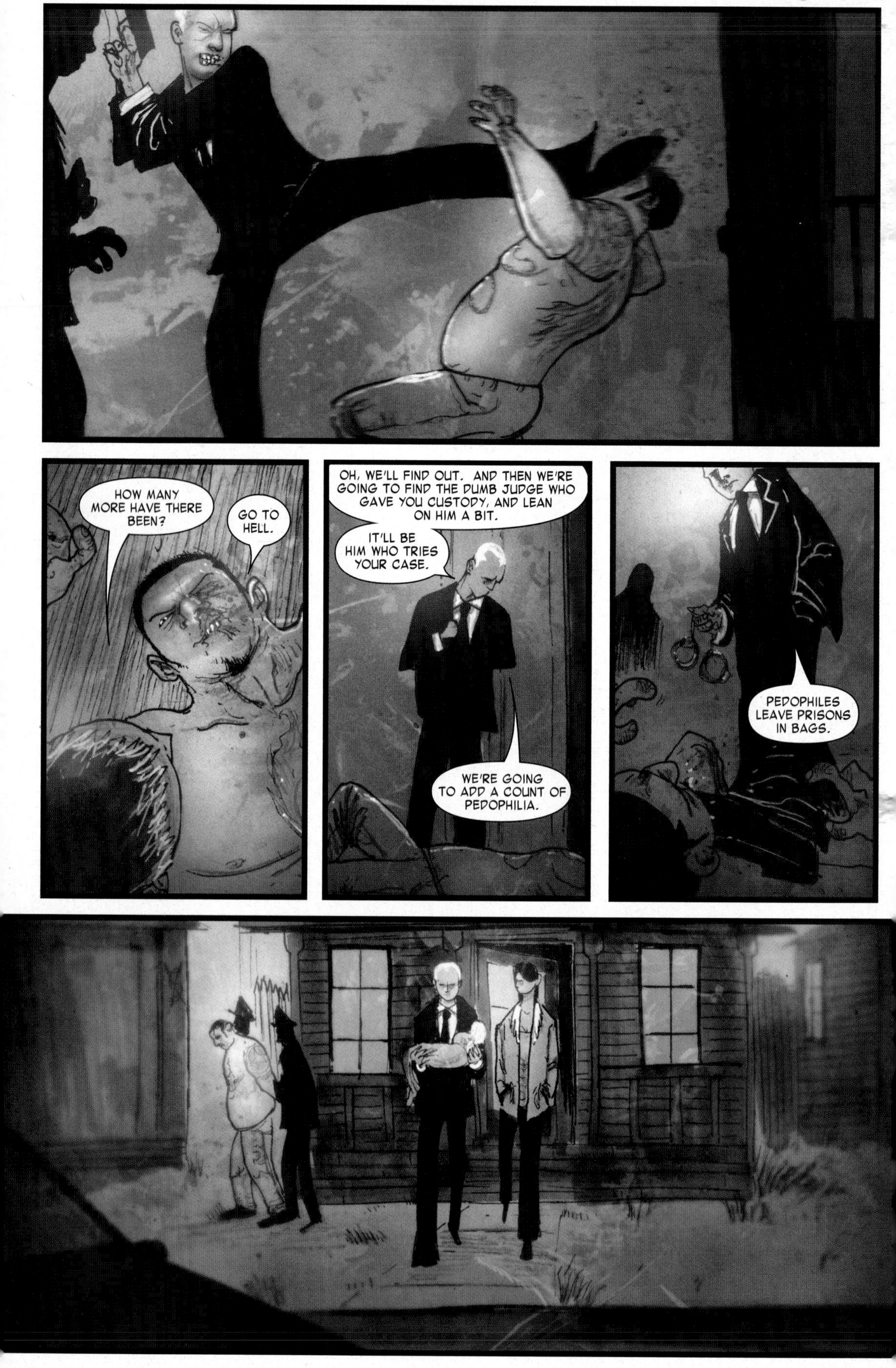
HOW MANY MORE HAVE THERE BEEN?
GO TO HELL.
OH, WE'LL FIND OUT. AND THEN WE'RE GOING TO FIND THE DUMB JUDGE WHO GAVE YOU CUSTODY, AND LEAN ON HIM A BIT.
IT'LL BE HIM WHO TRIES YOUR CASE.
WE'RE GOING TO ADD A COUNT OF PEDOPHILIA.
PEDOPHILES LEAVE PRISONS IN BAGS.

GIVE HER TO ME!

YOU'VE GOT NO GODDAMN RIGHT! SHE WAS GROWN FROM ME! SHE'S MINE!

BASTARDS!

FOR CHRIST'S SAKE--

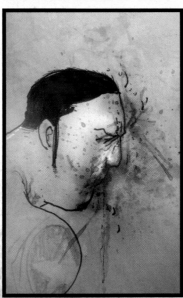

WILL YOU GET HIM UNDER CONTROL? HE'S TRYING TO KILL HIMSELF, YOU IDIOTS!

I DON'T GET IT.

MY FAULT. IT'S BECAUSE OF WHAT I SAID TO HIM. I WAS ANGRY.

YEAH, SOMETHING ABOUT PRISON AND BAGS?

PEDOPHILES DIE IN PRISON. THE OTHER PRISONERS KILL THEM.

NOT ONE OF THEM DIES WITH A SMILE ON HIS FACE, YOU KNOW?

WHERE'S YOUR CAMERA?

IN MY JACKET. WHY?

TAKE IT OUT.

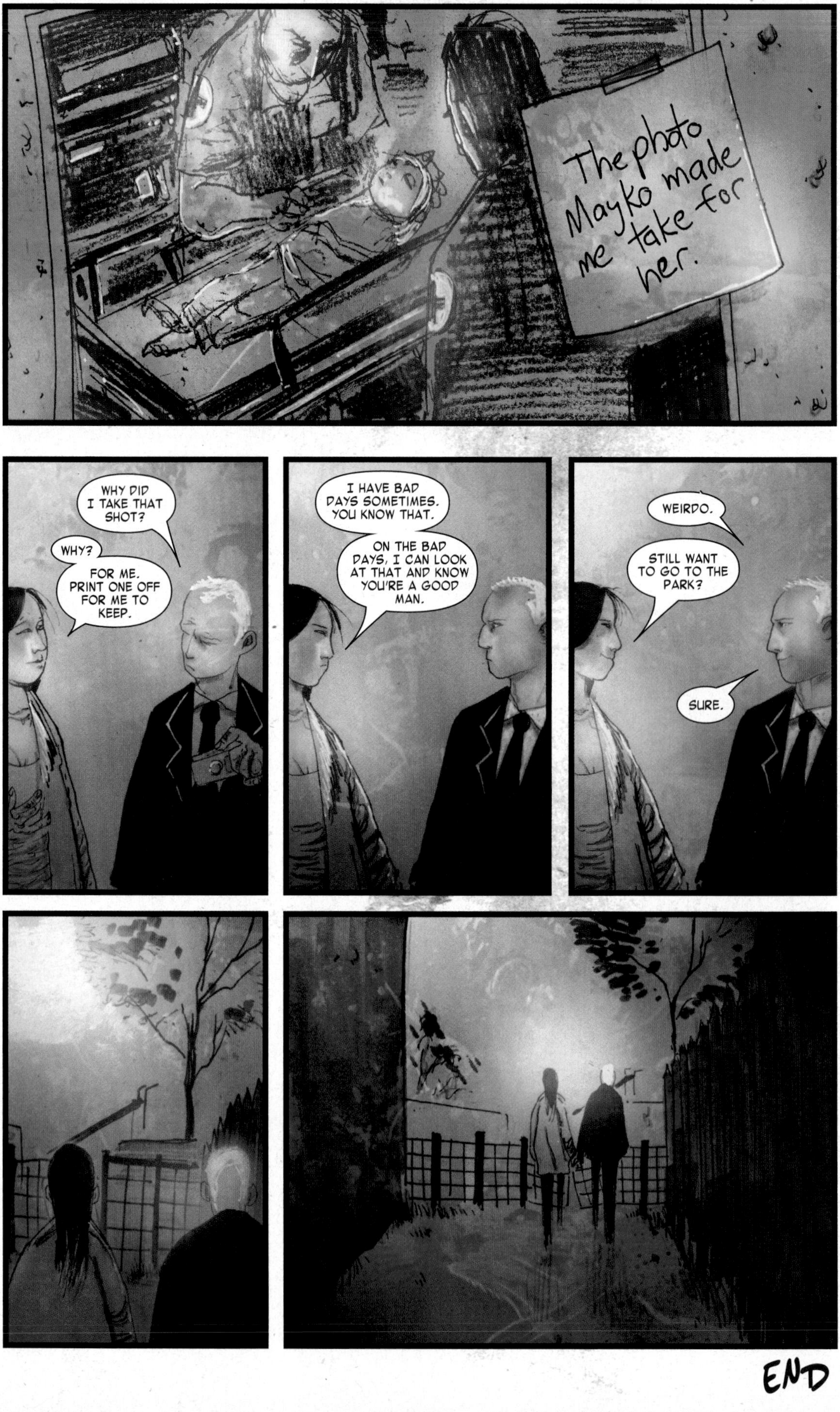
The photo Mayko made me take for her.
WHY DID I TAKE THAT SHOT?
WHY?
FOR ME. PRINT ONE OFF FOR ME TO KEEP.
I HAVE BAD DAYS SOMETIMES. YOU KNOW THAT.
ON THE BAD DAYS, I CAN LOOK AT THAT AND KNOW YOU'RE A GOOD MAN.
WEIRDO.
STILL WANT TO GO TO THE PARK?
SURE.
END

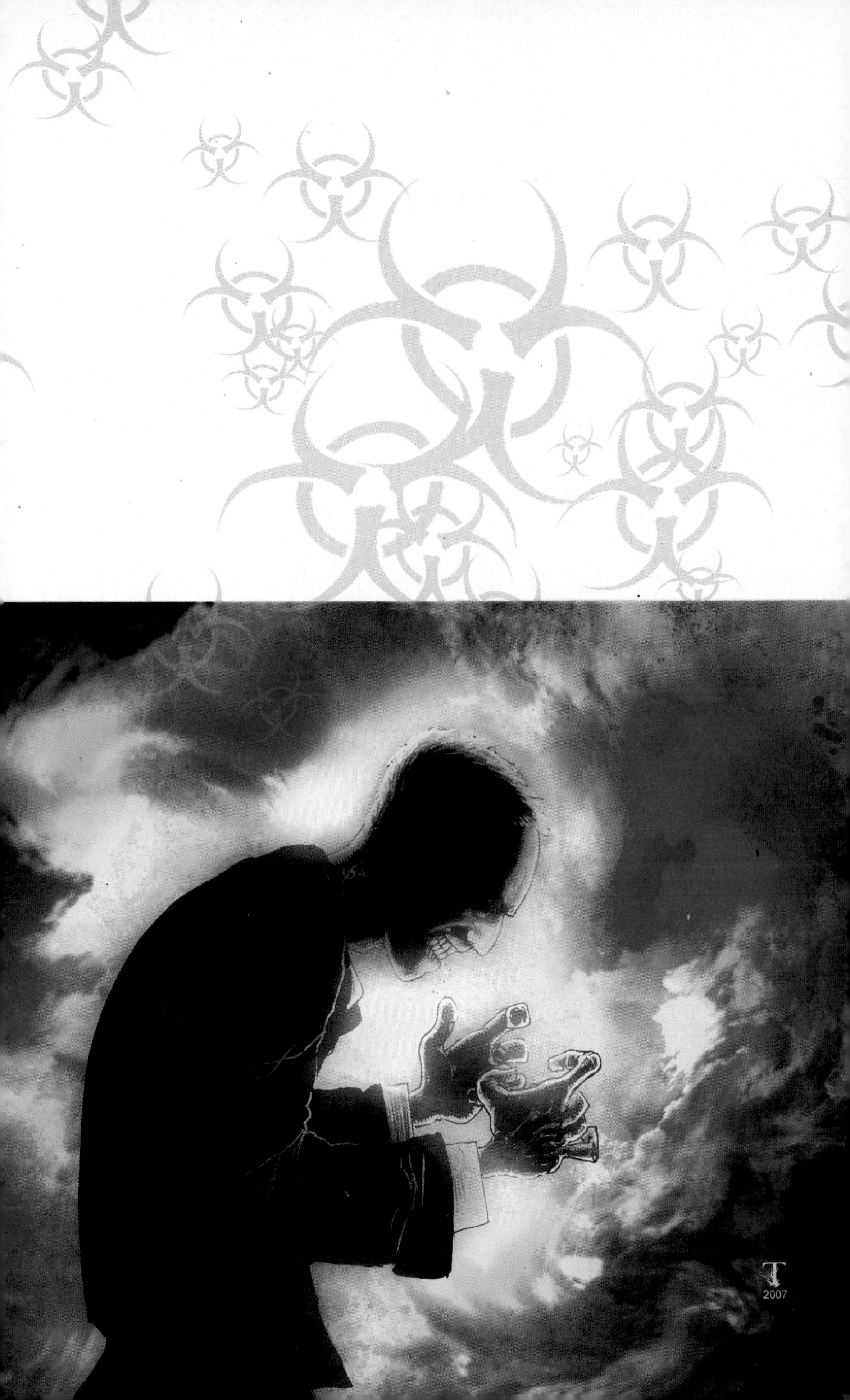
2007

# FE L L .

CHAPTER

7

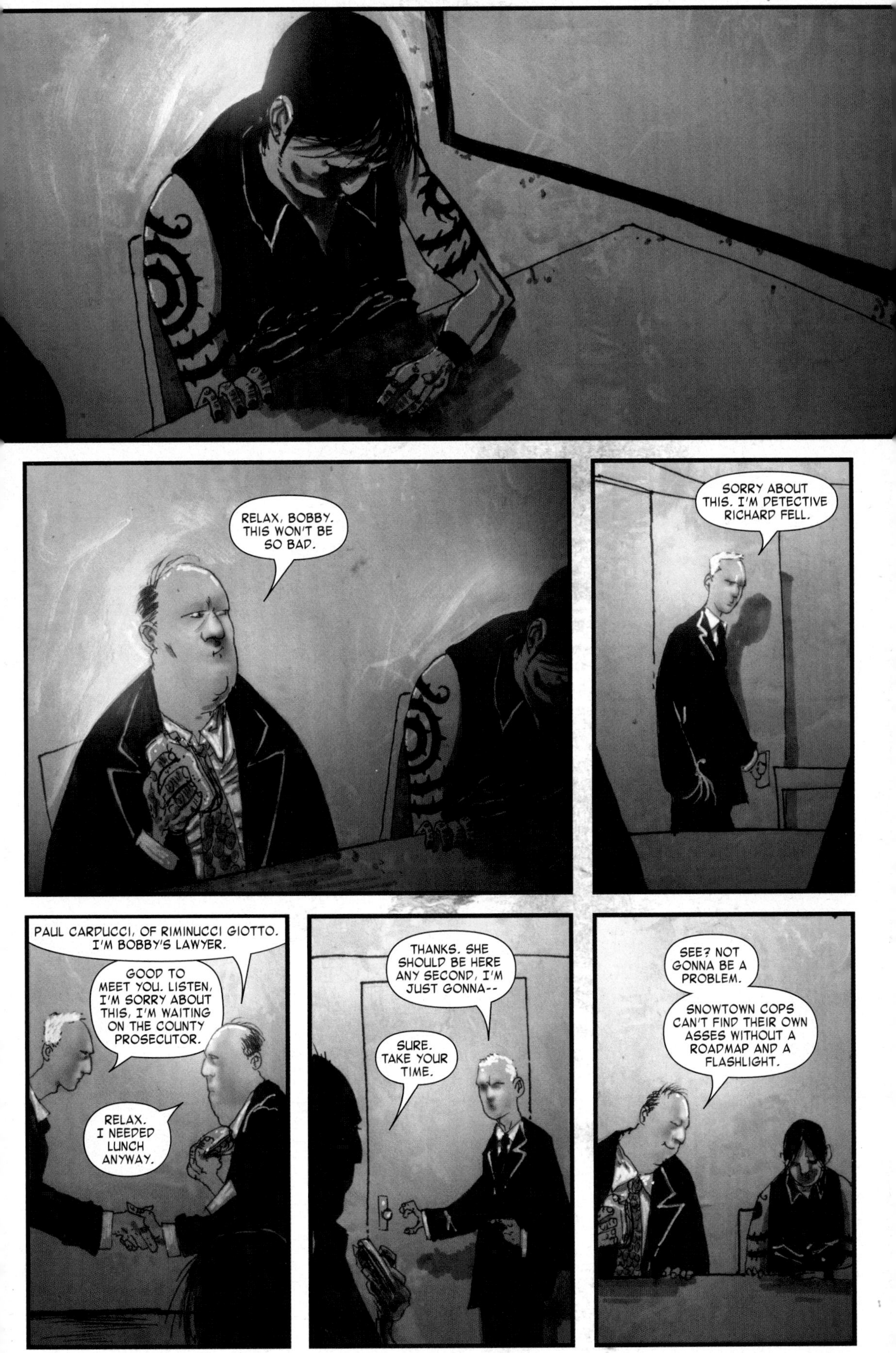
RELAX, BOBBY. THIS WON'T BE SO BAD.
SORRY ABOUT THIS. I'M DETECTIVE RICHARD FELL.
PAUL CARDUCCI, OF RIMINUCCI GIOTTO. I'M BOBBY'S LAWYER.
GOOD TO MEET YOU. LISTEN, I'M SORRY ABOUT THIS, I'M WAITING ON THE COUNTY PROSECUTOR.
RELAX. I NEEDED LUNCH ANYWAY.
THANKS. SHE SHOULD BE HERE ANY SECOND, I'M JUST GONNA--
SURE. TAKE YOUR TIME.
SEE? NOT GONNA BE A PROBLEM.
SNOWTOWN COPS CAN'T FIND THEIR OWN ASSES WITHOUT A ROADMAP AND A FLASHLIGHT.

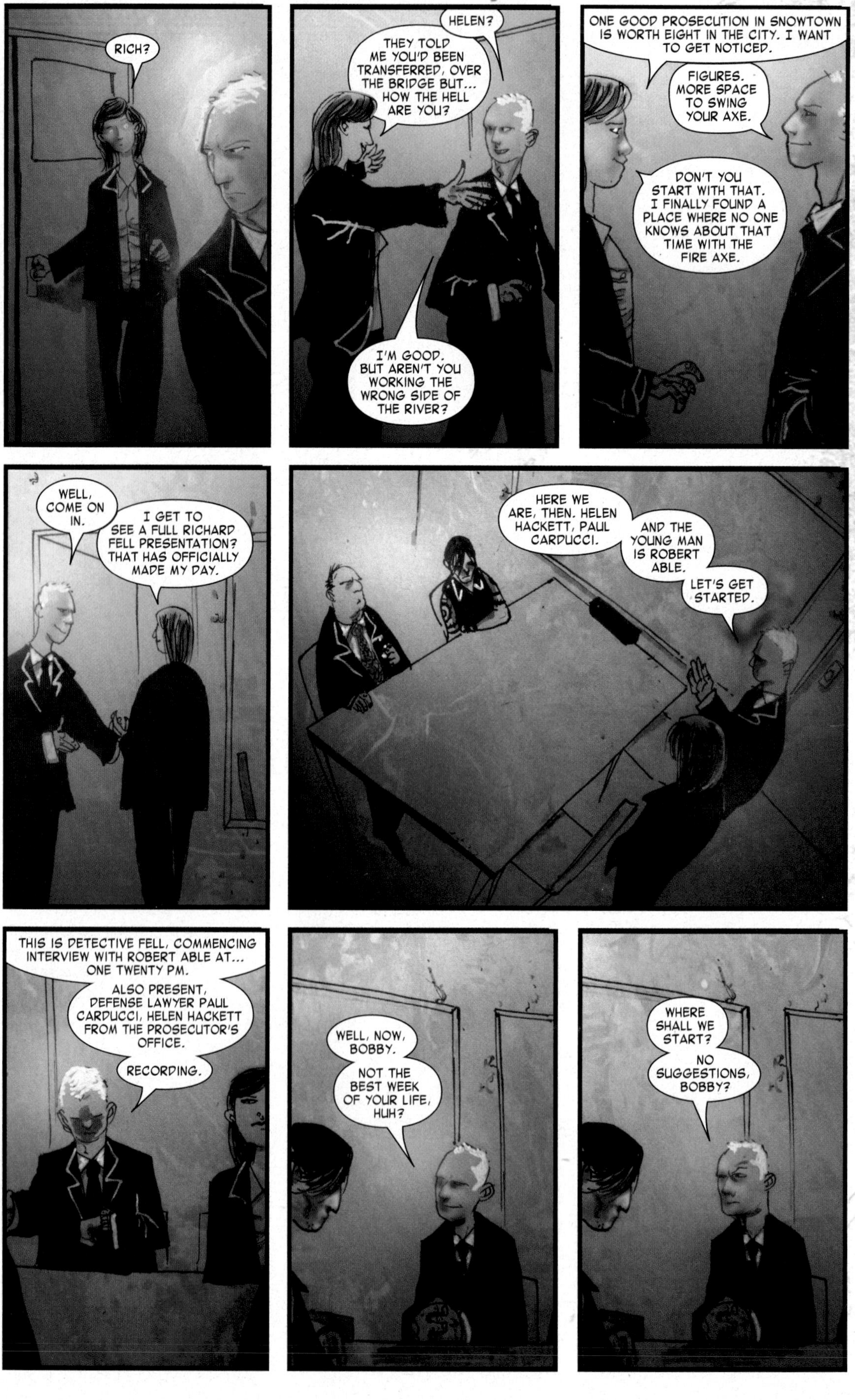
RICH?
HELEN?
THEY TOLD ME YOU'D BEEN TRANSFERRED, OVER THE BRIDGE BUT... HOW THE HELL ARE YOU?
I'M GOOD. BUT AREN'T YOU WORKING THE WRONG SIDE OF THE RIVER?
ONE GOOD PROSECUTION IN SNOWTOWN IS WORTH EIGHT IN THE CITY. I WANT TO GET NOTICED.
FIGURES. MORE SPACE TO SWING YOUR AXE.
DON'T YOU START WITH THAT. I FINALLY FOUND A PLACE WHERE NO ONE KNOWS ABOUT THAT TIME WITH THE FIRE AXE.
WELL, COME ON IN.
I GET TO SEE A FULL RICHARD FELL PRESENTATION? THAT HAS OFFICIALLY MADE MY DAY.
HERE WE ARE, THEN. HELEN HACKETT, PAUL CARDUCCI.
AND THE YOUNG MAN IS ROBERT ABLE.
LET'S GET STARTED.
THIS IS DETECTIVE FELL, COMMENCING INTERVIEW WITH ROBERT ABLE AT... ONE TWENTY PM.
ALSO PRESENT, DEFENSE LAWYER PAUL CARDUCCI, HELEN HACKETT FROM THE PROSECUTOR'S OFFICE.
RECORDING.
WELL, NOW, BOBBY.
NOT THE BEST WEEK OF YOUR LIFE, HUH?
WHERE SHALL WE START?
NO SUGGESTIONS, BOBBY?

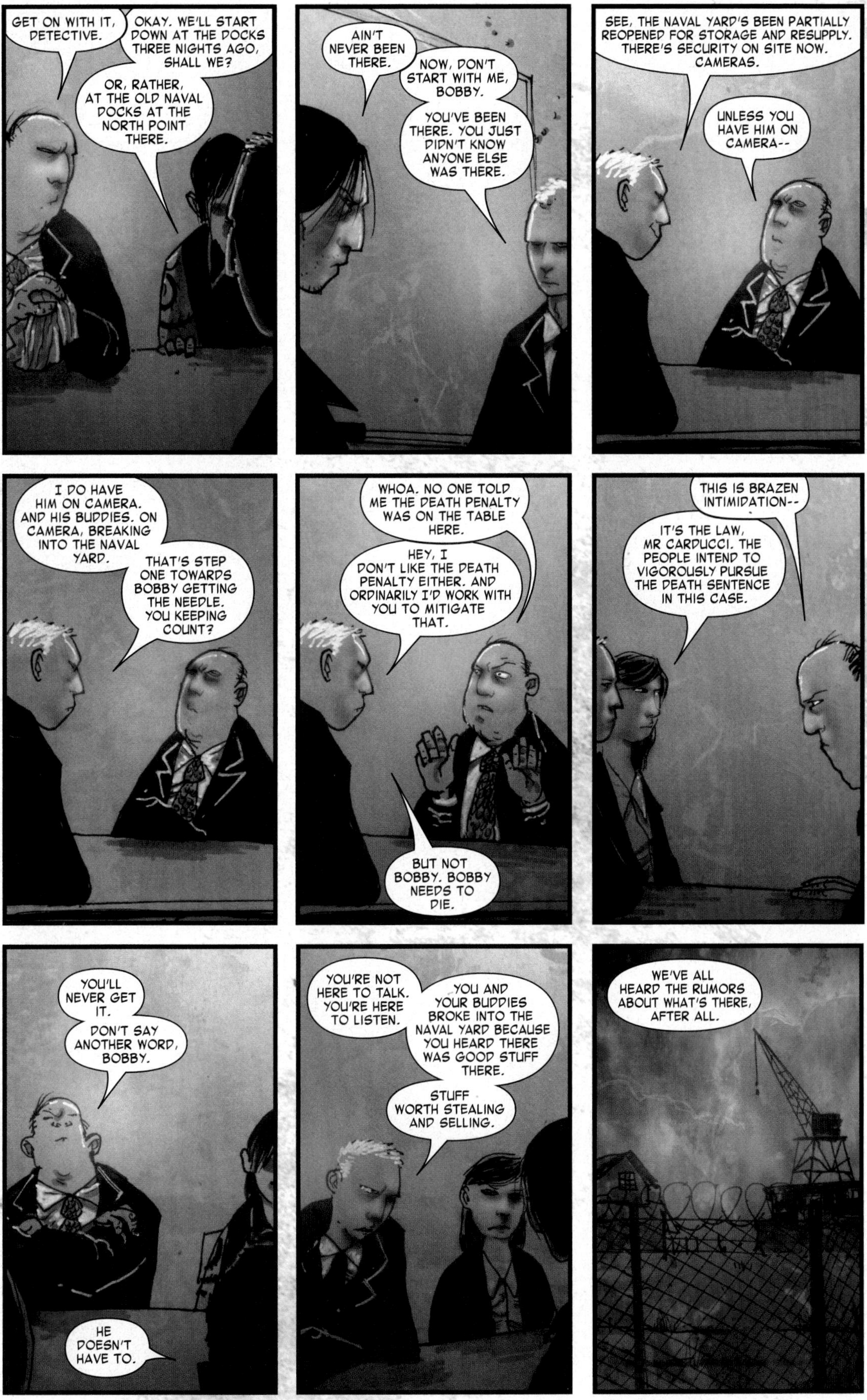
GET ON WITH IT, DETECTIVE.
OKAY. WE'LL START DOWN AT THE DOCKS THREE NIGHTS AGO, SHALL WE?
OR, RATHER, AT THE OLD NAVAL DOCKS AT THE NORTH POINT THERE.
AIN'T NEVER BEEN THERE.
NOW, DON'T START WITH ME, BOBBY.
YOU'VE BEEN THERE. YOU JUST DIDN'T KNOW ANYONE ELSE WAS THERE.
SEE, THE NAVAL YARD'S BEEN PARTIALLY REOPENED FOR STORAGE AND RESUPPLY. THERE'S SECURITY ON SITE NOW. CAMERAS.
UNLESS YOU HAVE HIM ON CAMERA--
I DO HAVE HIM ON CAMERA. AND HIS BUDDIES. ON CAMERA, BREAKING INTO THE NAVAL YARD.
THAT'S STEP ONE TOWARDS BOBBY GETTING THE NEEDLE. YOU KEEPING COUNT?
WHOA. NO ONE TOLD ME THE DEATH PENALTY WAS ON THE TABLE HERE.
HEY, I DON'T LIKE THE DEATH PENALTY EITHER. AND ORDINARILY I'D WORK WITH YOU TO MITIGATE THAT.
BUT NOT BOBBY. BOBBY NEEDS TO DIE.
THIS IS BRAZEN INTIMIDATION--
IT'S THE LAW, MR CARDUCCI. THE PEOPLE INTEND TO VIGOROUSLY PURSUE THE DEATH SENTENCE IN THIS CASE.
YOU'LL NEVER GET IT.
DON'T SAY ANOTHER WORD, BOBBY.
HE DOESN'T HAVE TO.
YOU'RE NOT HERE TO TALK. YOU'RE HERE TO LISTEN.
YOU AND YOUR BUDDIES BROKE INTO THE NAVAL YARD BECAUSE YOU HEARD THERE WAS GOOD STUFF THERE.
STUFF WORTH STEALING AND SELLING.
WE'VE ALL HEARD THE RUMORS ABOUT WHAT'S THERE, AFTER ALL.

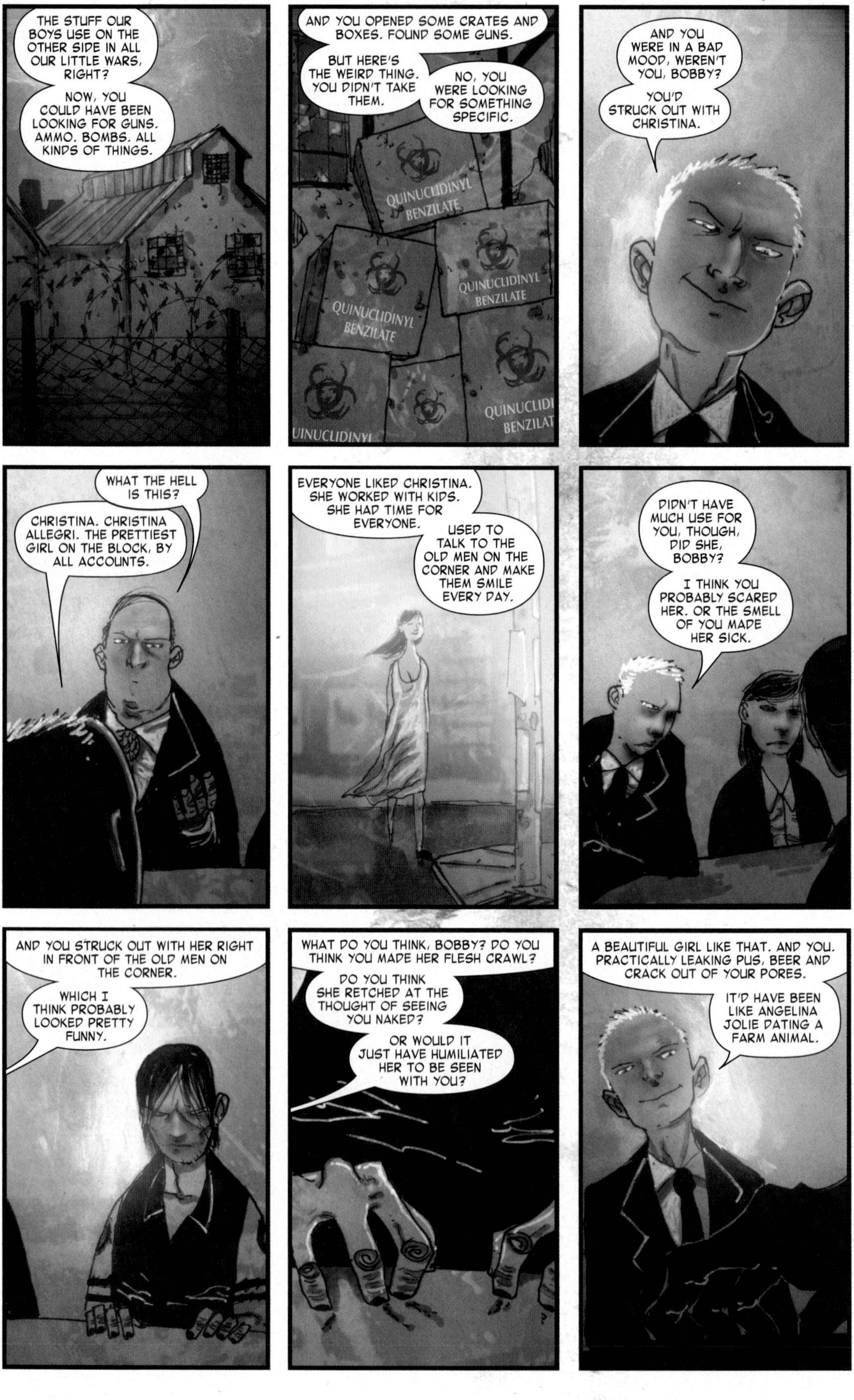
THE STUFF OUR BOYS USE ON THE OTHER SIDE IN ALL OUR LITTLE WARS, RIGHT?
NOW, YOU COULD HAVE BEEN LOOKING FOR GUNS. AMMO. BOMBS. ALL KINDS OF THINGS.
AND YOU OPENED SOME CRATES AND BOXES. FOUND SOME GUNS.
BUT HERE'S THE WEIRD THING. YOU DIDN'T TAKE THEM.
NO, YOU WERE LOOKING FOR SOMETHING SPECIFIC.
QUINUCLIDINYL BENZILATE
QUINUCLIDINYL BENZILATE
QUINUCLIDINYL BENZILATE
AND YOU WERE IN A BAD MOOD, WEREN'T YOU, BOBBY?
YOU'D STRUCK OUT WITH CHRISTINA.
WHAT THE HELL IS THIS?
CHRISTINA. CHRISTINA ALLEGRI. THE PRETTIEST GIRL ON THE BLOCK, BY ALL ACCOUNTS.
EVERYONE LIKED CHRISTINA. SHE WORKED WITH KIDS. SHE HAD TIME FOR EVERYONE.
USED TO TALK TO THE OLD MEN ON THE CORNER AND MAKE THEM SMILE EVERY DAY.
DIDN'T HAVE MUCH USE FOR YOU, THOUGH, DID SHE, BOBBY?
I THINK YOU PROBABLY SCARED HER. OR THE SMELL OF YOU MADE HER SICK.
AND YOU STRUCK OUT WITH HER RIGHT IN FRONT OF THE OLD MEN ON THE CORNER.
WHICH I THINK PROBABLY LOOKED PRETTY FUNNY.
WHAT DO YOU THINK, BOBBY? DO YOU THINK YOU MADE HER FLESH CRAWL?
DO YOU THINK SHE RETCHED AT THE THOUGHT OF SEEING YOU NAKED?
OR WOULD IT JUST HAVE HUMILIATED HER TO BE SEEN WITH YOU?
A BEAUTIFUL GIRL LIKE THAT. AND YOU. PRACTICALLY LEAKING PUS, BEER AND CRACK OUT OF YOUR PORES.
IT'D HAVE BEEN LIKE ANGELINA JOLIE DATING A FARM ANIMAL.

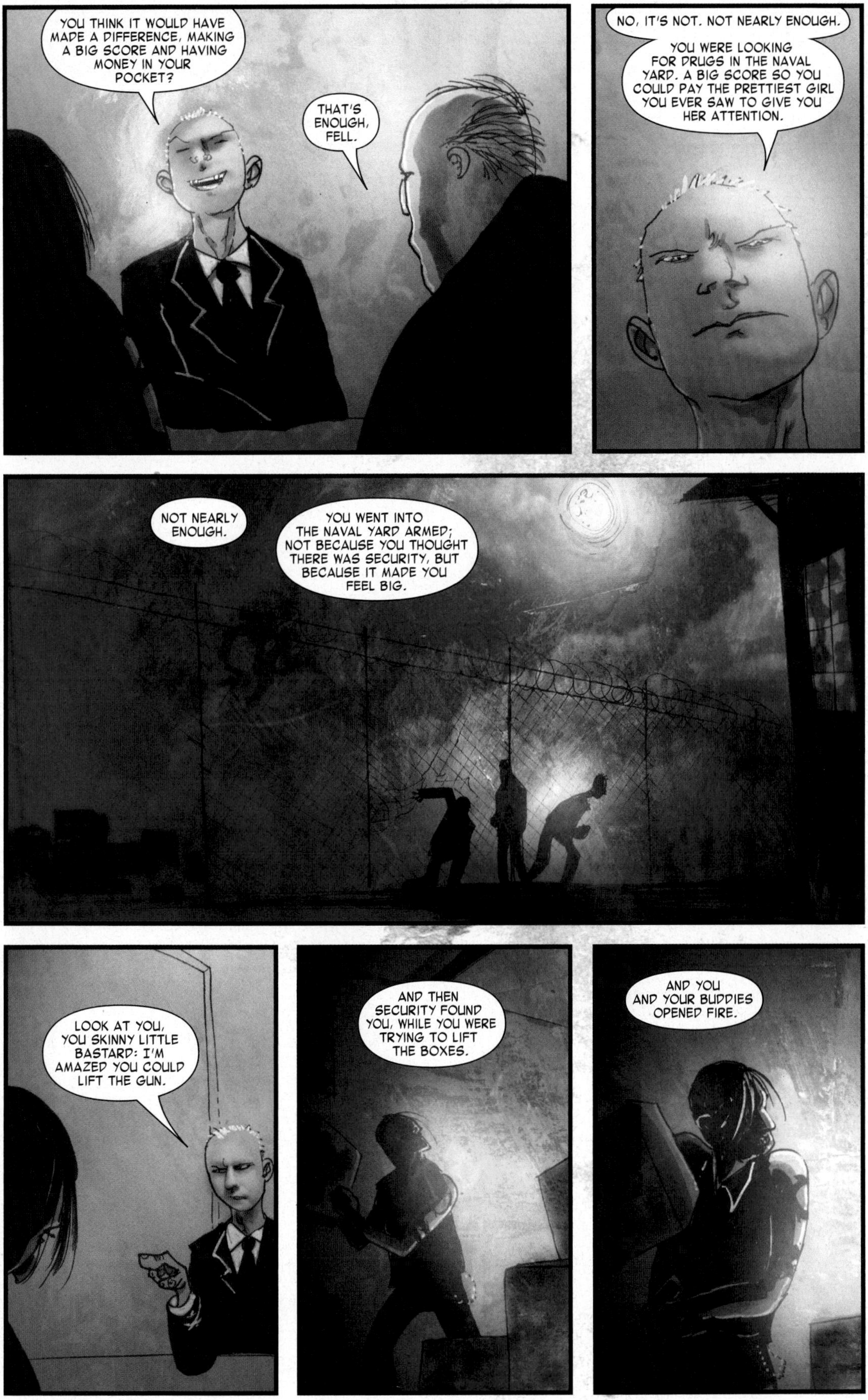
YOU THINK IT WOULD HAVE MADE A DIFFERENCE, MAKING A BIG SCORE AND HAVING MONEY IN YOUR POCKET?
THAT'S ENOUGH, FELL.
NO, IT'S NOT. NOT NEARLY ENOUGH.
YOU WERE LOOKING FOR DRUGS IN THE NAVAL YARD. A BIG SCORE SO YOU COULD PAY THE PRETTIEST GIRL YOU EVER SAW TO GIVE YOU HER ATTENTION.
NOT NEARLY ENOUGH.
YOU WENT INTO THE NAVAL YARD ARMED; NOT BECAUSE YOU THOUGHT THERE WAS SECURITY, BUT BECAUSE IT MADE YOU FEEL BIG.
LOOK AT YOU, YOU SKINNY LITTLE BASTARD: I'M AMAZED YOU COULD LIFT THE GUN.
AND THEN SECURITY FOUND YOU, WHILE YOU WERE TRYING TO LIFT THE BOXES.
AND YOU AND YOUR BUDDIES OPENED FIRE.

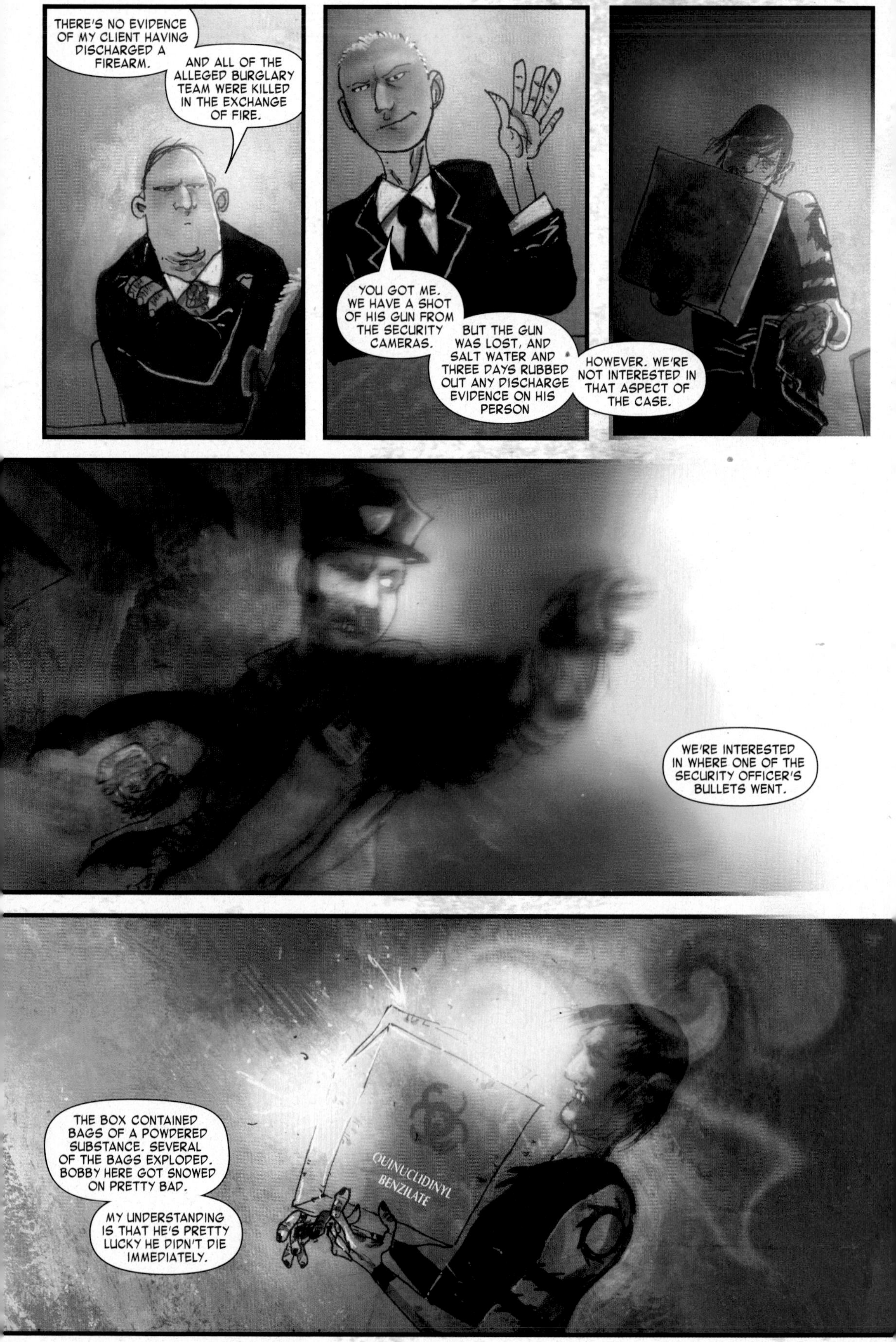
THERE'S NO EVIDENCE OF MY CLIENT HAVING DISCHARGED A FIREARM.
AND ALL OF THE ALLEGED BURGLARY TEAM WERE KILLED IN THE EXCHANGE OF FIRE.
YOU GOT ME. WE HAVE A SHOT OF HIS GUN FROM THE SECURITY CAMERAS.
BUT THE GUN WAS LOST, AND SALT WATER AND THREE DAYS RUBBED OUT ANY DISCHARGE EVIDENCE ON HIS PERSON
HOWEVER. WE'RE NOT INTERESTED IN THAT ASPECT OF THE CASE.
WE'RE INTERESTED IN WHERE ONE OF THE SECURITY OFFICER'S BULLETS WENT.
THE BOX CONTAINED BAGS OF A POWDERED SUBSTANCE. SEVERAL OF THE BAGS EXPLODED. BOBBY HERE GOT SNOWED ON PRETTY BAD.
QUINUCLIDINYL BENZILATE
MY UNDERSTANDING IS THAT HE'S PRETTY LUCKY HE DIDN'T DIE IMMEDIATELY.

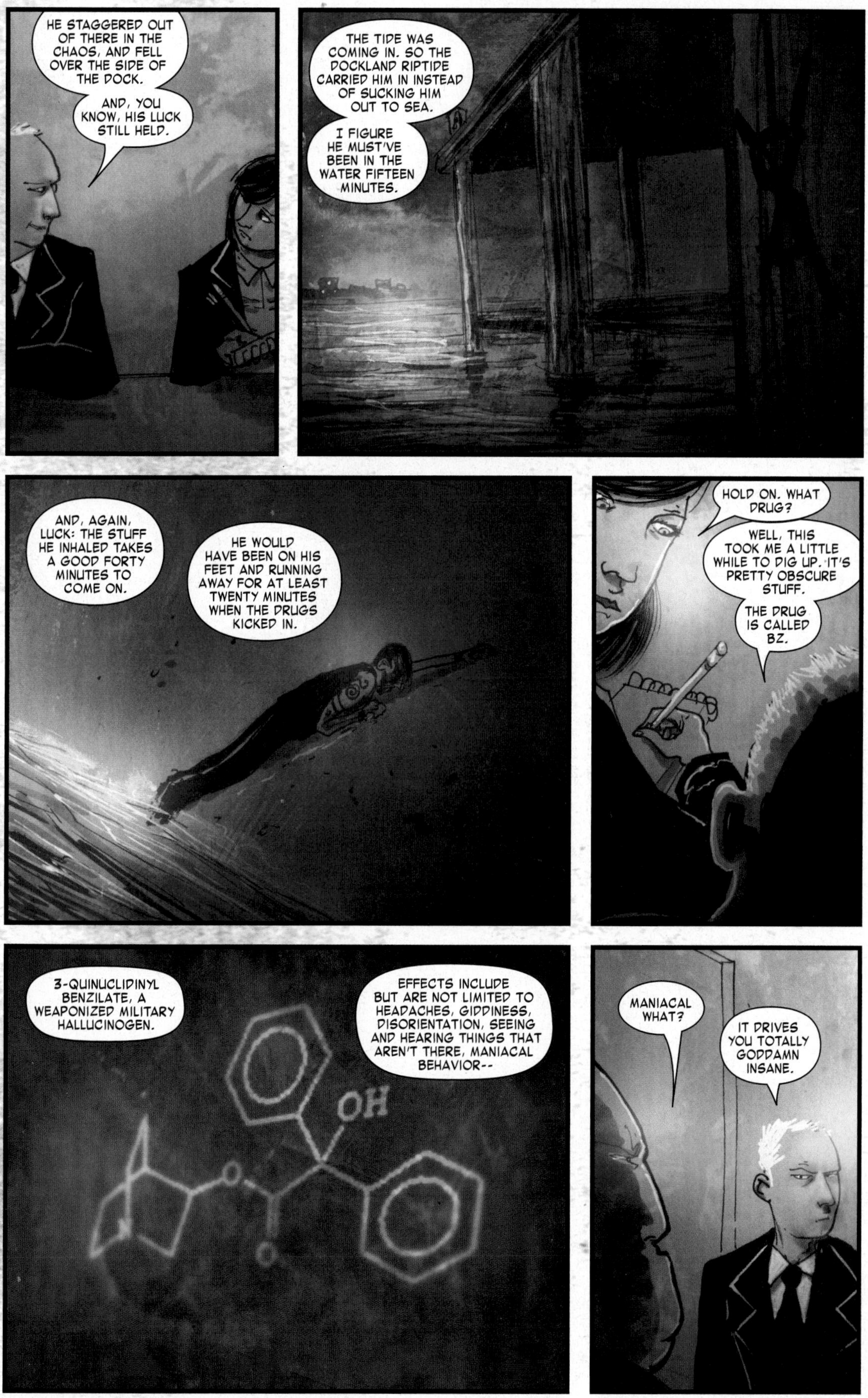
HE STAGGERED OUT OF THERE IN THE CHAOS, AND FELL OVER THE SIDE OF THE DOCK.
AND, YOU KNOW, HIS LUCK STILL HELD.
THE TIDE WAS COMING IN. SO THE DOCKLAND RIPTIDE CARRIED HIM IN INSTEAD OF SUCKING HIM OUT TO SEA.
I FIGURE HE MUST'VE BEEN IN THE WATER FIFTEEN MINUTES.
AND, AGAIN, LUCK: THE STUFF HE INHALED TAKES A GOOD FORTY MINUTES TO COME ON.
HE WOULD HAVE BEEN ON HIS FEET AND RUNNING AWAY FOR AT LEAST TWENTY MINUTES WHEN THE DRUGS KICKED IN.
HOLD ON. WHAT DRUG?
WELL, THIS TOOK ME A LITTLE WHILE TO DIG UP. IT'S PRETTY OBSCURE STUFF.
THE DRUG IS CALLED BZ.
3-QUINUCLIDINYL BENZILATE, A WEAPONIZED MILITARY HALLUCINOGEN.
EFFECTS INCLUDE BUT ARE NOT LIMITED TO HEADACHES, GIDDINESS, DISORIENTATION, SEEING AND HEARING THINGS THAT AREN'T THERE, MANIACAL BEHAVIOR--
OH
MANIACAL WHAT?
IT DRIVES YOU TOTALLY GODDAMN INSANE.

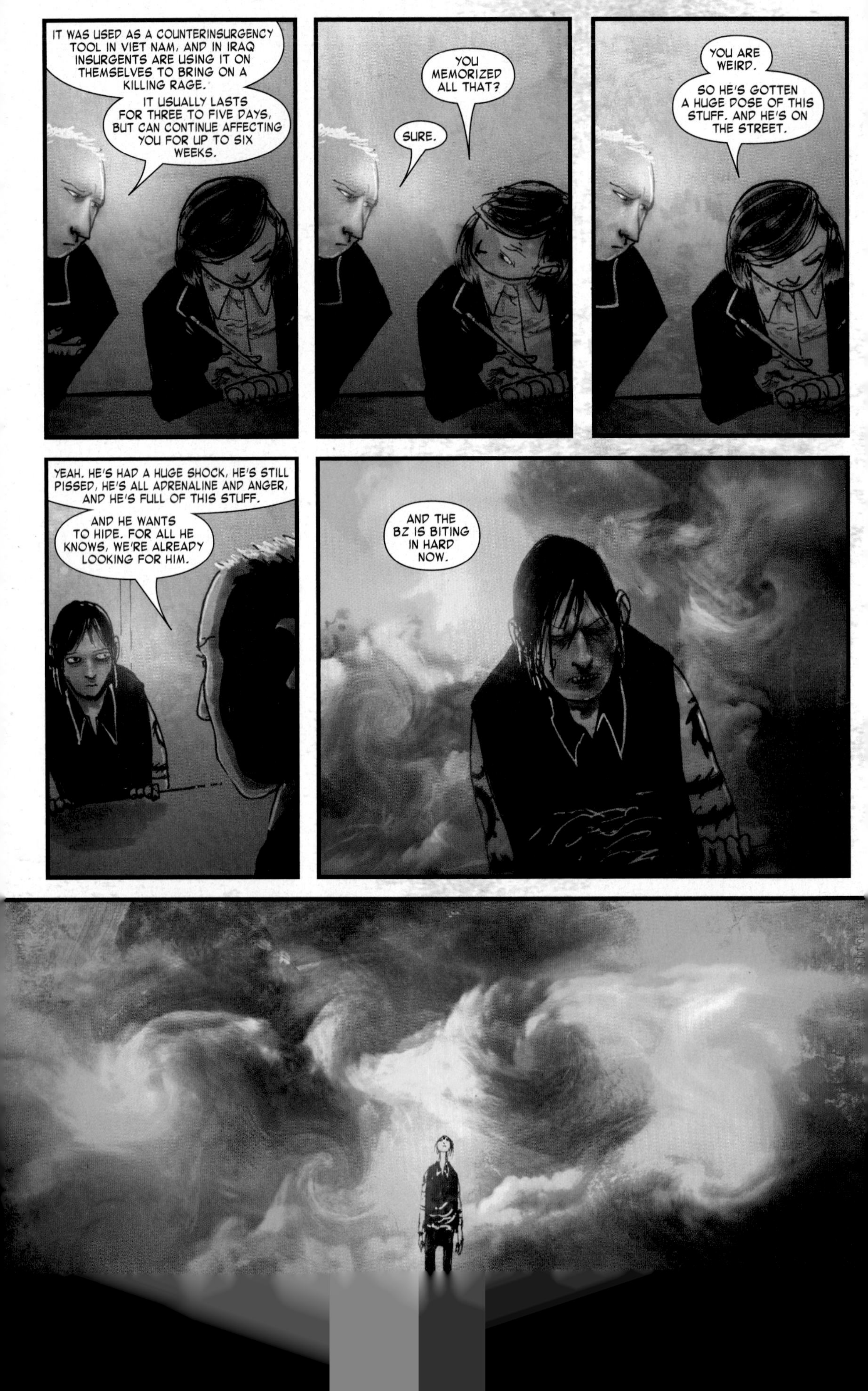
IT WAS USED AS A COUNTERINSURGENCY TOOL IN VIET NAM, AND IN IRAQ INSURGENTS ARE USING IT ON THEMSELVES TO BRING ON A KILLING RAGE.
IT USUALLY LASTS FOR THREE TO FIVE DAYS, BUT CAN CONTINUE AFFECTING YOU FOR UP TO SIX WEEKS.
YOU MEMORIZED ALL THAT?
SURE.
YOU ARE WEIRD.
SO HE'S GOTTEN A HUGE DOSE OF THIS STUFF. AND HE'S ON THE STREET.
YEAH. HE'S HAD A HUGE SHOCK, HE'S STILL PISSED, HE'S ALL ADRENALINE AND ANGER, AND HE'S FULL OF THIS STUFF.
AND HE WANTS TO HIDE. FOR ALL HE KNOWS, WE'RE ALREADY LOOKING FOR HIM.
AND THE BZ IS BITING IN HARD NOW.

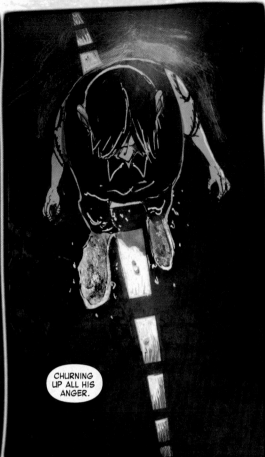

CHURNING UP ALL HIS ANGER.

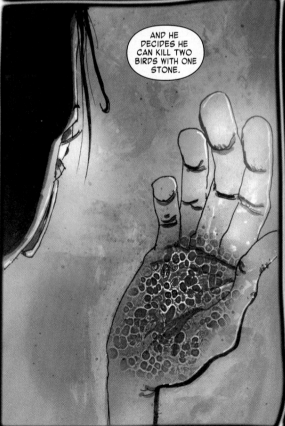

AND HE DECIDES HE CAN KILL TWO BIRDS WITH ONE STONE.

HE GOES DIRECTLY TO CHRISTINA'S APARTMENT.

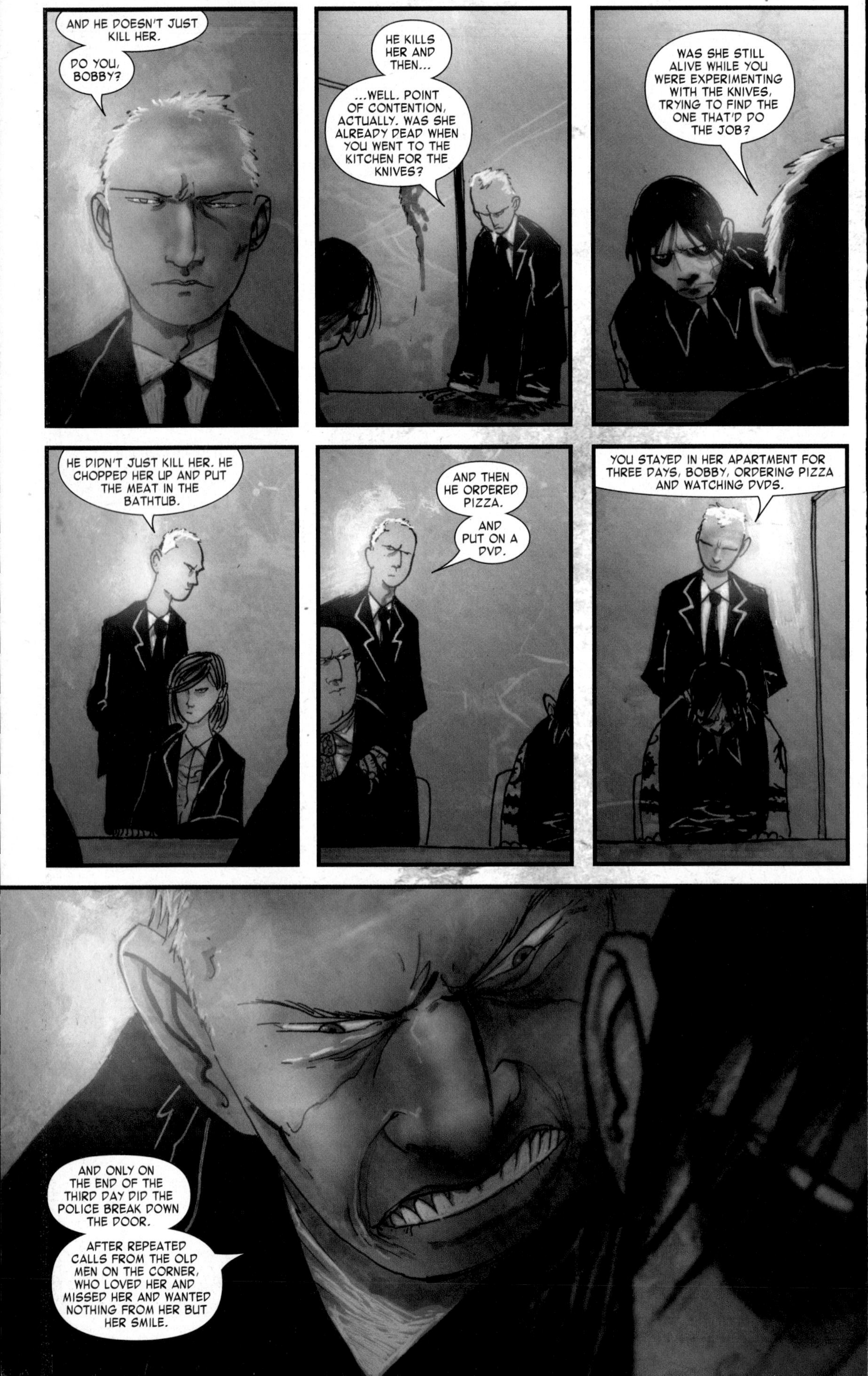
AND HE DOESN'T JUST KILL HER.
DO YOU, BOBBY?
HE KILLS HER AND THEN...
...WELL. POINT OF CONTENTION, ACTUALLY. WAS SHE ALREADY DEAD WHEN YOU WENT TO THE KITCHEN FOR THE KNIVES?
WAS SHE STILL ALIVE WHILE YOU WERE EXPERIMENTING WITH THE KNIVES, TRYING TO FIND THE ONE THAT'D DO THE JOB?
HE DIDN'T JUST KILL HER. HE CHOPPED HER UP AND PUT THE MEAT IN THE BATHTUB.
AND THEN HE ORDERED PIZZA.
AND PUT ON A DVD.
YOU STAYED IN HER APARTMENT FOR THREE DAYS, BOBBY, ORDERING PIZZA AND WATCHING DVDS.
AND ONLY ON THE END OF THE THIRD DAY DID THE POLICE BREAK DOWN THE DOOR.
AFTER REPEATED CALLS FROM THE OLD MEN ON THE CORNER, WHO LOVED HER AND MISSED HER AND WANTED NOTHING FROM HER BUT HER SMILE.

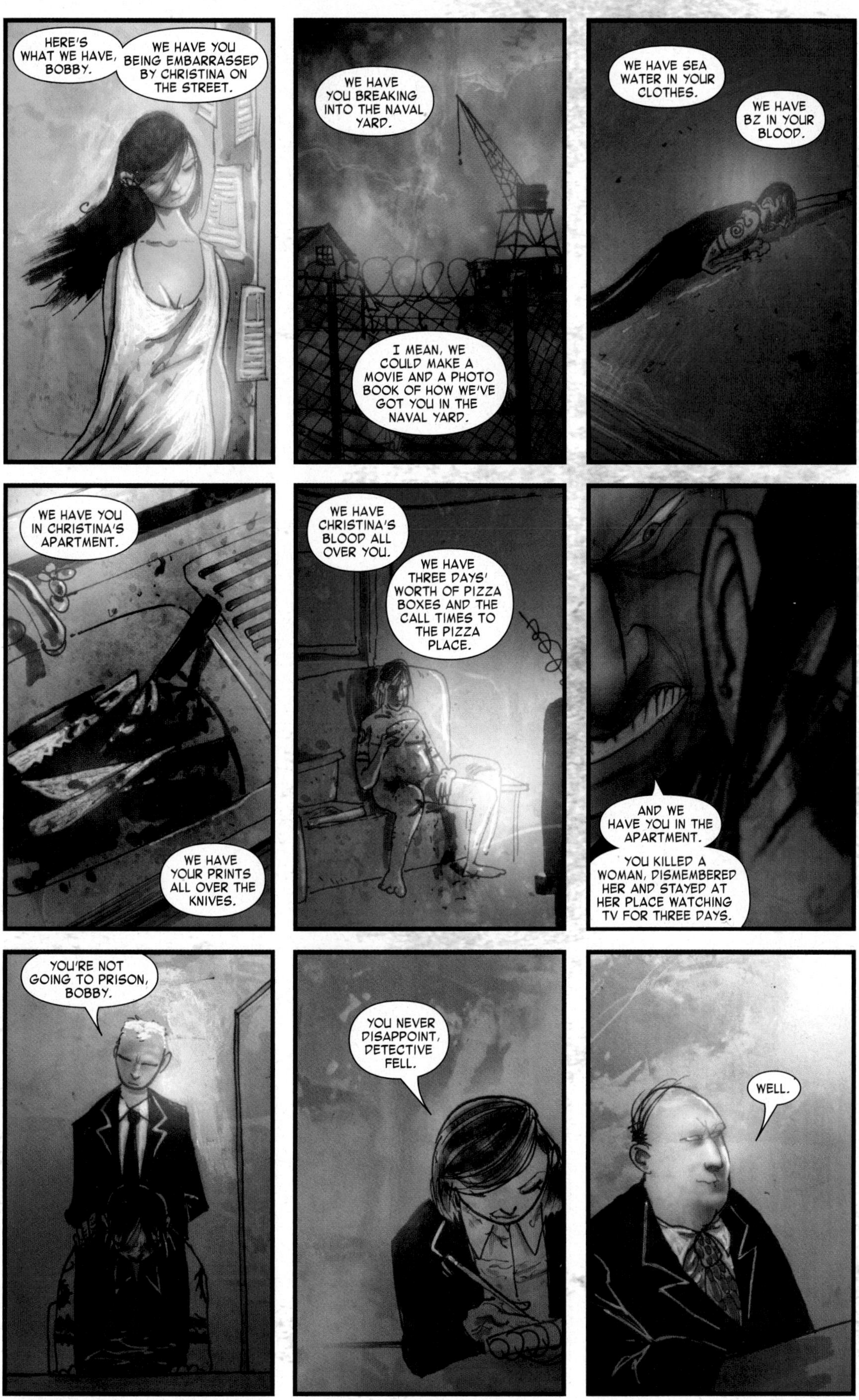
HERE'S WHAT WE HAVE, BOBBY.
WE HAVE YOU BEING EMBARRASSED BY CHRISTINA ON THE STREET.
WE HAVE YOU BREAKING INTO THE NAVAL YARD.
I MEAN, WE COULD MAKE A MOVIE AND A PHOTO BOOK OF HOW WE'VE GOT YOU IN THE NAVAL YARD.
WE HAVE SEA WATER IN YOUR CLOTHES.
WE HAVE BZ IN YOUR BLOOD.
WE HAVE YOU IN CHRISTINA'S APARTMENT.
WE HAVE YOUR PRINTS ALL OVER THE KNIVES.
WE HAVE CHRISTINA'S BLOOD ALL OVER YOU.
WE HAVE THREE DAYS' WORTH OF PIZZA BOXES AND THE CALL TIMES TO THE PIZZA PLACE.
AND WE HAVE YOU IN THE APARTMENT.
YOU KILLED A WOMAN, DISMEMBERED HER AND STAYED AT HER PLACE WATCHING TV FOR THREE DAYS.
YOU'RE NOT GOING TO PRISON, BOBBY.
YOU NEVER DISAPPOINT, DETECTIVE FELL.
WELL.

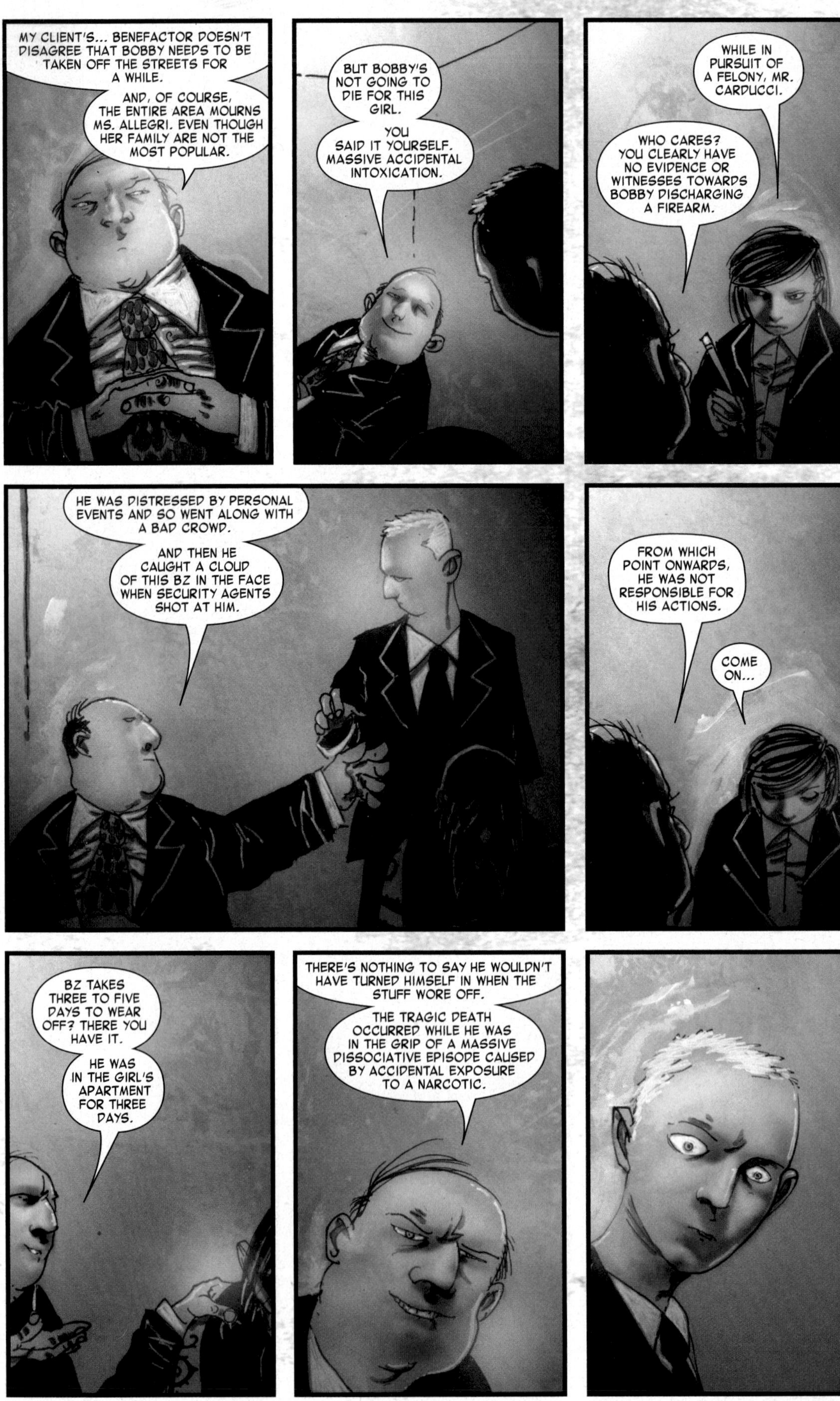
MY CLIENT'S... BENEFACTOR DOESN'T DISAGREE THAT BOBBY NEEDS TO BE TAKEN OFF THE STREETS FOR A WHILE.
AND, OF COURSE, THE ENTIRE AREA MOURNS MS. ALLEGRI. EVEN THOUGH HER FAMILY ARE NOT THE MOST POPULAR.
BUT BOBBY'S NOT GOING TO DIE FOR THIS GIRL.
YOU SAID IT YOURSELF. MASSIVE ACCIDENTAL INTOXICATION.
WHILE IN PURSUIT OF A FELONY, MR. CARDUCCI.
WHO CARES? YOU CLEARLY HAVE NO EVIDENCE OR WITNESSES TOWARDS BOBBY DISCHARGING A FIREARM.
HE WAS DISTRESSED BY PERSONAL EVENTS AND SO WENT ALONG WITH A BAD CROWD.
AND THEN HE CAUGHT A CLOUD OF THIS BZ IN THE FACE WHEN SECURITY AGENTS SHOT AT HIM.
FROM WHICH POINT ONWARDS, HE WAS NOT RESPONSIBLE FOR HIS ACTIONS.
COME ON...
BZ TAKES THREE TO FIVE DAYS TO WEAR OFF? THERE YOU HAVE IT.
HE WAS IN THE GIRL'S APARTMENT FOR THREE DAYS.
THERE'S NOTHING TO SAY HE WOULDN'T HAVE TURNED HIMSELF IN WHEN THE STUFF WORE OFF.
THE TRAGIC DEATH OCCURRED WHILE HE WAS IN THE GRIP OF A MASSIVE DISSOCIATIVE EPISODE CAUSED BY ACCIDENTAL EXPOSURE TO A NARCOTIC.

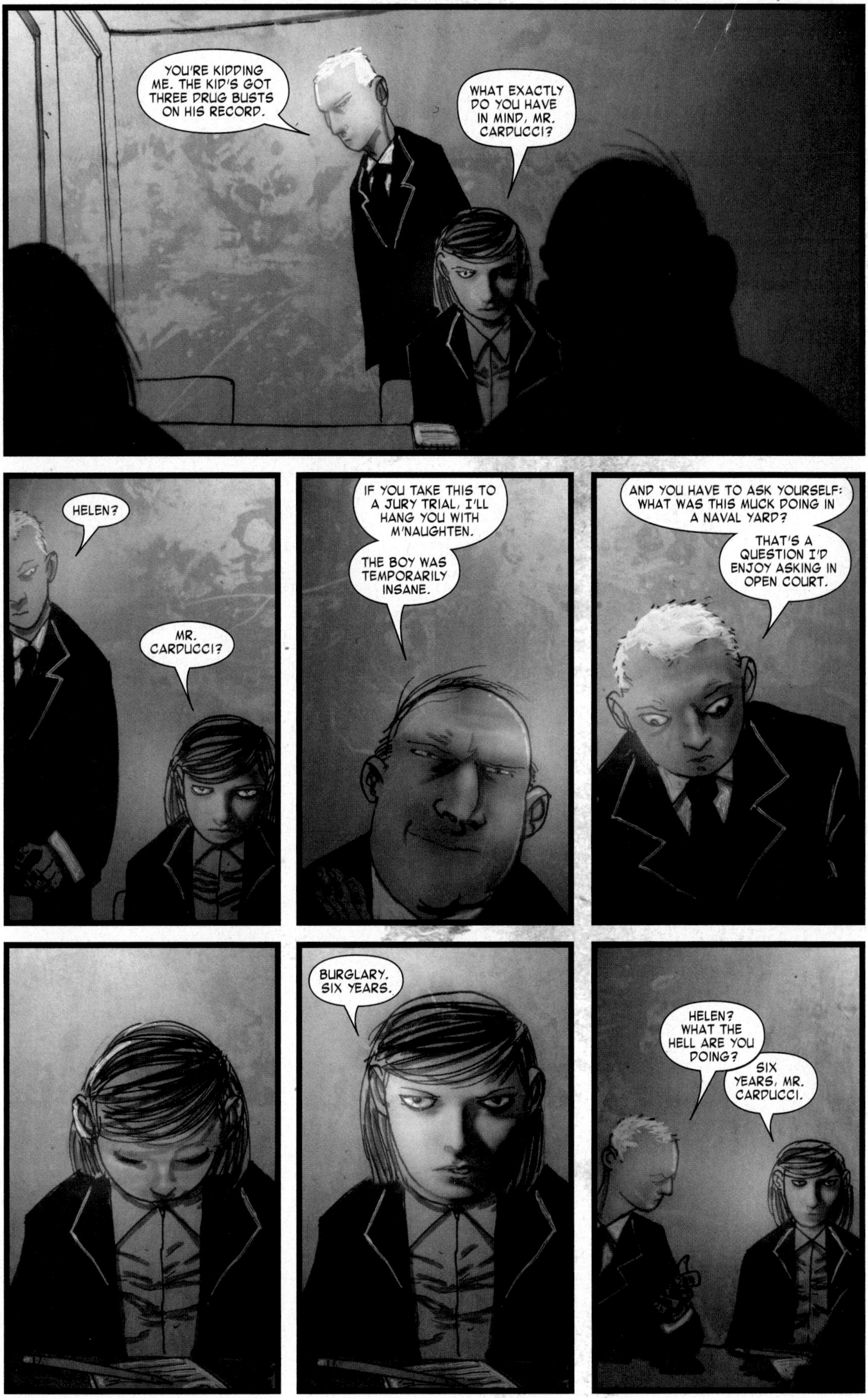
YOU'RE KIDDING ME. THE KID'S GOT THREE DRUG BUSTS ON HIS RECORD.
WHAT EXACTLY DO YOU HAVE IN MIND, MR. CARDUCCI?
HELEN?
MR. CARDUCCI?
IF YOU TAKE THIS TO A JURY TRIAL, I'LL HANG YOU WITH M'NAUGHTEN.
THE BOY WAS TEMPORARILY INSANE.
AND YOU HAVE TO ASK YOURSELF: WHAT WAS THIS MUCK DOING IN A NAVAL YARD?
THAT'S A QUESTION I'D ENJOY ASKING IN OPEN COURT.
BURGLARY. SIX YEARS.
HELEN? WHAT THE HELL ARE YOU DOING?
SIX YEARS, MR. CARDUCCI.

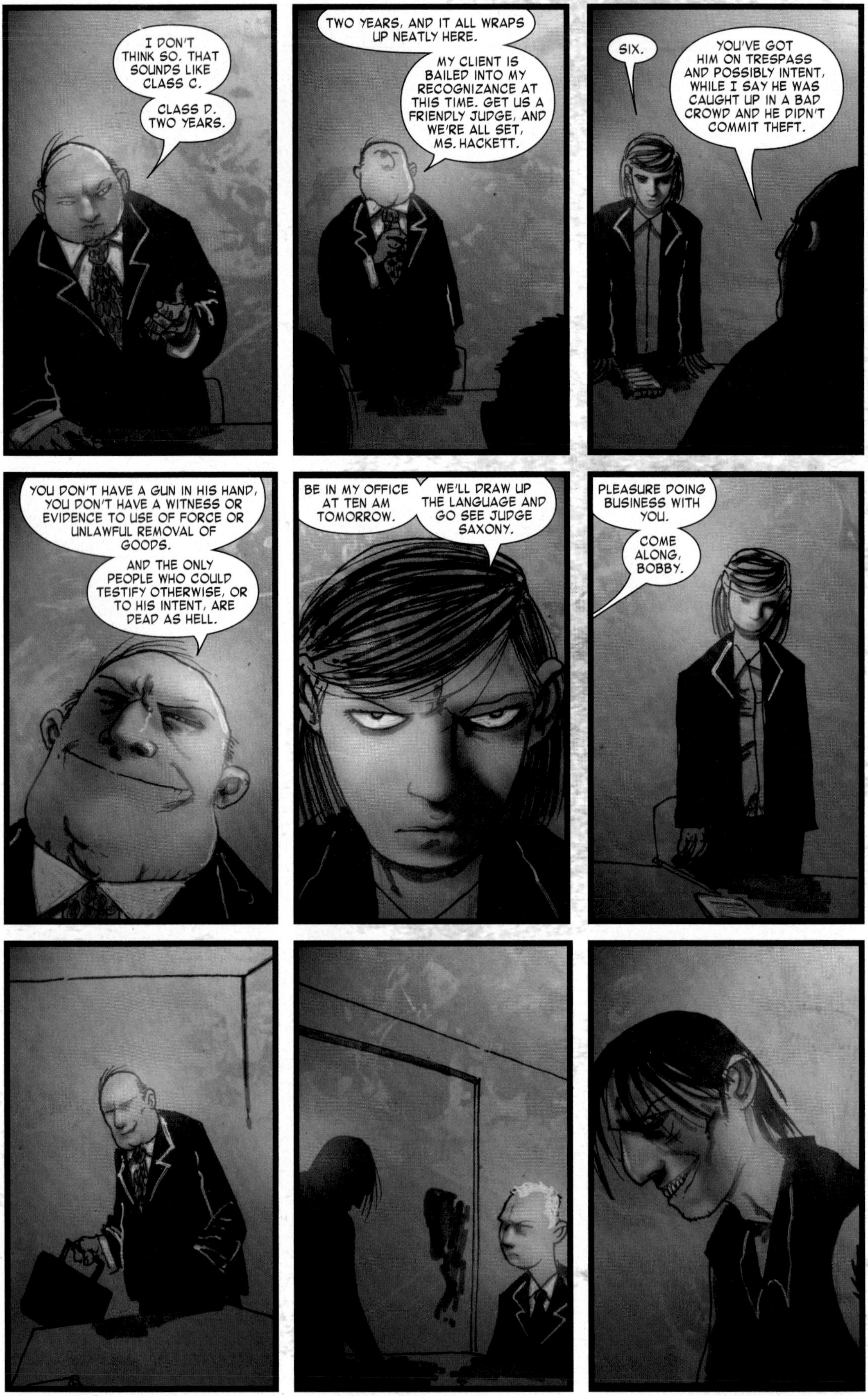
I DON'T THINK SO. THAT SOUNDS LIKE CLASS C.
CLASS D. TWO YEARS.
TWO YEARS, AND IT ALL WRAPS UP NEATLY HERE.
MY CLIENT IS BAILED INTO MY RECOGNIZANCE AT THIS TIME. GET US A FRIENDLY JUDGE, AND WE'RE ALL SET, MS. HACKETT.
SIX.
YOU'VE GOT HIM ON TRESPASS AND POSSIBLY INTENT, WHILE I SAY HE WAS CAUGHT UP IN A BAD CROWD AND HE DIDN'T COMMIT THEFT.
YOU DON'T HAVE A GUN IN HIS HAND, YOU DON'T HAVE A WITNESS OR EVIDENCE TO USE OF FORCE OR UNLAWFUL REMOVAL OF GOODS.
AND THE ONLY PEOPLE WHO COULD TESTIFY OTHERWISE, OR TO HIS INTENT, ARE DEAD AS HELL.
BE IN MY OFFICE AT TEN AM TOMORROW.
WE'LL DRAW UP THE LANGUAGE AND GO SEE JUDGE SAXONY.
PLEASURE DOING BUSINESS WITH YOU.
COME ALONG, BOBBY.

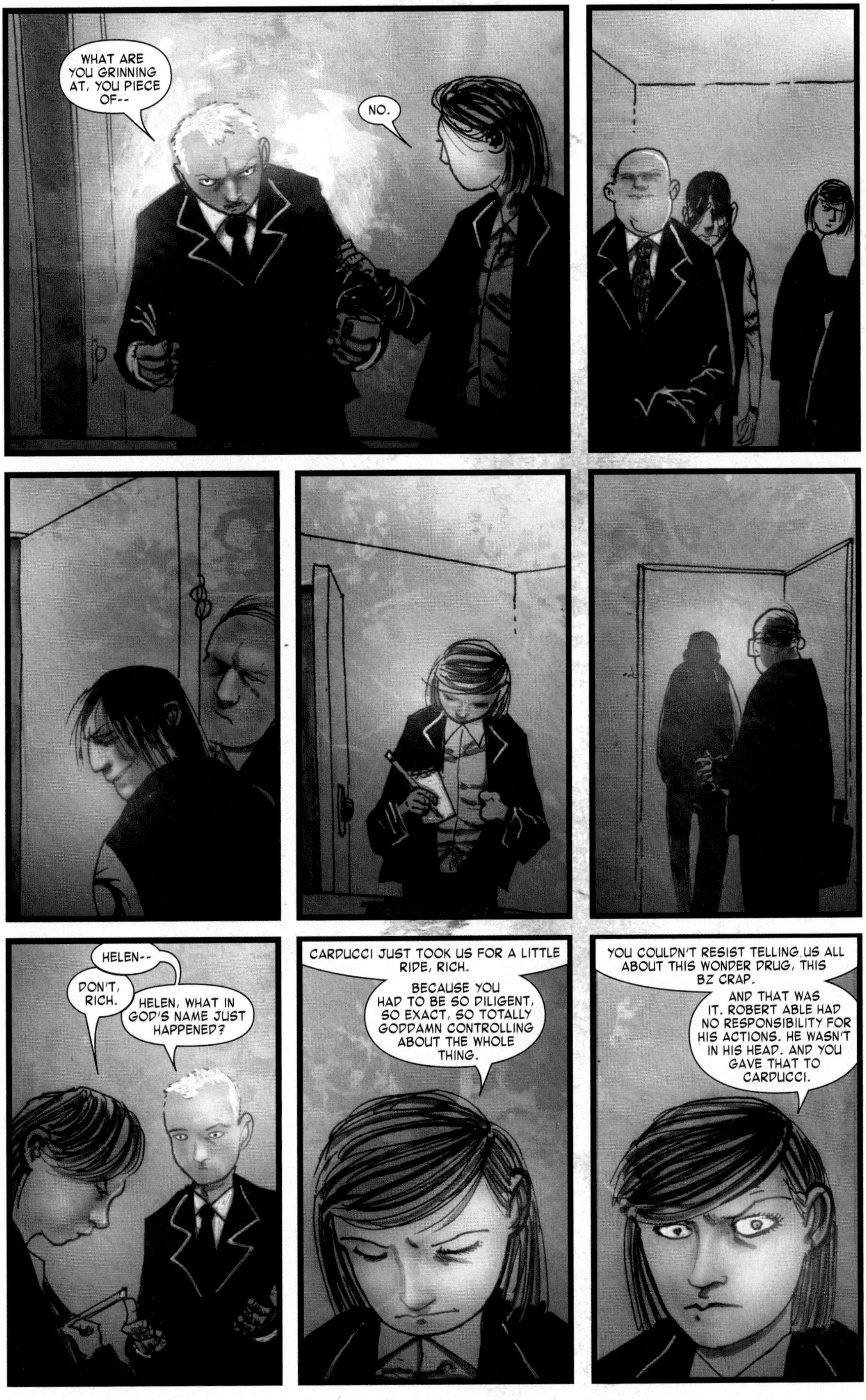
WHAT ARE YOU GRINNING AT, YOU PIECE OF--
NO.
HELEN--
DON'T, RICH.
HELEN, WHAT IN GOD'S NAME JUST HAPPENED?
CARDUCCI JUST TOOK US FOR A LITTLE RIDE, RICH.
BECAUSE YOU HAD TO BE SO DILIGENT, SO EXACT, SO TOTALLY GODDAMN CONTROLLING ABOUT THE WHOLE THING.
YOU COULDN'T RESIST TELLING US ALL ABOUT THIS WONDER DRUG, THIS BZ CRAP.
AND THAT WAS IT. ROBERT ABLE HAD NO RESPONSIBILITY FOR HIS ACTIONS. HE WASN'T IN HIS HEAD. AND YOU GAVE THAT TO CARDUCCI.

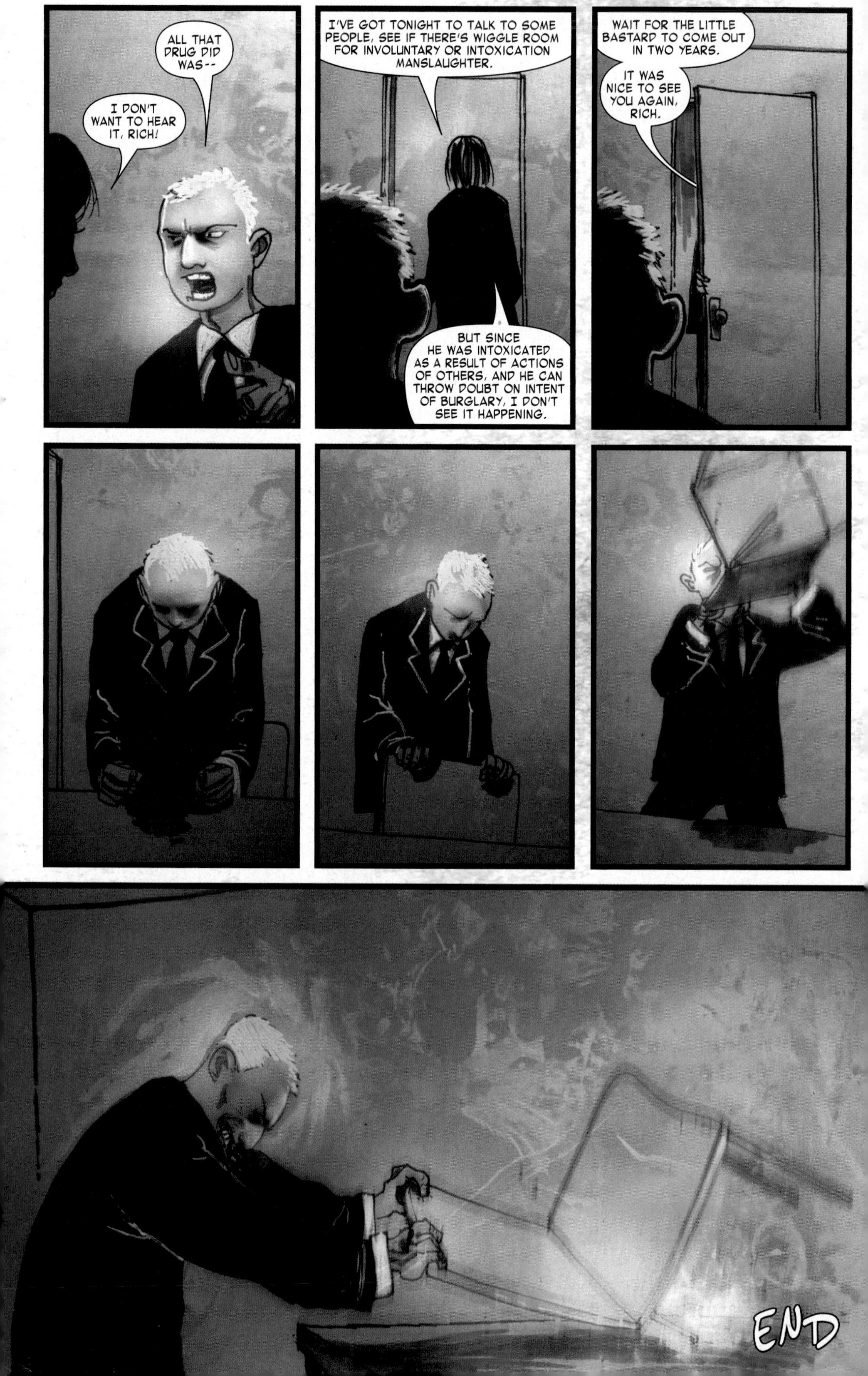
ALL THAT DRUG DID WAS--
I DON'T WANT TO HEAR IT, RICH!
I'VE GOT TONIGHT TO TALK TO SOME PEOPLE, SEE IF THERE'S WIGGLE ROOM FOR INVOLUNTARY OR INTOXICATION MANSLAUGHTER.
BUT SINCE HE WAS INTOXICATED AS A RESULT OF ACTIONS OF OTHERS, AND HE CAN THROW DOUBT ON INTENT OF BURGLARY, I DON'T SEE IT HAPPENING.
WAIT FOR THE LITTLE BASTARD TO COME OUT IN TWO YEARS.
IT WAS NICE TO SEE YOU AGAIN, RICH.
END

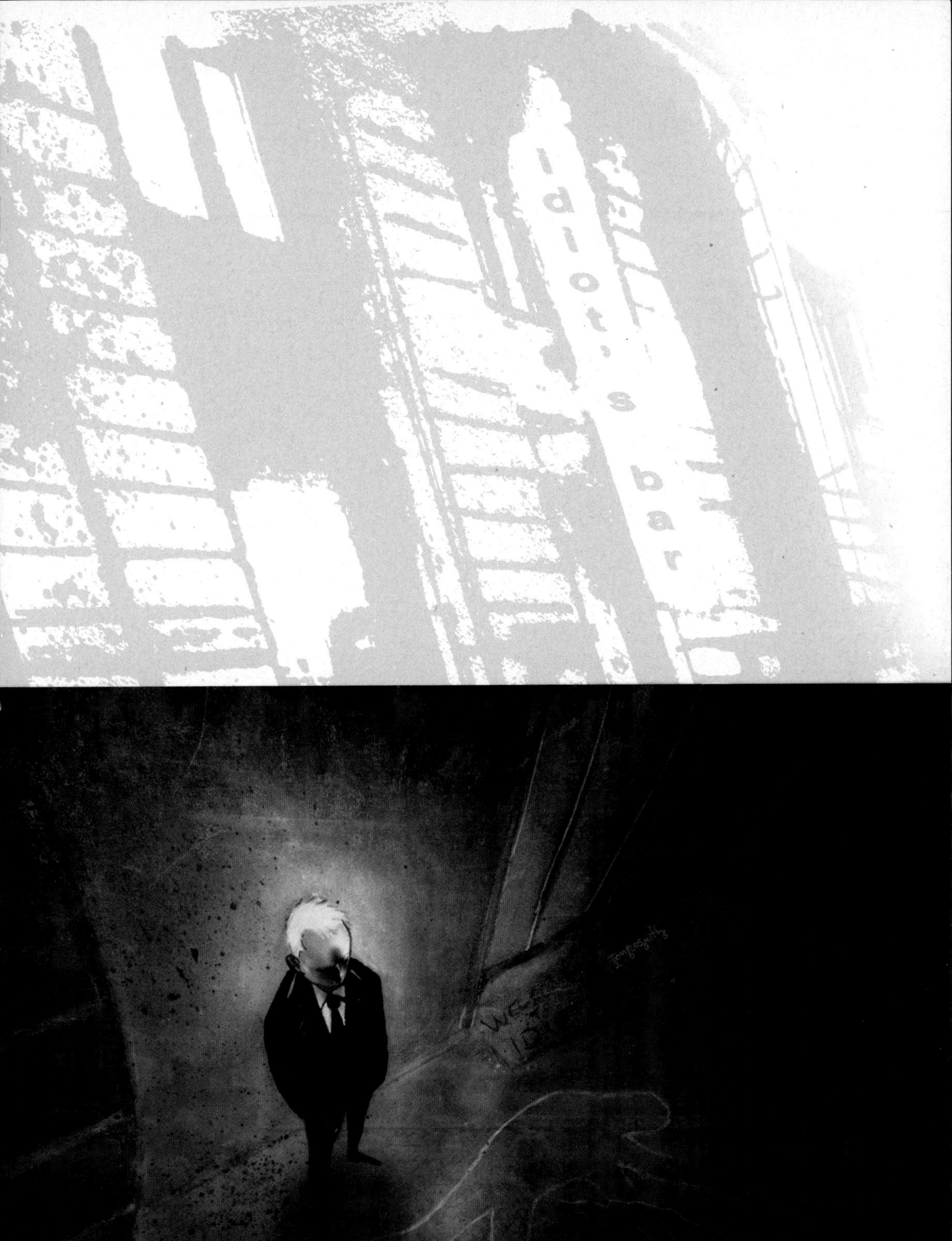
idiot's bar

# FELL.™

## CHAPTER 8

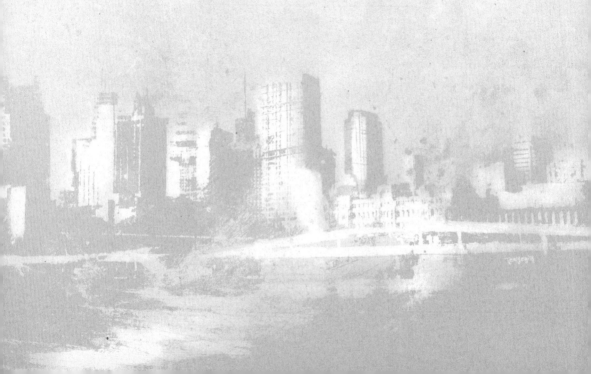

Y'KNOW, DETECTIVE FELL, THE GUY'S NOT GOING TO POSE FOR YOU.

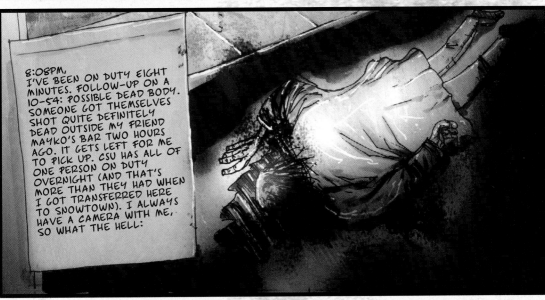

8:08PM,
I'VE BEEN ON DUTY EIGHT MINUTES. FOLLOW-UP ON A 10-54: POSSIBLE DEAD BODY. SOMEONE GOT THEMSELVES SHOT QUITE DEFINITELY DEAD OUTSIDE MY FRIEND MAYKO'S BAR TWO HOURS AGO. IT GETS LEFT FOR ME TO PICK UP. CSU HAS ALL OF ONE PERSON ON DUTY OVERNIGHT (AND THAT'S MORE THAN THEY HAD WHEN I GOT TRANSFERRED HERE TO SNOWTOWN). I ALWAYS HAVE A CAMERA WITH ME, SO WHAT THE HELL:

MAYKO'S ANNOYED, BUT NOT BY THIS. SHE'S ANNOYED BY HAVING TO CLOSE THE BAR FOR AN HOUR (ANYWHERE ELSE AND IT'D BE CLOSED FOR THE NIGHT), SHE'S ANNOYED THAT WORD WILL GET AROUND ABOUT THE SHOOTING IN A NEIGHBORHOOD WHERE MAKING ENOUGH MONEY TO LIVE ON IS ALREADY TOUGH ENOUGH, AND ANNOYED BY ME TAKING A PHOTO OF HER.

THE CRIME SCENE UNIT GUY IS SO STONED THAT IT TAKES HIM EIGHT TRIES TO PLUCK A BULLET THAT, LET'S FACE IT, ISN'T MOVING AROUND OUT OF THE NOTORIOUSLY SNEAKY AND EVASIVE MEDIUM OF SIDEWALK. GOD KNOWS HOW HE DROVE HERE WITHOUT KILLING ANYONE. PARAMEDICS TAKE THE BODY AWAY (THAT NEVER MADE SENSE TO ME). I'VE GOT ALL I NEED. LOCAL SMALL-TIME DRUG DEALER, CRAZY CUSTOMER (IN DEBT?): IT'LL KEEP 'TIL MORNING.

NIGHTS IN SNOWTOWN ALWAYS TURN INTO A NUMBERS GAME. THE TIRED, LONELY DISPATCHER, DRAWLING OUT CODES AND ADDRESSES.

8:46PM,
I GET PULLED INTO A BURGLARY, 459, THAT IS AMENDED EN ROUTE TO 5150--MENTAL CASE. I KNOW WHO THIS IS IMMEDIATELY.

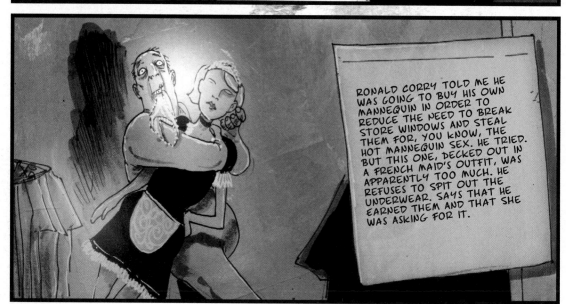

RONALD CORRY TOLD ME HE WAS GOING TO BUY HIS OWN MANNEQUIN IN ORDER TO REDUCE THE NEED TO BREAK STORE WINDOWS AND STEAL THEM FOR, YOU KNOW, THE HOT MANNEQUIN SEX. HE TRIED. BUT THIS ONE, DECKED OUT IN A FRENCH MAID'S OUTFIT, WAS APPARENTLY TOO MUCH. HE REFUSES TO SPIT OUT THE UNDERWEAR. SAYS THAT HE EARNED THEM AND THAT SHE WAS ASKING FOR IT.

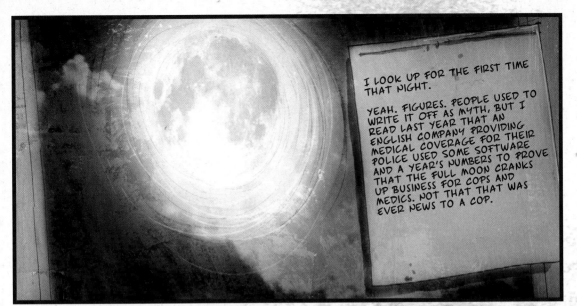

I LOOK UP FOR THE FIRST TIME THAT NIGHT.

YEAH. FIGURES. PEOPLE USED TO WRITE IT OFF AS MYTH, BUT I READ LAST YEAR THAT AN ENGLISH COMPANY PROVIDING MEDICAL COVERAGE FOR THEIR POLICE USED SOME SOFTWARE AND A YEAR'S NUMBERS TO PROVE THAT THE FULL MOON CRANKS UP BUSINESS FOR COPS AND MEDICS. NOT THAT THAT WAS EVER NEWS TO A COP.

CORRY'S GOING TO PULL TIME FOR THIS ONE. SOME DUTY LAWYER'S NOT GOING TO GIVE A DAMN; MIGHT EVEN BE HAPPY TO PUT THE POOR CRAZY BASTARD "IN THE SYSTEM." HE COULD BE LOOKING AT AS MUCH AS THIRTEEN YEARS.

9:12PM,
10-62 AND THE LATE-NIGHT SPEEDMART ON 18TH AND CROSS IS CLOSING EARLY. THE FIRST FRESH FRUIT THEY'VE HAD IN STOCK IN THREE DAYS, AND SOMEONE'S ADULTERATED IT. I LEAVE AN EAGER YOUNG UNIFORM OFFICER TO GO THROUGH THE STORE'S SECURITY TAPES. POINTLESS CALLING THE CSU GUY. WHAT'S WRONG IN OUR BRAINS THAT WE DON'T NOTICE SOME FREAK HUNCHED OVER THE FRUIT STAND WEAPONIZING BANANAS?

10:10PM.
GRAB A DEATH COFFEE FROM MR. YANG, THE FOOD PERVERT. HE MELTS A HERSHEY BAR INTO A POT OF FILTER COFFEE, POURS A 16OZ AND THEN DROPS A DEPTH-CHARGE OF ESPRESSO ON IT. AND MAYBE CRYSTAL METH. I DON'T KNOW ANYMORE WHAT FEELS WORSE: HAVING ONE DEATH COFFEE A DAY, OR SKIPPING IT. I CAN ALREADY FEEL MY INTERNAL ORGANS GOING INTO CRISIS MODE. AT THE END OF MY SHIFT THE WORLD'S GOING TO FALL OUT OF MY BUTT.

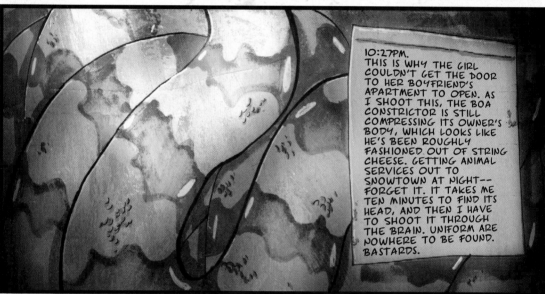

10:27PM.
THIS IS WHY THE GIRL COULDN'T GET THE DOOR TO HER BOYFRIEND'S APARTMENT TO OPEN. AS I SHOOT THIS, THE BOA CONSTRICTOR IS STILL COMPRESSING ITS OWNER'S BODY, WHICH LOOKS LIKE HE'S BEEN ROUGHLY FASHIONED OUT OF STRING CHEESE. GETTING ANIMAL SERVICES OUT TO SNOWTOWN AT NIGHT-- FORGET IT. IT TAKES ME TEN MINUTES TO FIND ITS HEAD, AND THEN I HAVE TO SHOOT IT THROUGH THE BRAIN. UNIFORM ARE NOWHERE TO BE FOUND. BASTARDS.

THE PARAMEDICS MADE ME TAKE THIS SHOT FOR THEM.

PARAMEDICS ARE ALL CRAZY.

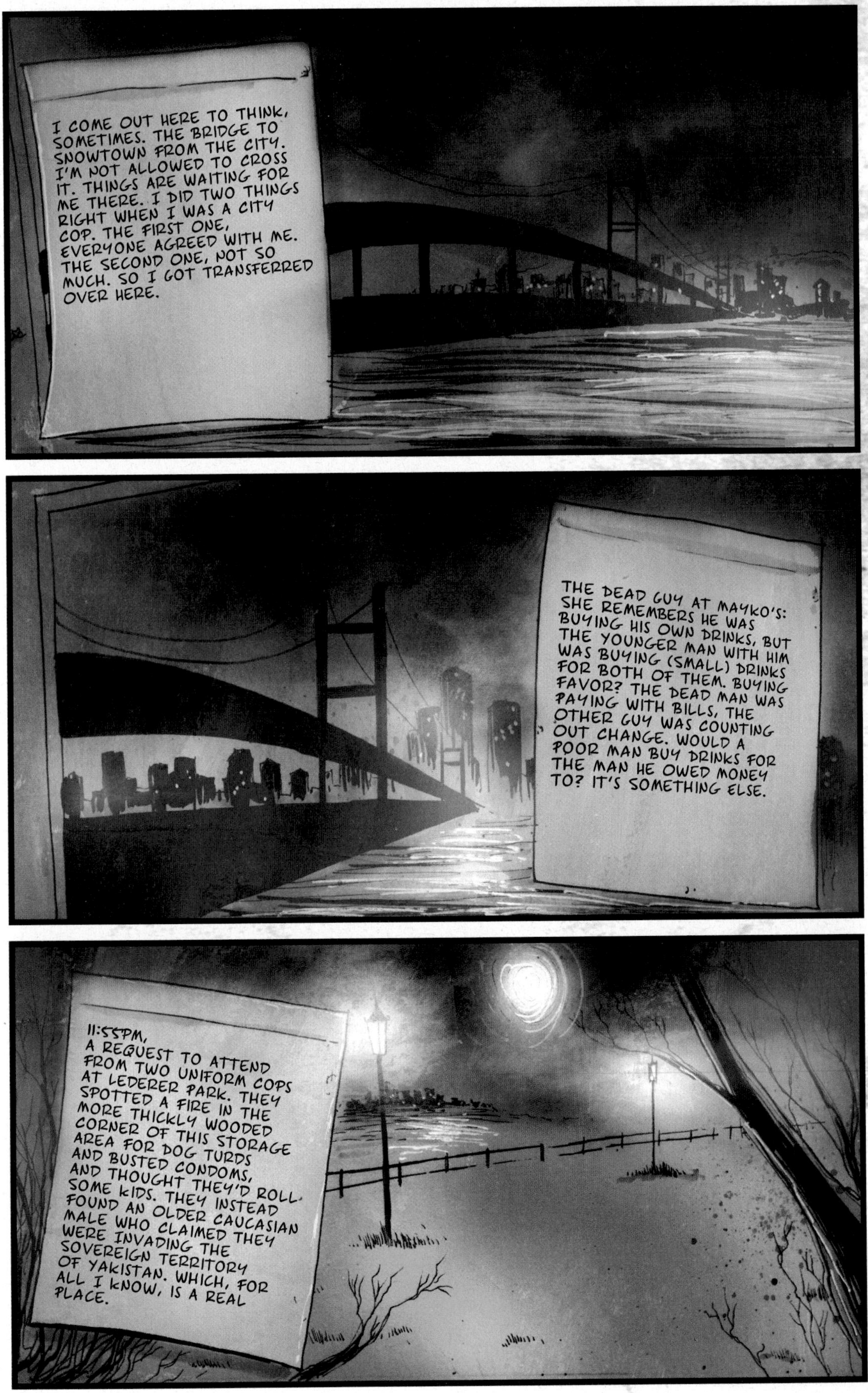
I COME OUT HERE TO THINK, SOMETIMES. THE BRIDGE TO SNOWTOWN FROM THE CITY. I'M NOT ALLOWED TO CROSS IT. THINGS ARE WAITING FOR ME THERE. I DID TWO THINGS RIGHT WHEN I WAS A CITY COP. THE FIRST ONE, EVERYONE AGREED WITH ME. THE SECOND ONE, NOT SO MUCH. SO I GOT TRANSFERRED OVER HERE.
THE DEAD GUY AT MAYKO'S: SHE REMEMBERS HE WAS BUYING HIS OWN DRINKS, BUT THE YOUNGER MAN WITH HIM WAS BUYING (SMALL) DRINKS FOR BOTH OF THEM. BUYING FAVOR? THE DEAD MAN WAS PAYING WITH BILLS, THE OTHER GUY WAS COUNTING OUT CHANGE. WOULD A POOR MAN BUY DRINKS FOR THE MAN HE OWED MONEY TO? IT'S SOMETHING ELSE.
11:55PM, A REQUEST TO ATTEND FROM TWO UNIFORM COPS AT LEDERER PARK. THEY SPOTTED A FIRE IN THE MORE THICKLY WOODED CORNER OF THIS STORAGE AREA FOR DOG TURDS AND BUSTED CONDOMS, AND THOUGHT THEY'D ROLL SOME KIDS. THEY INSTEAD FOUND AN OLDER CAUCASIAN MALE WHO CLAIMED THEY WERE INVADING THE SOVEREIGN TERRITORY OF YAKISTAN. WHICH, FOR ALL I KNOW, IS A REAL PLACE.

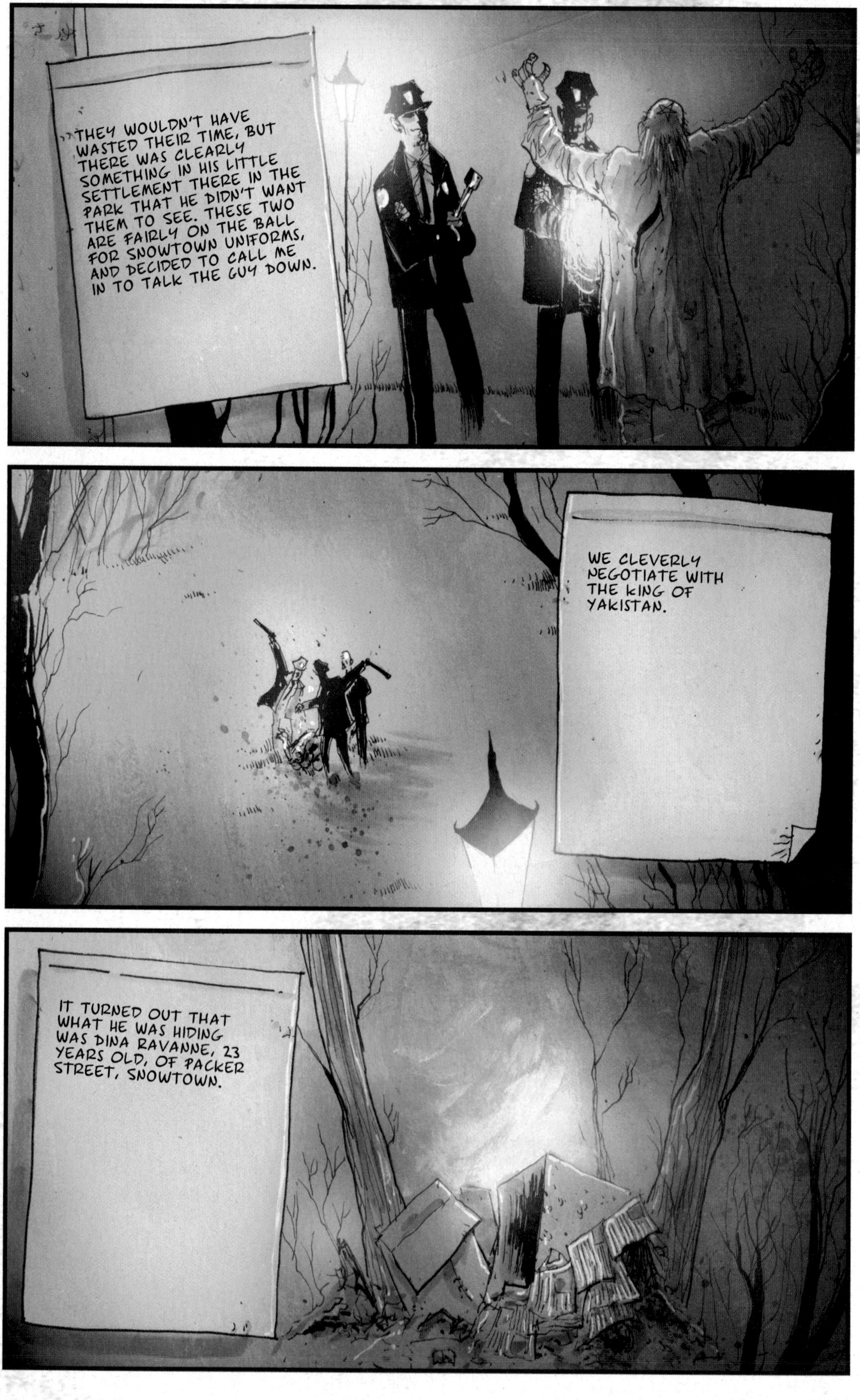
THEY WOULDN'T HAVE WASTED THEIR TIME, BUT THERE WAS CLEARLY SOMETHING IN HIS LITTLE SETTLEMENT THERE IN THE PARK THAT HE DIDN'T WANT THEM TO SEE. THESE TWO ARE FAIRLY ON THE BALL FOR SNOWTOWN UNIFORMS, AND DECIDED TO CALL ME IN TO TALK THE GUY DOWN.
WE CLEVERLY NEGOTIATE WITH THE KING OF YAKISTAN.
IT TURNED OUT THAT WHAT HE WAS HIDING WAS DINA RAVANNE, 23 YEARS OLD, OF PACKER STREET, SNOWTOWN.

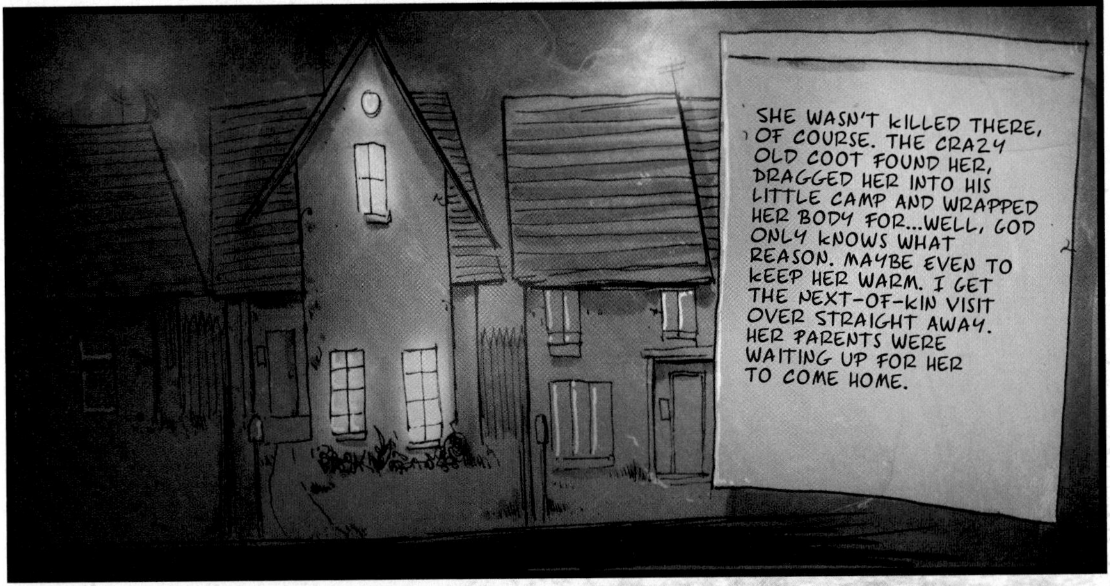
SHE WASN'T KILLED THERE, OF COURSE. THE CRAZY OLD COOT FOUND HER, DRAGGED HER INTO HIS LITTLE CAMP AND WRAPPED HER BODY FOR...WELL, GOD ONLY KNOWS WHAT REASON. MAYBE EVEN TO KEEP HER WARM. I GET THE NEXT-OF-KIN VISIT OVER STRAIGHT AWAY. HER PARENTS WERE WAITING UP FOR HER TO COME HOME.

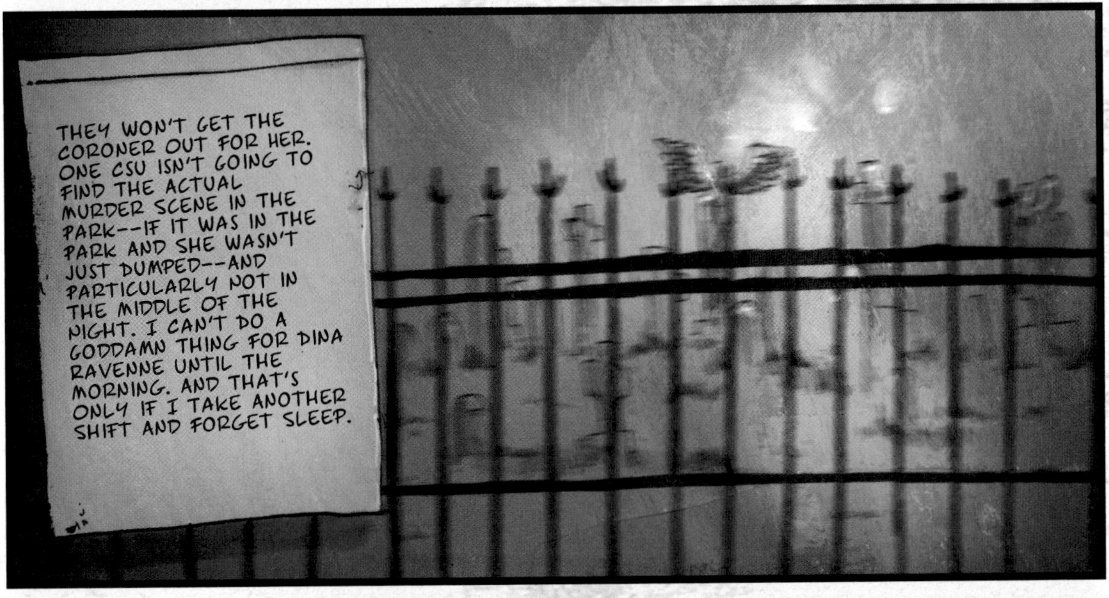
THEY WON'T GET THE CORONER OUT FOR HER. ONE CSU ISN'T GOING TO FIND THE ACTUAL MURDER SCENE IN THE PARK--IF IT WAS IN THE PARK AND SHE WASN'T JUST DUMPED--AND PARTICULARLY NOT IN THE MIDDLE OF THE NIGHT. I CAN'T DO A GODDAMN THING FOR DINA RAVENNE UNTIL THE MORNING. AND THAT'S ONLY IF I TAKE ANOTHER SHIFT AND FORGET SLEEP.

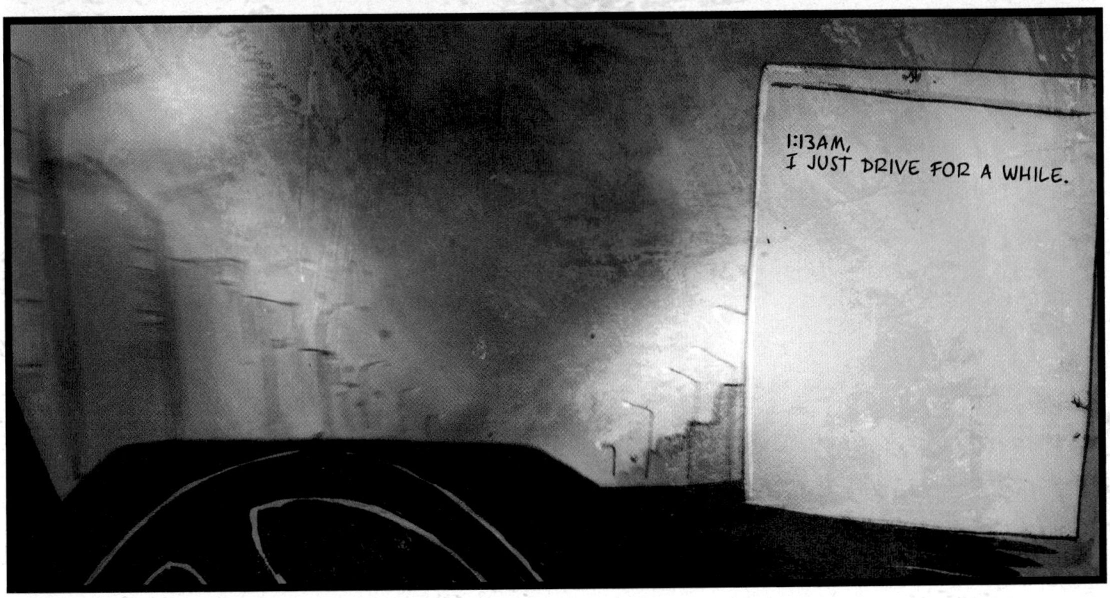
1:13AM,
I JUST DRIVE FOR A WHILE.

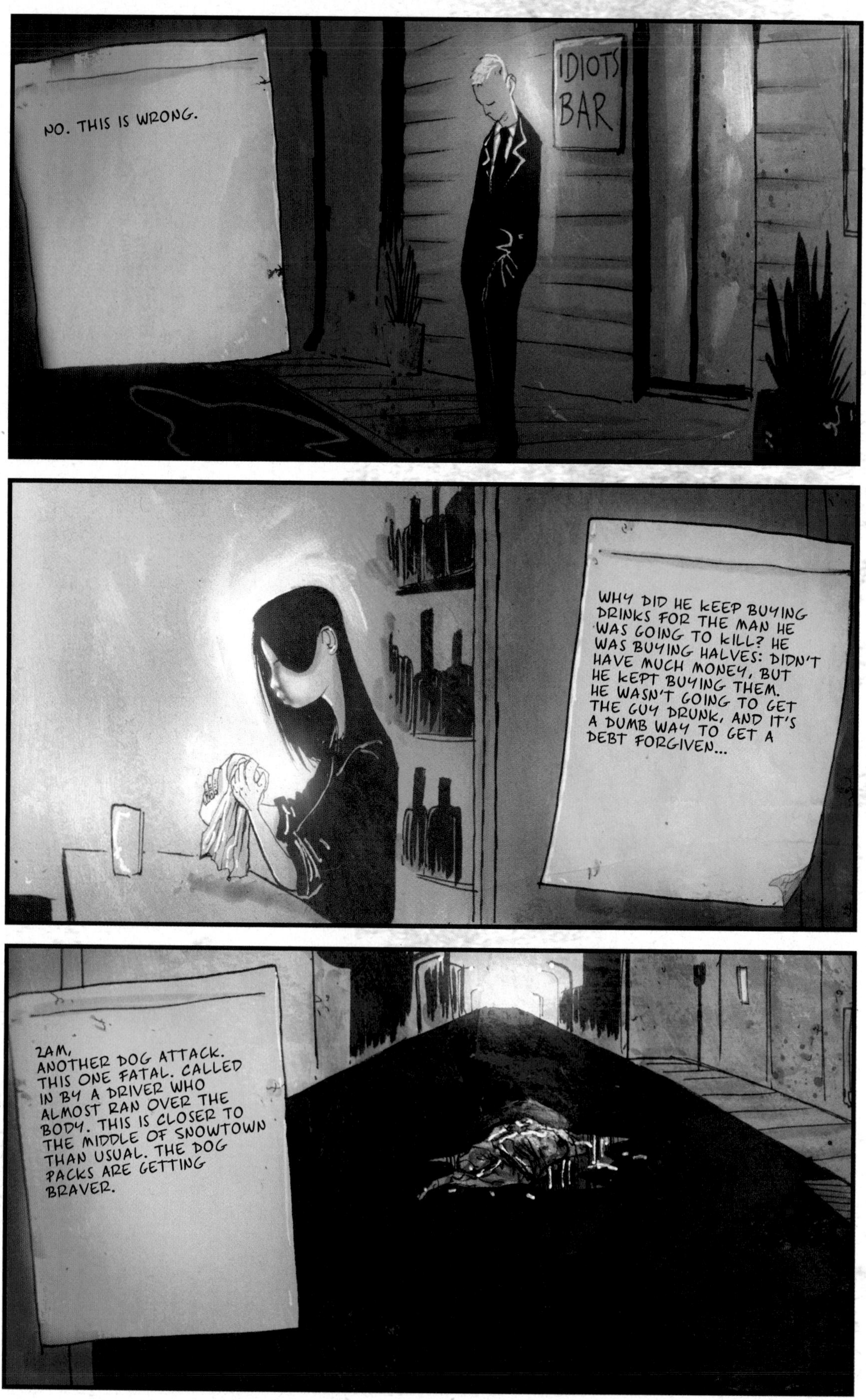
NO. THIS IS WRONG.
IDIOTS BAR
WHY DID HE KEEP BUYING DRINKS FOR THE MAN HE WAS GOING TO KILL? HE WAS BUYING HALVES: DIDN'T HAVE MUCH MONEY, BUT HE KEPT BUYING THEM. HE WASN'T GOING TO GET THE GUY DRUNK, AND IT'S A DUMB WAY TO GET A DEBT FORGIVEN...
2AM, ANOTHER DOG ATTACK. THIS ONE FATAL. CALLED IN BY A DRIVER WHO ALMOST RAN OVER THE BODY. THIS IS CLOSER TO THE MIDDLE OF SNOWTOWN THAN USUAL. THE DOG PACKS ARE GETTING BRAVER.

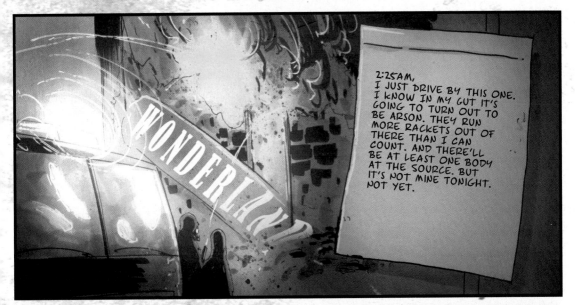

2:25AM,
I JUST DRIVE BY THIS ONE. I KNOW IN MY GUT IT'S GOING TO TURN OUT TO BE ARSON. THEY RUN MORE RACKETS OUT OF THERE THAN I CAN COUNT. AND THERE'LL BE AT LEAST ONE BODY AT THE SOURCE. BUT IT'S NOT MINE TONIGHT. NOT YET.

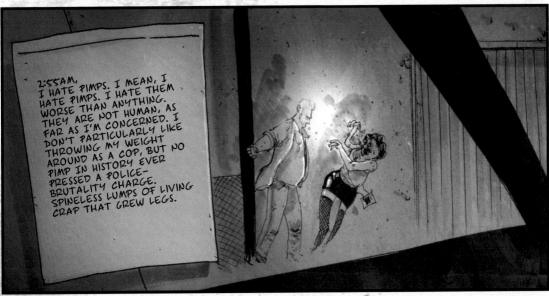

2:55AM,
I HATE PIMPS. I MEAN, I HATE PIMPS. I HATE THEM WORSE THAN ANYTHING. THEY ARE NOT HUMAN, AS FAR AS I'M CONCERNED. I DON'T PARTICULARLY LIKE THROWING MY WEIGHT AROUND AS A COP, BUT NO PIMP IN HISTORY EVER PRESSED A POLICE-BRUTALITY CHARGE. SPINELESS LUMPS OF LIVING CRAP THAT GREW LEGS.

TURNS OUT MY CAMERA'S PRETTY TOUGH FOR A CHEAP DIGITAL. BUT ISN'T THAT ALWAYS THE WAY? SPEND A GRAND ON A TOP-END GADGET AND IT BREAKS WHEN YOU BREATH ON IT, BUT SOME PIECE OF TEN-DOLLAR JUNK KEEPS WORKING EVEN IF YOU DROP IT ON THE STREET AND A PIMP FALLS ON IT A FEW TIMES.

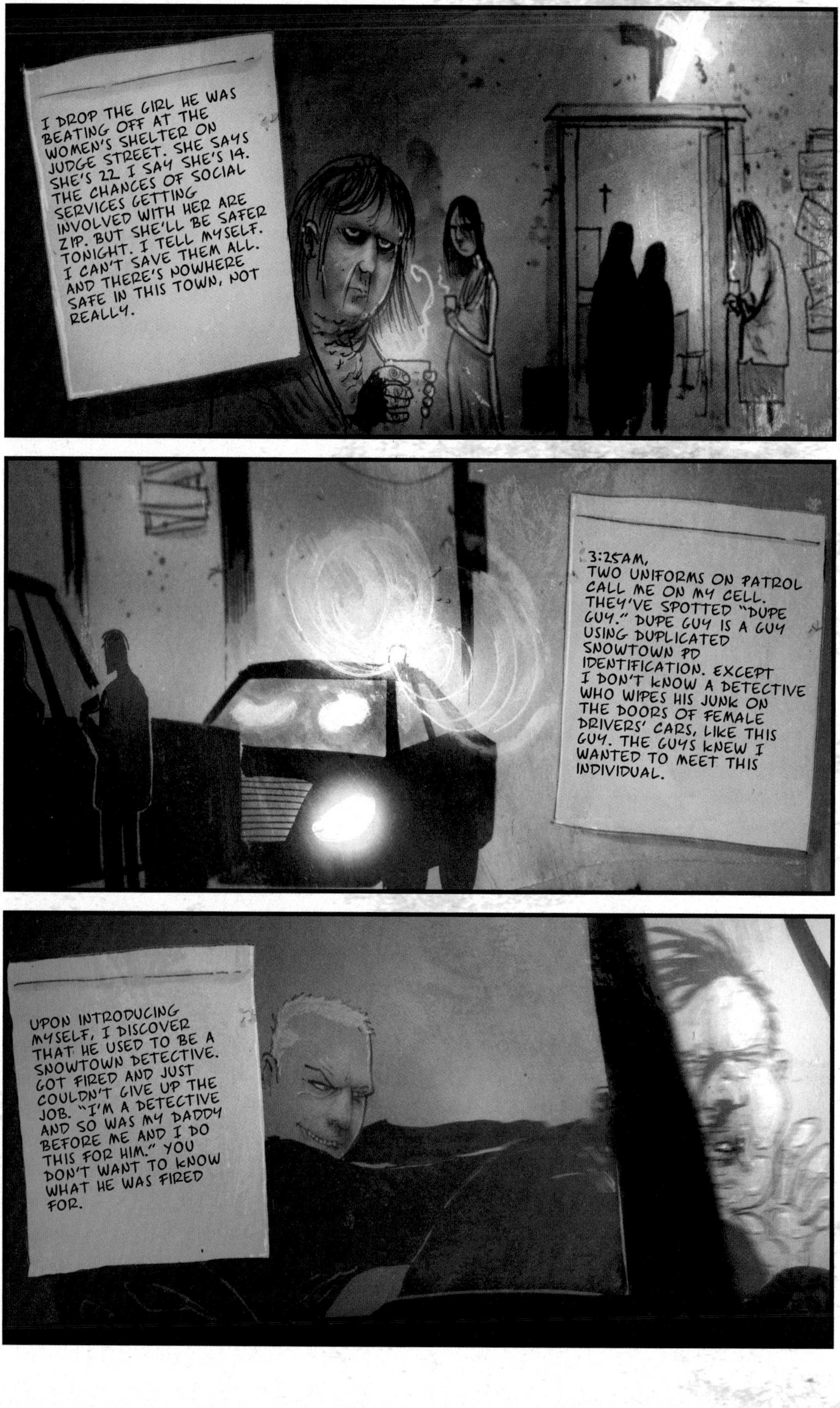
I DROP THE GIRL HE WAS BEATING OFF AT THE WOMEN'S SHELTER ON JUDGE STREET. SHE SAYS SHE'S 22. I SAY SHE'S 14. THE CHANCES OF SOCIAL SERVICES GETTING INVOLVED WITH HER ARE ZIP. BUT SHE'LL BE SAFER TONIGHT. I TELL MYSELF. I CAN'T SAVE THEM ALL. AND THERE'S NOWHERE SAFE IN THIS TOWN, NOT REALLY.
3:25AM,
TWO UNIFORMS ON PATROL CALL ME ON MY CELL. THEY'VE SPOTTED "DUPE GUY." DUPE GUY IS A GUY USING DUPLICATED SNOWTOWN PD IDENTIFICATION. EXCEPT I DON'T KNOW A DETECTIVE WHO WIPES HIS JUNK ON THE DOORS OF FEMALE DRIVERS' CARS, LIKE THIS GUY. THE GUYS KNEW I WANTED TO MEET THIS INDIVIDUAL.
UPON INTRODUCING MYSELF, I DISCOVER THAT HE USED TO BE A SNOWTOWN DETECTIVE. GOT FIRED AND JUST COULDN'T GIVE UP THE JOB. "I'M A DETECTIVE AND SO WAS MY DADDY BEFORE ME AND I DO THIS FOR HIM." YOU DON'T WANT TO KNOW WHAT HE WAS FIRED FOR.

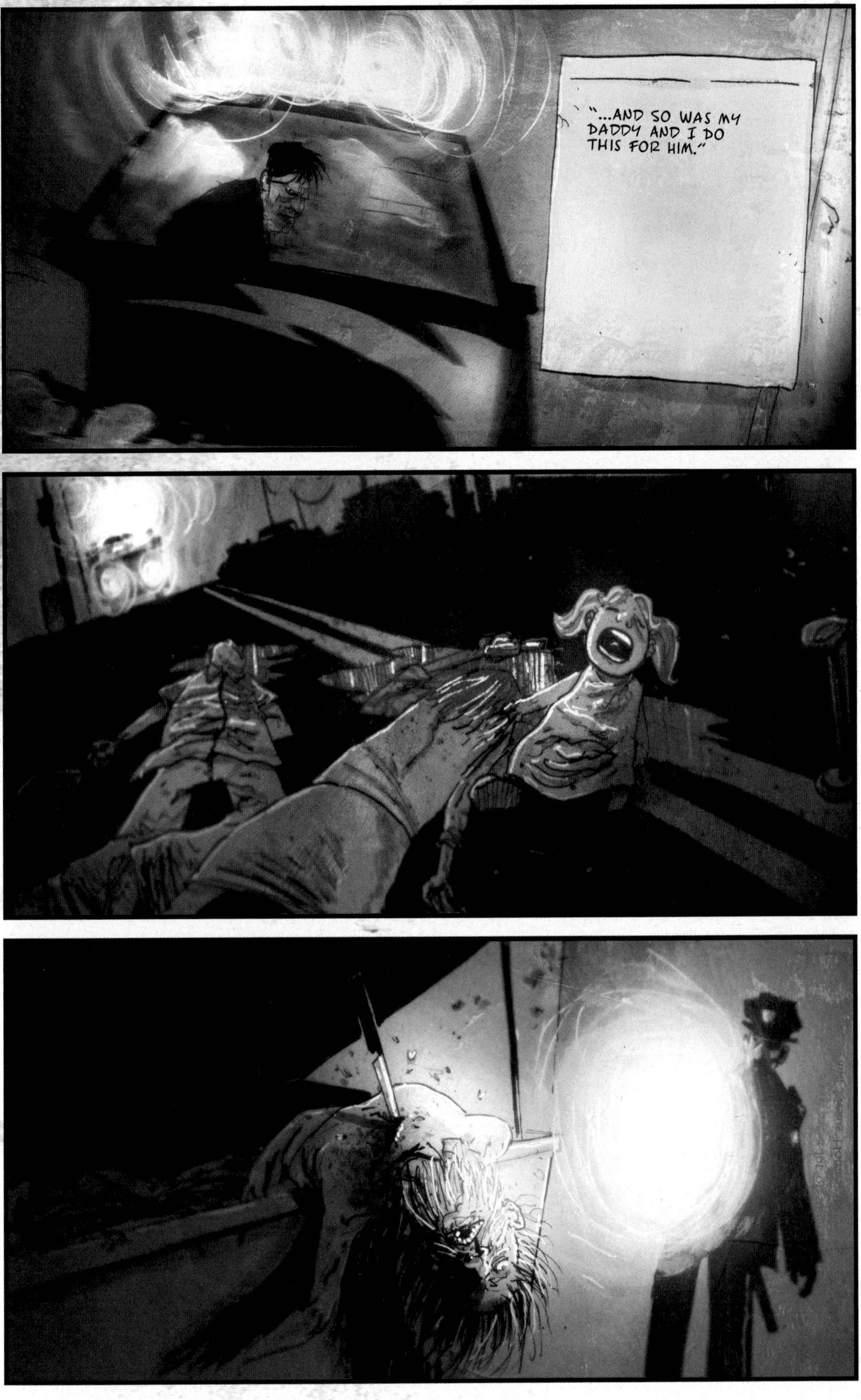
"...AND SO WAS MY DADDY AND I DO THIS FOR HIM."

4AM,
AND THE BIG TRUCKS START TRICKLING INTO SNOWTOWN, BRINGING IN WHATEVER GOODS AND PRODUCE THE CITY CAN BE ASSUMED TO AFFORD. I SHOULD BE HEADED BACK TO THE STATION AND THEN HOME.

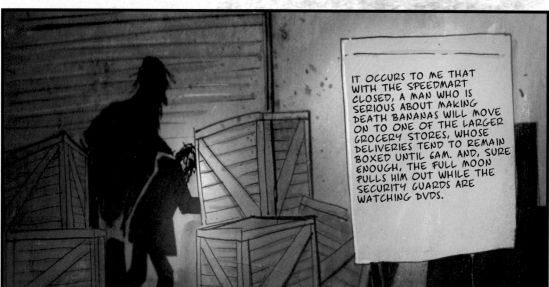

IT OCCURS TO ME THAT WITH THE SPEEDMART CLOSED, A MAN WHO IS SERIOUS ABOUT MAKING DEATH BANANAS WILL MOVE ON TO ONE OF THE LARGER GROCERY STORES, WHOSE DELIVERIES TEND TO REMAIN BOXED UNTIL 6AM. AND, SURE ENOUGH, THE FULL MOON PULLS HIM OUT WHILE THE SECURITY GUARDS ARE WATCHING DVDS.

I DECIDE TO BE A JERK AND TAKE HIS PHOTO AFTER I, AH, TOOK STEPS TO PREVENT HIS ESCAPE. IT WAS A GOOD SHOOTING. THE GUY WAS ARMED, AFTER ALL. WITH DEATH BANANAS.

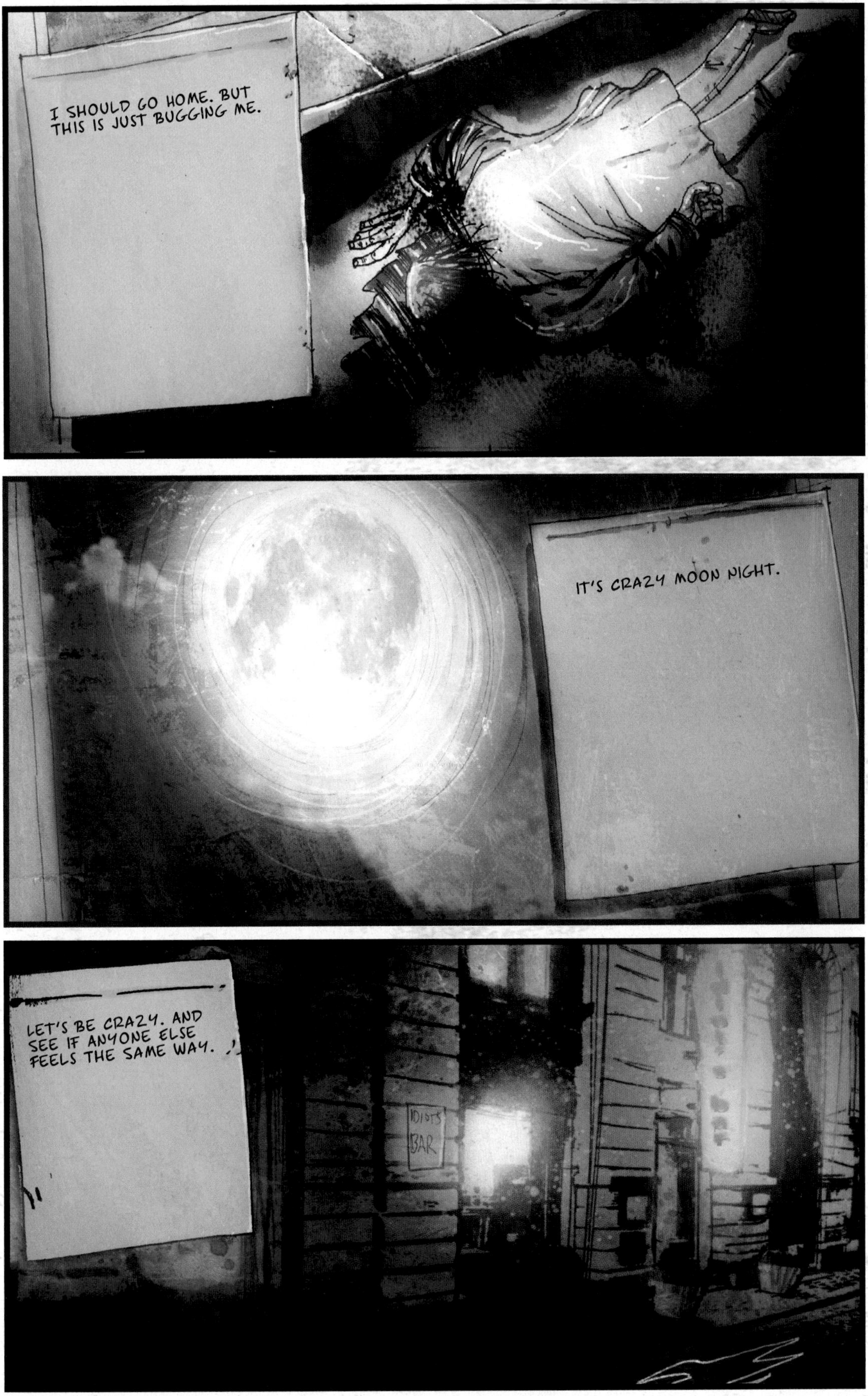
I SHOULD GO HOME. BUT THIS IS JUST BUGGING ME.
IT'S CRAZY MOON NIGHT.
LET'S BE CRAZY. AND SEE IF ANYONE ELSE FEELS THE SAME WAY.
IDIOTS BAR

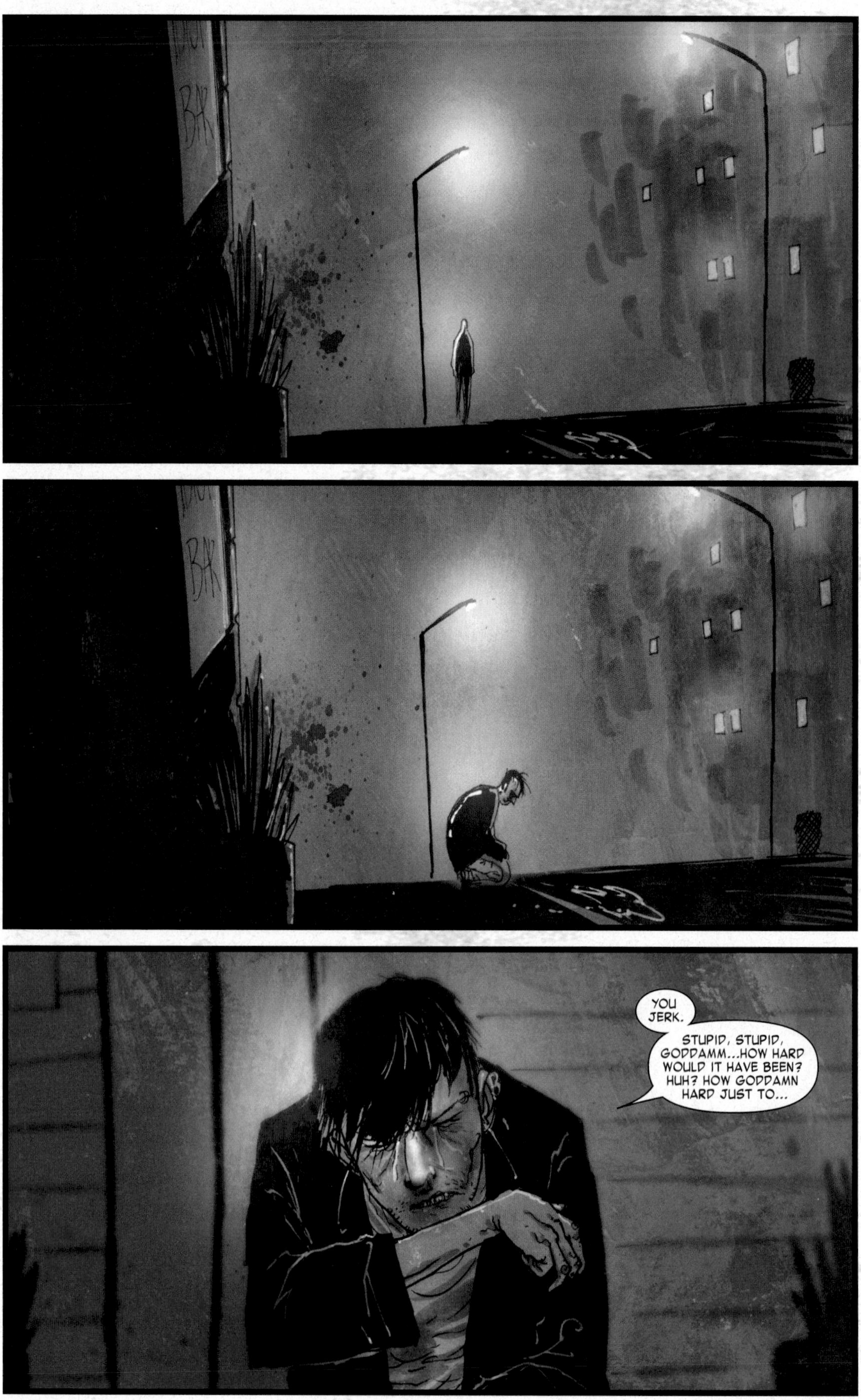
YOU JERK.
STUPID, STUPID, GODDAMM...HOW HARD WOULD IT HAVE BEEN? HUH? HOW GODDAMN HARD JUST TO...

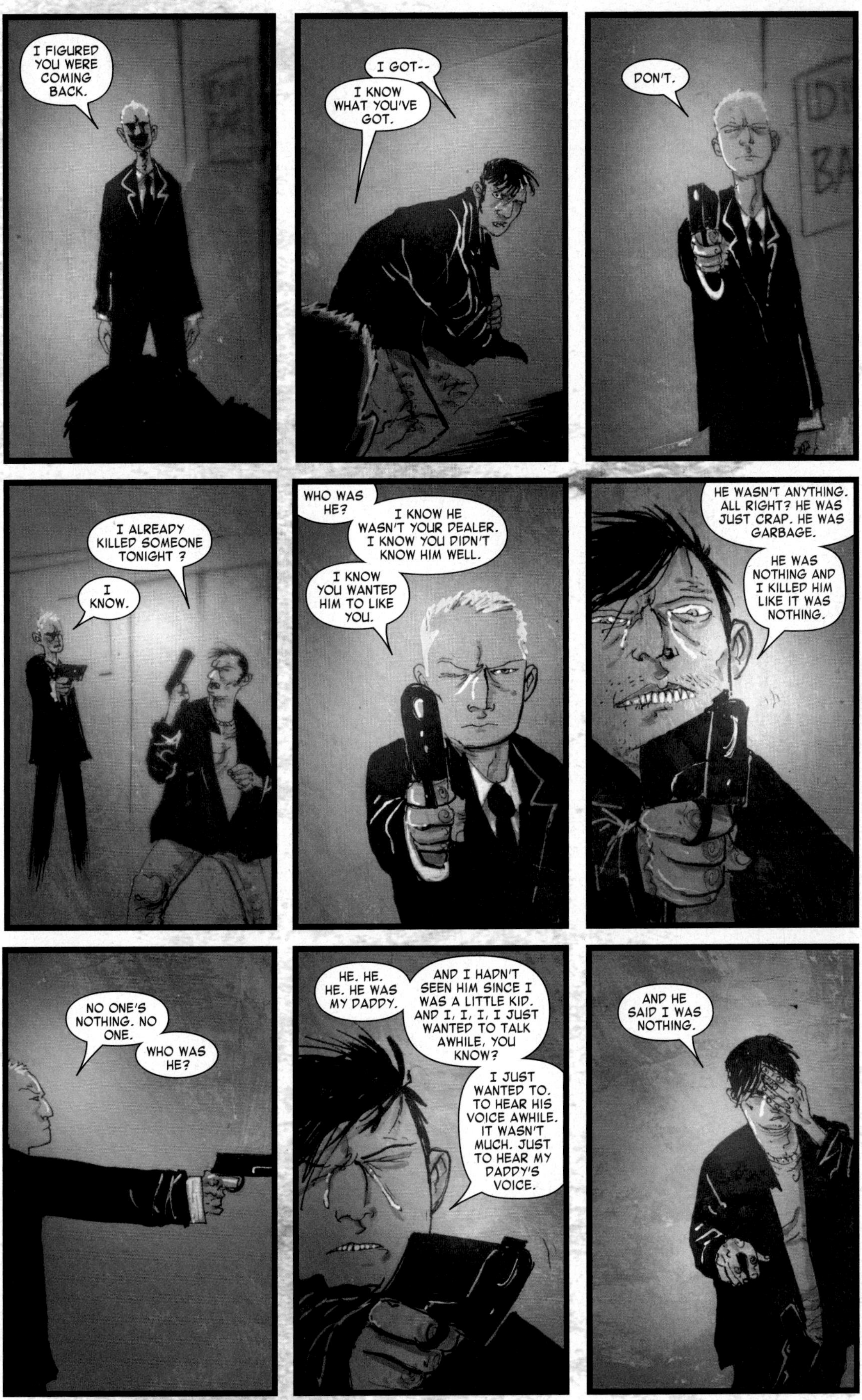
I FIGURED YOU WERE COMING BACK.
I GOT--
I KNOW WHAT YOU'VE GOT.
DON'T.
I ALREADY KILLED SOMEONE TONIGHT ?
I KNOW.
WHO WAS HE?
I KNOW HE WASN'T YOUR DEALER. I KNOW YOU DIDN'T KNOW HIM WELL.
I KNOW YOU WANTED HIM TO LIKE YOU.
HE WASN'T ANYTHING. ALL RIGHT? HE WAS JUST CRAP. HE WAS GARBAGE.
HE WAS NOTHING AND I KILLED HIM LIKE IT WAS NOTHING.
NO ONE'S NOTHING. NO ONE.
WHO WAS HE?
HE. HE. HE. HE WAS MY DADDY.
AND I HADN'T SEEN HIM SINCE I WAS A LITTLE KID. AND I, I, I, I JUST WANTED TO TALK AWHILE, YOU KNOW?
I JUST WANTED TO. TO HEAR HIS VOICE AWHILE. IT WASN'T MUCH. JUST TO HEAR MY DADDY'S VOICE.
AND HE SAID I WAS NOTHING.

7AM,
THIS IS WHERE I LIVE
NOW.
NONE OF YOU ARE
NOTHING TO ME.
T
2007
END

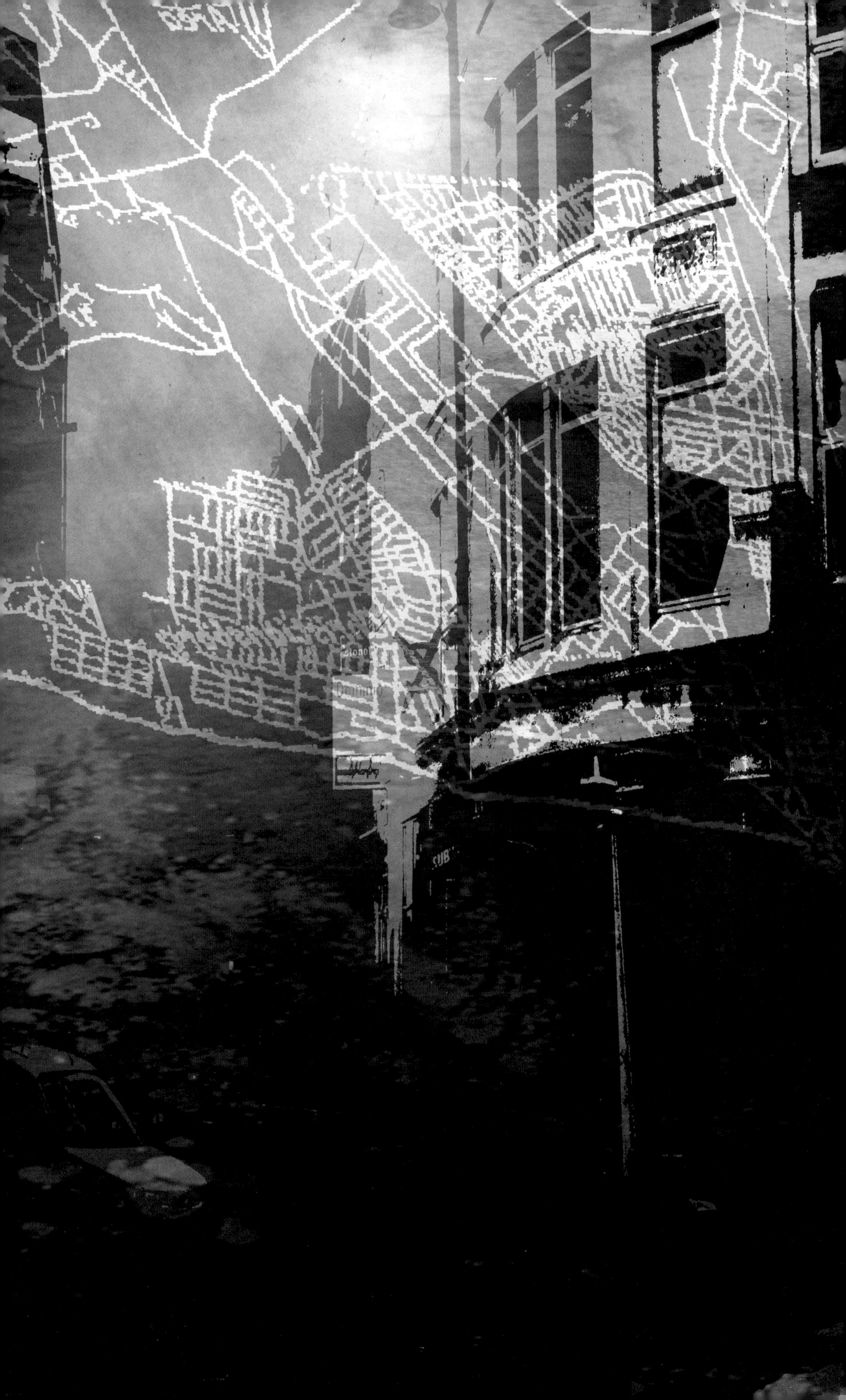

# MORE GREAT TITLES FRO

MINISTRY OF SPACE
ELLIS · WESTON · MARTIN

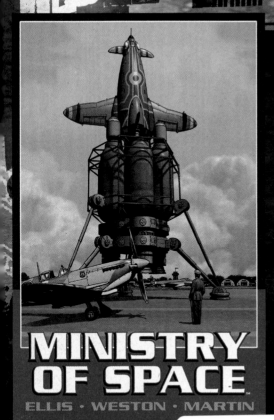

## MINISTRY OF SPACE

WRITTEN BY **WARREN ELLIS**
ART BY **CHRIS WESTON**
COLORS BY **LAURA MARTIN**

THIS IS THE STORY OF HOW THE BRITISH COULD HAVE GONE TO SPACE. MAYBE *HOW* WE SHOULD HAVE GONE TO SPACE. THIS IS THE STORY OF THE MINISTRY OF SPACE. IN 2000, THE END OF THE GOLDEN AGE, AS AMERICA AND RUSSIA BEGIN MOVING INTO SPACE. THE SECRET REVEALED, AND THE DESTRUCTION OF A MAN WHO SACRIFICED HIMSELF FOR THE MINISTRY OF SPACE.

ISBN: **978-1-58240-423-3**
**$12.99** USD

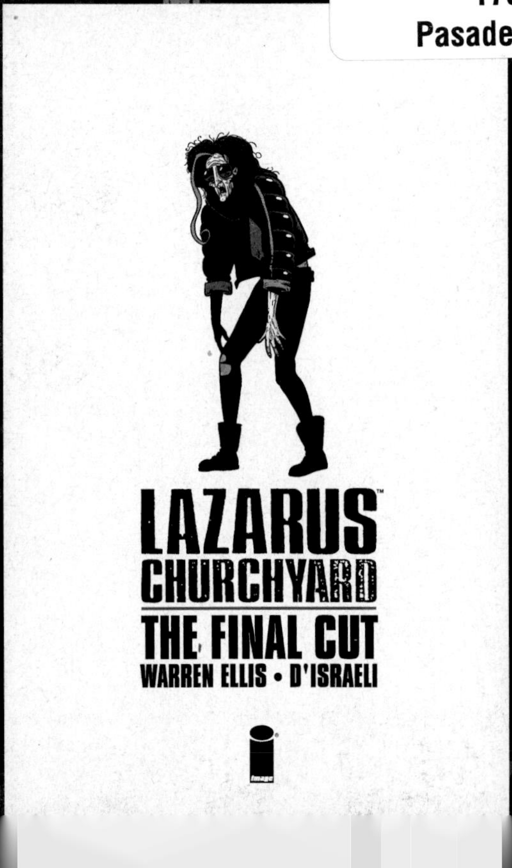

LAZARUS CHURCHYARD
THE FINAL CUT
WARREN ELLIS • D'ISRAELI

## LAZARUS CHURCHYARD THE FINAL CUT

WRITTEN BY **WARREN ELLIS**
ART BY **D'ISRAELI**

MEET LAZARUS CHURCHYARD, A JUNKIE TRAPPED IN A MISERABLE FUTURE WHO WANTS NOTHING MORE THAN TO DIE. CATCH IS, HE CAN'T. WRITER WARREN ELLIS TAKES YOU ON A DARK, TWISTED, VIOLENT AND MORBIDLY FUNNY TRIP THROUGH THE WORLD OF LAZARUS CHURCHYARD WITH TWISTED CYBERPUNK ARTWORK FROM THE INIMITABLE D'ISRAELI.

ISBN: **978-1-58240-108-5**
**$14.95** USD

# WARREN ELLIS & IMAGE COMICS

## CITY OF SILENCE

WRITTEN BY **WARREN ELLIS**
ART BY **GARY ERSKINE**

THE FUTURE IS BAD FOR YOU. IN A PLACE WHERE EVERYONE HAS THE TECHNOLOGY TO CREATE BRAND-NEW, WEIRD SCIENCES TEN TIMES A DAY, THERE ARE POLICEMEN WHO WILL HUNT YOU DOWN FOR HAVING A BAD IDEA. THEY ARE THE SILENCERS. AND THE INVESTIGATION OF A DEAD KID WITH A SILICON PENTAGRAM ON HIS NECK OPENS UP A WHOLE BOX OF BAD IDEAS UPON A CITY THAT ONLY SURVIVES THROUGH SILENCE...

ISBN: **978-1-58240-367-0**
**$9.95** USD

warren ellis • gary erskine
CITY OF SILENCE

## TOP COW'S BEST OF WARREN ELLIS: DOWN & TALES OF THE WITCHBLADE

WRITTEN BY **WARREN ELLIS**
ART BY **TONY HARRIS, CULLY HAMNER & BILLY TAN**

FOLLOW THE ADVENTURES OF DETECTIVE DEANNA RANSOM AS SHE GOES DEEP UNDERVOER TO BRING BACK A COP GONE BAD. ALSO INCLUDES A STORY OF THE WITCHBLADE FROM THE NOT SO DISTANT FUTURE!

ISBN: **978-1-58240-423-3**
**$15.99** USD

Top Cow's Best of: Warren Ellis
DOWN
&
Tales of the Witchblade

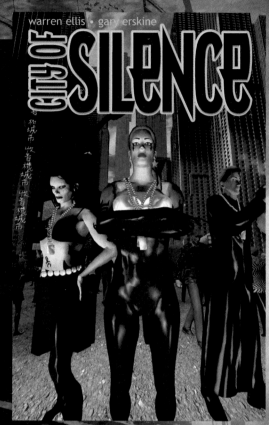

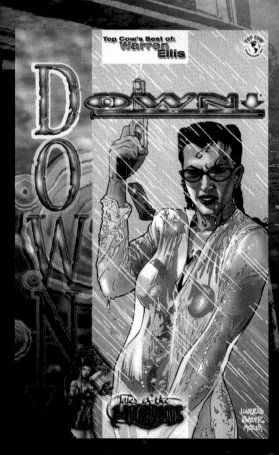

**24SEVEN, VOL. 1 TP**
ISBN: 978-1-58240-636-7
$24.99

**BASTARD SAMURAI TP**
ISBN: 978-1-58240-746-3
$12.99

**BLOOD RIVER GN**
ISBN: 978-1-58240-509-4
$7.99

**CASANOVA, VOL. 1:
LUXURIA HC**
ISBN: 978-1-58240-698-5
$24.99

**CROSS BRONX, VOL. 1: TP**
ISBN: 978-1-58240-690-9
$14.99

**DIORAMAS, A LOVE STORY GN**
ISBN: 978-1-58240-359-5
$12.95

**FIRE: THE DEFINITIVE
COLLECTION TP**
ISBN: 978-1-58240-071-6
$9.95

**THE FIVE FISTS OF SCIENCE
GN**
ISBN: 978-1-58240-605-3
$12.99

## GIRLS
**VOL. 1: CONCEPTION TP**
ISBN: 978-1-58240-529-2
$14.99
**VOL. 2: ERMERGENCE TP**
ISBN: 978-1-58240-608-4
$14.99
**VOL. 3: SURVIVAL TP**
ISBN: 978-1-58240-703-6
$14.99
**VOL. 4: EXTINCTION**
ISBN: 978-1-58240-753-1
$14.99

**GOLDFISH: THE DEFINITIVE
COLLECTION TP**
ISBN: 978-1-58240-195-9
$19.95

**HAMMER OF THE GODS,
VOL. 1: MORTAL ENEMY TP**
ISBN: 978-1-58240-271-0
$18.95

## HAWAIIAN DICK
**VOL. 1: BYRD OF PARADISE TP**
ISBN: 978-1-58240-317-5
$14.95
**VOL. 2: THE LAST RESORT TP**
ISBN: 978-1-58240-644-0
$14.99

**HELLSHOCK: THE DEFINITIVE
COLLECTION TP**
ISBN: 978-1-58240-504-9
19.99

**JINX: THE DEFINITIVE
COLLECTION TP**
ISBN: 978-1-58240-179-9
$24.95

## KABUKI
**VOL. 1: CIRCLE OF BLOOD TP**
ISBN: 978-1-88727-980-1
$19.95

**VOL. 2: DREAMS TP**
ISBN: 978-1-58240-277-2
$12.95
**VOL. 3: MASKS OF NOH TP**
ISBN: 978-1-58240-108-9
$12.95
**VOL. 4: SKIN DEEP TP**
ISBN: 978-1-58240-000-6
$12.95
**VOL. 5: METAMORPHOSIS TP**
ISBN: 978-1-58240-203-1
$24.99
**VOL. 6: SCARAB TP**
ISBN: 978-1-58240-258-1
$19.95

## KANE
**VOL. 1:
GREETINGS FROM NEW EDEN TP**
ISBN: 978-1-88727-340-3
$19.95
**VOL. 2: RABBIT HUNT TP**
ISBN: 978-1-58240-355-7
$12.95
**VOL. 3: HISTORIES TP**
ISBN: 978-1-58240-382-3
$12.95
**VOL. 4: THIRTY NINTH TP**
ISBN: 978-1-58240-422-6
$12.95
**VOL. 5: THE UNTOUCHABLE
RICO COSTAS AND OTHER SHORT
STORIES TP**
ISBN: 978-1-58240-551-3
$24.99
**VOL. 6: PARTNERS TP**
ISBN: 978-1-58240-704-3
$19.95

**MIDNIGHT NATION TP**
ISBN: 978-1-58240-460-8
$24.99

**NOWHERESVILLE TP**
ISBN: 978-1-58240-241-3
$14.95

**NYC MECH, VOL. 1:
LET'S ELECTRIFY TP**
ISBN: 978-1-58240-558-2
$14.99

**PARLIAMENT OF JUSTICE**
$5.95

**PHONOGRAM, VOL. 1:
RUE BRITANNIA TP**
ISBN: 978-1-58240-694-7
$14.99

## POWERS
**VOL. 1: WHO KILLED RETRO
GIRL? TP**
ISBN: 978-1-58240-669-5
$21.99
**VOL. 2: ROLEPLAY TP**
ISBN: 978-1-58240-695-4
$13.99
**VOL. 3: LITTLE DEATHS TP**
ISBN: 978-1-58240-670-181
$19.99
**VOL. 4: SUPERGROUP TP**
ISBN: 978-1-58240-671-5
$21.99
**VOL. 5: ANARCHY TP**
ISBN: 978-1-58240-331-7
$14.95
**POWERS SCRIPTBOOK**
ISBN: 978-1-58240-233-8
$19.95

**PUT THE BOOK BACK ON
THE SHELF: A BELLE AND
SEBASTIAN ANTHOLOGY**
ISBN: 978-1-58240-600-8
$14.99

**QUIXOTE NOVEL**
ISBN: 978-1-58240-434-9
$9.95

## RISING STARS
**VOL. 1: BORN IN FIRE TP**
ISBN: 978-1-58240-172-0
$19.95
**VOL. 2: POWER TP**
ISBN: 978-1-58240-226-0
$19.95
**VOL. 3: FIRE & ASH TP**
ISBN: 978-1-58240-491-2
$19.99

## RUULE
**VOL. 1:
GANGLORDS OF CHINATOWN TP**
ISBN: 978-1-58240-566-7
$19.99
**VOL. 2: KISS & TELL**
ISBN: 978-1-58240-540-7
$19.99

**SIX GN**
ISBN: 978-1-58240-398
$5.95

**TORSO: THE DEFINITIVE
COLLECTION TP**
ISBN: 978-1-58240-174
$21.95

**TOTAL SELL OUT TP**
ISBN: 978-1-58240-287
$14.95

**ULTRA: SEVEN DAYS TP**
ISBN: 978-1-58240-483
$17.95

## THE WALKING D
**VOL. 1: DAYS GONE BY**
ISBN: 978-1-58240-67
$9.99
**VOL. 2: MILES BEHIND US T**
ISBN: 978-1-58240-413-4
$12.95
**VOL. 3:
SAFETY BEHIND BARS TP**
ISBN: 978-1-58240-805-7
$12.99
**VOL. 4:
THE HEART'S DESIRE TP**
ISBN: 978-1-58240-753-1
$12.99
**VOL. 5: THE BEST DEFENSE TP**
ISBN: 978-1-58240-612-1
$12.99
**VOL. 6:
THIS SORROWFUL LIFE TP**
ISBN: 978-1-58240-684-8
$12.99
**BOOK ONE HC**
ISBN: 978-1-58240-619-0
$29.99
**BOOK TWO HC**
ISBN: 978-1-58240-759-3
$29.99

**WANTED TP**
ISBN: 978-1-58240-497-4
$19.99

**WINGS OF ANASI GN**
$6.99

TO FIND YOUR ... IMAGE TIELS, CALL TOLL-FREE: **1-800-COMIC-BOOK**